FUNCTIONAL HEARING

A CONTEXTUAL

METHOD FOR

EAR TRAINING

Arthur
Gottschalk

&

Phillip
Kloeckner

THE SHEPHERD
SCHOOL OF MUSIC

RICE
UNIVERSITY

ARDSLEY HOUSE,
PUBLISHERS, INC.
NEW YORK

Address orders and editorial
correspondence to:
Ardsley House, Publishers, Inc.
320 Central Park West
New York, NY 10025

ISBN: 1-880157-51-9

Printed in the United States of America

10 9 8 7 6 5 4 3 2 1

To Paul Cooper: friend, mentor, composer

A.G.

• • • • •

To my family

P.K.

The artworks that appear on the cover and area openers were created by the eclectic David Adickes. He is a sculptor, painter, clarinetist, composer, and playwright, whose travels have taken him from the first "happening" at Houston's legendary Love Street Light Circus to the Atelier F. Leger School in Paris. His art is in the collections of the Louvre, the Prado, the Uffizi, the Philadelphia Museum of Art, and other institutions. His works have also been exhibited at the Metroplitan Museum of Art. His sculpture of George Bush, "The Winds of Change," will soon grace the Bush Presidential Library at Texas A&M University.

•••Contents•••••••••••••••••••••••••••••••

AREA II *Hearing Quality, Function, and Inversion in Triads* ∿ 115

AREA **II** *Hearing Quality, Function, and Inversion in Seventh Chords* ～ 175

*F*unctional Hearing: A Contextual Method for Ear Training presents a unique method of comprehensive ear training. It has been refined over two decades in response to the realization that many of our students (as well as many professionals), despite great talent and the ability to perform competently, were not acquiring the aural acuity they needed to comprehend effectively the melodic, harmonic, and rhythmic contexts of the music they perform.

We initially searched for a textbook that would go beyond the simplistic presentation of melodies for sight-singing found in the majority of texts used in ear-training classes. We sought in vain. Those few texts that do attempt to address issues of larger melodic, harmonic, and rhythmic contexts fail to present specific and effective techniques that students can follow—both in class and on their own—to develop truly effective and serviceable aural skills.

The present textbook seeks to fill this void. In addition to presenting melodies for dictation and sight-singing, we instruct students in *how* to develop the skills and strategies to hear and sight-sing unfamiliar music. In addition to presenting harmonic and rhythmic dictations, students are shown *how* to listen and use their theoretical knowledge to comprehend the harmonic and rhythmic contexts in which they are listening.

Going far beyond traditional topics and approaches, *Functional Hearing* incorporates numerous unique and groundbreaking ways to train the ears of developing musicians and to encourage them to acquire a high level of aural skill. Principal among these features are:

◆ An integrated approach, strongly dependent upon the perception and awareness of tendency and function, in which ear training and sight-singing are taught within specific diatonic contexts

◆ Separate units devoted exclusively to teaching specific techniques for taking melodic, harmonic, and rhythmic dictation

◆ Pitch puzzles, pitch patterns, and error detections that help students bridge the gap between their cognitive and aural perception of intervals

◆ Use of familiar melodies as a means of remembering the sounds of intervals and establishing a diatonic context

◆ Detailed explanations of composite rhythms: how to perceive and notate them, including the use of the least-common-multiples method

- Unique home exercises that challenge students to think about and practice the skills presented and drilled in class

- Several units devoted to hearing, analyzing, and performing sequences

- A logical and systematic approach to transposing at sight and reading standard instrumental clefs that relates these skills to each other

- Careful descriptions of asymmetric meters and subdivisions

- Specialized instructions for writing, hearing, and performing canons, hockets, and catches

- An organizational plan that facilitates coordination with the general outline of most undergraduate theory courses

- Compatibility with all commonly used syllable systems

- A convenient lay-flat binding that allows the book to stay open on a music stand

- Generous amounts of blank staves bound on perforated pages for convenient use in class and homework assignments

• • • • •

The importance of the discipline of aural skills is reflected by its inclusion in virtually every college music curriculum in the country. Though the teaching of aural skills is one of the most important tasks facing the college-level music educator, it is often one of the most problematic, sometimes the most feared. Some of this apprehension undoubtedly arises from the lack of effective pedagogical tools that can reliably and more completely address the needs of the discipline. An organized text with clear goals and the solid and proven pedagogical methods to achieve them is of critical importance to teachers and students alike.

As the result of our observations and analyses of the challenges facing our students in preparing for careers as teachers and per-formers at all levels of these professions, we have devised an approach to teaching aural skills that is both effective and exciting, based on the concept of "functional hearing." This concept holds that musical sounds are relatively meaningless when separated from a specific musical context. The most likely context in which students will initially attempt to hear sounds is a tonal one, since this is the context in which they have the greatest number of musical experiences. If none other is provided by the instructor, students will naturally furnish a tonal context for the sounds they hear. And because the greater part of their post-secondary educa-tion also emphasizes tonal music, one should encourage and re-ward such a contextual association, rather than ignore it, fight it, or pretend that it doesn't exist. Furthermore, the appreciation and comprehension of nontonal contexts can actually be heightened through a thorough awareness of tonality, since twentieth-century nontonal systems are, for the most part, built upon the great Western European tonal tradition.

Functional Hearing is intended to be used in any aural skills sequence lasting from two to seven semesters, depending on the time available (or allocated) and the abilities of the students being taught. The book should also be considered for use as a companion text in most traditional courses in music theory. We have found that students are very receptive to an approach that closely links the development of theoretical knowledge with the development of the ability to hear and perceive internally that which is being studied and analyzed.

The material in *Functional Hearing* is divided into seven areas. Each area is organized around a broad category of related skills, which, in turn, are drilled and mastered in numerous units that progress cumulatively to the end while focusing on short, readily accomplished tasks. It has been shown repeatedly that students achieve the greatest success when they are given the opportunity to progress in small, well-defined steps. As instructors of aural skills, we know that this approach also makes our teaching more focused.

● ● ● ● ●

In Area I, students are asked to hear, recognize, and identify scale degrees and their tendencies within the context of the most familiar major and minor scales. Next, **intervals** are introduced with continual reference to the scales from which they spring, since the "meaning" of any particular interval (and thus its "sound") is not the result of its quality alone, but also arises from the characteristics of the scale degrees of which it is made. The vast majority of these exercises and examples are accomplished within a tonal context.

Octaves and perfect fifths are introduced first, as they are the most important functionally and therefore are the most natural and the easiest to hear and sing. After introducing the concept of interval inversion (unisons and perfect fourths), we proceed along the natural overtone series to thirds (with sixths) and seconds (with sevenths), and finally introduce the more "artificial" augmented and diminished intervals that result from seven-note scales and well-tempered tuning systems. Intervals are approached melodically (horizontally) at first, to instill confidence in students when they are called upon to recognize and perform the scalar components.

Throughout Area I, in preparation for the practice of **sight-singing**, students are asked to study, analyze, and learn "melodic constructs," created specifically for this text, which progressively incorporate intervals in the order being studied and drilled, according to their basic functional character. Our melodic constructs are best understood as etudes that must be mastered before one attempts to sight-sing from the literature.

Our conviction, confirmed through considerable experience, is that even though melodies consisting of the smallest intervals may seem *easier* to sight-sing at first, they do not ultimately work to produce an effective aural perception of the functional aspects of the individual scale degrees in tonal melodies. This has given us the confidence to break with past traditions of presenting intervals according to increasing size rather than according to functional significance. The ultimate result is greater accuracy and success in sight-singing, which students practice for the first time in Unit 24.

Triads are introduced in Area II, again in a functional context. Students are trained to listen for quality, function, and, later, inversion of the triads they hear. Hearing and knowing the quality of a triad is a valuable and necessary skill for any musician, but being able to hear concurrently the *function* of a particular triad is much more valuable. Knowing that one is listening to V rather than I or IV is far more descriptive than simply knowing one is hearing a major triad. Students are first taught how to hear triads and their inversions in the context of relatively brief harmonic progressions. From this point we develop the students' abilities to comprehend the sounds of more complex harmonies as we consider, in Areas III and IV, **seventh chords**, chords with secondary functions, and modulations. Suggestions on how to identify certain sonorities and relate them to others are made throughout the text.

Dictation of four-part homophony is introduced in Area V after students have developed the aural acuity to hear and identify multiple aspects of harmonic progressions, as has been outlined. The decision of when to introduce the process of writing down four parts from dictation was also informed by our classroom experience. In general, we feel that this activity is undertaken prematurely in most schools—that is, long before students can easily hear the function and quality of the chords they encounter in progressions. To attempt the writing of four parts before achieving that level of aural discernment inevitably forces most students to guess about the inner voices without a concrete method for listening to and perceiving four-part textures. Furthermore, by the time students have made their way through Areas III and IV and have encountered seventh chords, secondary functions, and modulations, their ears should be more experienced and more sensitive to subtleties of different sounds so that actually predicting and hearing inner parts should be much easier.

In Area VI, the identification of both functional and nonfunctional **chromaticism** (modal borrowing, decorative chromaticism, altered harmony) is introduced and drilled with techniques similar to those used earlier in the text until the students' aural skills are sufficiently honed to permit the step into the less-familiar complexities of the late nineteenth and early twentieth centuries in Area VII.

The study of **rhythm** is also presented in a progressively graded way throughout the text and is seldom considered without reference to pitch. One- and two-part rhythmic studies that incorporate such diverse devices as syncopation, threes against twos, dual-identity divisions, asymmetric meters, and asymmetric subdivisions are gradually introduced in the text after the student has encountered a wide variety of uncomplicated rhythmic patterns in all of the common simple and compound meters. Specific techniques for accurately performing rhythms and writing them down from dictation, as well as understanding polyrhythms, are given. The concept of hearing and writing the composite rhythm of two or more simultaneously sounding parts is stressed throughout.

● ● ● ● ●

Despite theories and misconceptions to the contrary, with few exceptions, every student can develop his or her aural skills well beyond their innate levels. The principal goal of *Functional Hearing* is to make this development not only possible but probable by providing effective new avenues into the processes of learning and developing aural skills.

Supplemental Resources

Instructor's Manual

An Instructor's Manual (ISBN: 1-880157-58-6) is available to accompany *Functional Hearing*. In addition to containing a keyboard score for each dictation called for in the student text, the instructor's manual has answers for every exercise requiring a student response, detailed explanations of the purposes and desired effects of many exercises, discussions of the rhetorical and specific questions posed in the text, and numerous suggestions for presenting the material. Any of the dictations provided in the Instructor's Manual may be adapted for use as a quiz, using the format of a class drill, a home exercise, or that of the instructor's choosing. Sufficient examples exist for the instructor to give multiple drills and exercises in class and still have fresh material at hand for testing.

Software

Knowing that many teachers and students appreciate having the option of using interactive software to supplement their class work and homework, the authors have arranged for special adaptations of two frequently used ear training programs, **MacGAMUT**™ and **Practica Musica**™. These are versatile and user-friendly Macintosh-compatible programs which work well with personal computers in a variety of configurations. (Ars Nova has indicated that a Windows '95 version of Practica Musica™ is being prepared and may be ready before the end of 1997.) Both software companies have agreed to make available on the Internet a set of supplemental materials for their programs that will make them more directly compatible with the methods of instruction encountered in *Functional Hearing*.

MacGAMUT™ Music Software International may be contacted by phone at 800-305-8731 or by fax at 614-263-9359. Information about Practica Musica™ may be obtained from Ars Nova Software at 800-445-4866, by fax at 206-889-8699, or from the World Wide Web at http://www.ars-nova.com.

Information from the Internet

Important information about many aspects of this text, including ordering the text and obtaining the supplemental software materials may be found on the Web page for Functional Hearing at http://www.ruf.rice.edu/~gottsch/functional. To ask questions or to offer comments about *Functional Hearing,* please contact the authors at gottsch@rice.edu or contact the publisher at the address given on the copyright page.

Acknowledgments

Numerous students, colleagues, mentors, and friends have unknowingly contributed to the substance and form of this text as it evolved over a period of several years: through a casual comment or a penetrating question, they helped us to focus our thoughts and to define our purposes in bringing this text into being. We would like to thank them for their valuable assistance.

We wish to express special appreciation to a number of people who were pivotal in helping us to shape our ideas and methods: Hali Fieldman, University of Massachusetts; Gerald Frank, Oklahoma State University at Stillwater; Reed Holmes, University of Texas at San Antonio; Ann McNamee, Swarthmore College; and Samuel Magrill, University of Central Oklahoma. These colleagues read the manuscript at various stages of its development and offered wonderfully creative and perspicacious ideas about how to improve what was presented to them.

Thanks are also warmly extended to: Mary Sieber, who with grace and perseverance helped us in the proofreading of galley and page proofs; George Burt, Pierre Jalbert, Samuel Jones, Richard Lavenda, and Ellsworth Milburn, our colleagues in the Composition/ Theory Department of the Shepherd School of Music, who supported us with their continuing interest and advice; Rick Russell, Reynaldo Ochoa, and the Art Institute of Houston who provided expert technical assistance; and Berry Bowen, Paul English, Stephen R. Ganns, Mary Gottschalk, Ann Kloeckner, Fred Modica, and Elissa Palacios, family members and friends who gave unstintingly of their time and encouragement throughout the writing and publishing process.

To David Adickes goes our inestimable gratitude for his unrestricted permission to use his paintings, which enliven and dignify this book.

AREA

I

UNITS 1–24

*Hearing
the
Essential
Elements
of
Music*

Fundamentals

UNIT 1

Major and Minor Scales

*T*he concept of **scale** plays a significant role in the music of all cultures, both Western and non-Western. There is a wide variety of scales, each describing the intervallic relationships among the **pitches** of any given composition. Thus, a scale is a theoretical tool, derived from music itself, which helps us to organize and understand the musical elements of a particular composition, genre, style, or tradition.

The Chromatic Scale

In the Western tradition, most of our music can be described by the twelve **half steps** (**semitones**) that make up the **chromatic scale**. For example, if we choose the chromatic scale beginning on C (and we could choose any one of the twelve half steps as our **tonic** or central pitch), the letter names of this scale, ascending and descending, would be as shown in Table I.1.

By assigning a different syllable to each half step in the chromatic scale, the movable-*do* **solfège system** allows us to reinforce the distinct **functional** character of each pitch in the scale. The functional character of each pitch depends on the specific tonal context under consideration. In Table I.2, solfège syllables are given for the letter names.

The most common scales in **tonal** music—the **major** and **minor** scales—are made up of varying numbers of half steps between each

TABLE I.1 *The chromatic scale beginning on* C, *ascending and descending*

Ascending →												
C	C♯	D	D♯	E	F	F♯	G	G♯	A	A♯	B	(C)
								← Descending				
(C)	D♭	D	E♭	E	F	G♭	G	A♭	A	B♭	B	C

TABLE I.2 *Solfège syllables for the chromatic scale beginning on* C

Ascending →												
C	C♯	D	D♯	E	F	F♯	G	G♯	A	A♯	B	(C)
do	*di*	*re*	*ri*	*mi*	*fa*	*fi*	*so*	*si*	*la*	*li*	*ti*	*(do)*
								← Descending				
(C)	D♭	D	E♭	E	F	G♭	G	A♭	A	B♭	B	C
(do)	*ra*	*re*	*me*	*mi*	*fa*	*se*	*so*	*le*	*la*	*te*	*ti*	*do*

C	D	E	F	G	A	B	C
do	*re*	*mi*	*fa*	*so*	*la*	*ti*	*do*
$\hat{1}$	$\hat{2}$	$\hat{3}$	$\hat{4}$	$\hat{5}$	$\hat{6}$	$\hat{7}$	$\hat{1}$ (or $\hat{8}$)

TABLE I.3 *The major scale*

step of the scale (**scale degree**). Carefully compare the major scale given in Table I.3 with the chromatic scale given in Table I.2 to see where they coincide and where they differ. Both ascending and descending forms are the same. With respect to *do*, we indicate the relative position of each scale step with an Arabic number. By placing a caret (^) above each of these numbers, we create a third way to refer to specific scale degrees in the major and minor scales. For example, $\hat{5}$ should be read "scale-degree five." This also helps to reduce confusion among the many other uses of Arabic numbers.

Thus, the familiar major scale is defined by two half steps (a **whole step**) between each scale degree except between $\hat{3}$ and $\hat{4}$ and between $\hat{7}$ and $\hat{8}$, in both of which pairs the scale degrees are separated by a single half step, as is indicated in Tables I.3 and I.4 by ⌄.

THE NATURAL MINOR SCALE

C	D	E♭	F	G	A♭	B♭	C
do	*re*	*me*	*fa*	*so*	*le*	*te*	*do*
$\hat{1}$	$\hat{2}$	$\hat{3}$	$\hat{4}$	$\hat{5}$	$\hat{6}$	$\hat{7}$	$\hat{1}$

THE HARMONIC MINOR SCALE

C	D	E♭	F	G	A♭	B	C
do	*re*	*me*	*fa*	*so*	*le*	*ti*	*do*
$\hat{1}$	$\hat{2}$	$\hat{3}$	$\hat{4}$	$\hat{5}$	$\hat{6}$	$\hat{7}$	$\hat{1}$

THE MELODIC MINOR SCALE

Ascending →

C	D	E♭	F	G	A	B	C
do	*re*	*me*	*fa*	*so*	*la*	*ti*	*do*
$\hat{1}$	$\hat{2}$	$\hat{3}$	$\hat{4}$	$\hat{5}$	$\hat{6}$	$\hat{7}$	$\hat{1}$

← *Descending*

C	D	E♭	F	G	A♭	B♭	C
do	*re*	*me*	*fa*	*so*	*le*	*te*	*do*
$\hat{1}$	$\hat{2}$	$\hat{3}$	$\hat{4}$	$\hat{5}$	$\hat{6}$	$\hat{7}$	$\hat{1}$

TABLE I.4 *Three forms of the minor scale*

SCALE DEGREE	FUNCTIONAL NAME
$\hat{1}$	Tonic
$\hat{2}$	Supertonic
$\hat{3}$	Mediant
$\hat{4}$	Subdominant
$\hat{5}$	Dominant
$\hat{6}$	Submediant
$\hat{7}$	Leading tone

TABLE I.5 *Common functional names of diatonic scale degrees*

The three forms of the minor scale—the **natural minor scale**, the **harmonic minor scale**, and the **melodic minor scale**—are each closely related to the major scale. In comparison with the structure of the major scale, all three forms of the minor scale share the lowered third scale degree, creating a whole step between $\hat{3}$ and $\hat{4}$ and a half step between $\hat{2}$ and $\hat{3}$. The varying forms of the minor scale differ in their sixth and seventh scale degrees, as shown in Table I.4.

These scales have been established over centuries by analyzing the music of the Western tonal tradition. The variations of the minor scale come directly from the ways in which composers have written their music in minor keys.

Music derived solely from the seven notes of a given major or minor scale is termed **diatonic** music. That is, diatonic music is made up exclusively of pitches with a distinct function in a given scale. As listed in Table I.5, each step of any of these scales, whether major or minor, is known by the special name indicating the function of that degree.

CLASS DRILLS & HOME EXERCISES

At the present time, you will be asked to concentrate exclusively on those sounds that constitute the diatonic tonal system. (Chromaticism of various types will be studied later in the text.) By *diatonic identity* we mean a scale degree, letter name, or solfège syllable.

1 Your instructor will play a series of pitches in a variety of **registers** at the keyboard. As quickly as you can, match each pitch with a **neutral syllable** (that is, a syllable without a diatonic association) in a register that is comfortable for you, and check for accuracy and intonation. Continue this exercise with a classmate outside of class, each student taking turns as "instructor," giving pitches at the keyboard or using any other instrument.

2 Using your knowledge of the structure of the major scale, sing ascending and descending major scales, starting on any pitch. Use whichever system of diatonic identification is suggested by your instructor. Be careful of your intonation, especially when singing the half steps. They will tend to be sharp or flat, depending on the direction in which you are singing the scale.

3 Choose any pitch and mentally assign to that pitch a particular diatonic position in the major scale. (For example, the pitch you have chosen might be assigned *la* or $\hat{6}$.) Beginning with that assigned identity of the chosen pitch, sing the ascending and descending major scales up to the octave above and down to the octave below the starting pitch. If your vocal range does not span two octaves, sing to the extent that you are comfortable.

4 Maintain the same pitch as in Exercise 3, but mentally reassign the diatonic identity of that pitch. (For example, the pitch chosen in Exercise 3 and given the diatonic identity of *la* or $\hat{6}$ should now be mentally reassigned as *re* or $\hat{2}$.) Beginning with the newly assigned identity of the chosen pitch, sing, in turn, the descending and ascending major scales down to the octave below, and then up to the octave above, the starting pitch. Repeat until the same pitch has been given seven different diatonic identities.

EXAMPLE I.1 *The C scale in a variety of major keys*

5 Repeat Exercises 2–4 utilizing all three forms of the minor scale.

6 After identifying a scale and establishing the tonic, your instructor will start on a pitch other than $\hat{1}$ and will play or sing scales or scale fragments, both ascending and descending. You should immediately sing back what you have just heard, using some form of diatonic identification (in the key of G major: B, C, D, E, or $\hat{3}$, $\hat{4}$, $\hat{5}$, $\hat{6}$, or *mi, fa, so, la*).

7 Your instructor will announce a scale (for example, G minor) and establish the tonic. He or she will then play or sing four contiguous pitches,

ascending or descending, in the given key. On staff paper, write the appropriate **clef** and **key signature**, and then write the scale fragment that was played.

8 With reference to any major or minor scale in either the **bass** or **treble clef**, mentally change the key signature and reinterpret the notes of the scale in the new key. Sing those notes in the "new" key with some form of diatonic identification. Some samples of this procedure are given in Examples I.1 and I.2. (In Example I.2, be certain to make the correct alterations to the appropriate pitches, according to the form of minor scale indicated for each line of music.)

EXAMPLE I.2 *The G scale in a variety of minor keys*

9 After identifying a scale and establishing the tonic, your instructor will play or sing a pitch. In a comfortable vocal register, match that pitch, using its diatonic identity. This can be repeated for all scale degrees, while changing the key and tonic from time to time.

10 Given the tonic pitch and mode of a scale, sing with its diatonic identity any pitch requested without audibly singing any intervening pitches. This can be repeated for all scale degrees, while changing the key and tonic from time to time.

11 Sing the following scale fragments, both forward (ascending) and backward (descending).

(a) Begin on a different pitch for each fragment.

(b) Begin on the same pitch for each fragment.

so	*la*	*ti*	*do*	*fa*	*so*	*le*	*ti*	*te*	*do*	*re*	*me*
$\hat{5}$	$\hat{6}$	$\hat{7}$	$\hat{1}$	$\hat{4}$	$\hat{5}$	$\hat{6}$	$\hat{7}$	$\hat{7}$	$\hat{1}$	$\hat{2}$	$\hat{3}$
le	*ti*	*do*	*re*	*so*	*le*	*ti*	*do*	*le*	*te*	*do*	*re*
$\hat{6}$	$\hat{7}$	$\hat{1}$	$\hat{2}$	$\hat{5}$	$\hat{6}$	$\hat{7}$	$\hat{1}$	$\hat{6}$	$\hat{7}$	$\hat{1}$	$\hat{2}$
la	*ti*	*do*	*re*	*me*	*fa*	*so*	*le*	*do*	*re*	*mi*	*fa*
$\hat{6}$	$\hat{7}$	$\hat{1}$	$\hat{2}$	$\hat{3}$	$\hat{4}$	$\hat{5}$	$\hat{6}$	$\hat{1}$	$\hat{2}$	$\hat{3}$	$\hat{4}$
so	*le*	*te*	*do*	*fa*	*so*	*le*	*te*	*re*	*mi*	*fa*	*so*
$\hat{5}$	$\hat{6}$	$\hat{7}$	$\hat{1}$	$\hat{4}$	$\hat{5}$	$\hat{6}$	$\hat{7}$	$\hat{2}$	$\hat{3}$	$\hat{4}$	$\hat{5}$
me	*fa*	*so*	*la*	*ti*	*do*	*re*	*mi*	*fa*	*so*	*la*	*ti*
$\hat{3}$	$\hat{4}$	$\hat{5}$	$\hat{6}$	$\hat{7}$	$\hat{1}$	$\hat{2}$	$\hat{3}$	$\hat{4}$	$\hat{5}$	$\hat{6}$	$\hat{7}$
ti	*do*	*re*	*me*	*re*	*me*	*fa*	*so*	*do*	*re*	*me*	*fa*
$\hat{7}$	$\hat{1}$	$\hat{2}$	$\hat{3}$	$\hat{2}$	$\hat{3}$	$\hat{4}$	$\hat{5}$	$\hat{1}$	$\hat{2}$	$\hat{3}$	$\hat{4}$
mi	*fa*	*so*	*la*								
$\hat{3}$	$\hat{4}$	$\hat{5}$	$\hat{6}$								

Rhythm

UNIT 2

Simple Duple and Triple Meters

*T*he traditional listing of the basic elements of all music— pitch, **rhythm**, and **timbre**—communicates the obvious importance of rhythm in any form of musical expression. Indeed, rhythm confers on pitch a temporal structure that transforms it into melody and reinforces its function.

Meter   As a means of emphasizing the distinction between rhythm and **meter**, a pattern of regularly occurring strong and weak pulses, upon which rhythm is based, our study of rhythm in this text will frequently be within the context of pitch. Although it is essential to be completely secure in the basic vocabulary of standard metrical patterns (on which true rhythm is based), your ultimate challenge will be to develop the ability to comprehend quickly and project effectively the larger rhythmic organization and **phrase** structure of the music we perform.

The authors believe that the study of metrical patterns within the context of pitch leads more quickly to the ability to perform with good rhythm and phrasing, and it reinforces the basic vocal and melodic character of most tonal music. Furthermore, singing metrical patterns and exercises helps one to develop a keen sense not only for the beginning of a note, but also for its end and for the character of its duration.

Standard metrical patterns are categorized according to the number of principal **beats** in each measure; **duple meters** are those with two or four principal beats per measure, and **triple meters** have three principal beats in each measure. As Table I.6 indicates, there is a variety of duple and triple meters, each characterized by different note values representing the principal beat. Each meter has a specific **time signature**, which describes the metrical structure of each measure.

As you know from your previous musical experience, time signatures resemble mathematical fractions (but without lines separating the numerators and denominators). In the simple meters listed in Table I.6, the denominator indicates the value of the note that receives the principal beat (2 = half; 4 = quarter; 8 = eighth). The numerator gives the number of beats per measure. (The case for compound meters is somewhat different; this will be discussed later.)

TIME SIGNATURE	VALUE OF BEAT	BEATS PER MEASURE	DIVISION OF BEAT	SUBDIVISION OF BEAT
2/2 (𝄵)	𝅗𝅥	2	𝅘𝅥 𝅘𝅥	𝅘𝅥𝅮 𝅘𝅥𝅮 𝅘𝅥𝅮 𝅘𝅥𝅮
4/2	𝅗𝅥	4	𝅘𝅥 𝅘𝅥	𝅘𝅥𝅮 𝅘𝅥𝅮 𝅘𝅥𝅮 𝅘𝅥𝅮
2/4	𝅘𝅥	2	𝅘𝅥𝅮 𝅘𝅥𝅮	𝅘𝅥𝅯 𝅘𝅥𝅯 𝅘𝅥𝅯 𝅘𝅥𝅯
4/4 (𝄴)	𝅘𝅥	4	𝅘𝅥𝅮 𝅘𝅥𝅮	𝅘𝅥𝅯 𝅘𝅥𝅯 𝅘𝅥𝅯 𝅘𝅥𝅯
2/8	𝅘𝅥𝅮	2	𝅘𝅥𝅯 𝅘𝅥𝅯	𝅘𝅥𝅰 𝅘𝅥𝅰 𝅘𝅥𝅰 𝅘𝅥𝅰
4/8	𝅘𝅥𝅮	4	𝅘𝅥𝅯 𝅘𝅥𝅯	𝅘𝅥𝅰 𝅘𝅥𝅰 𝅘𝅥𝅰 𝅘𝅥𝅰
3/2	𝅗𝅥	3	𝅘𝅥 𝅘𝅥	𝅘𝅥𝅮 𝅘𝅥𝅮 𝅘𝅥𝅮 𝅘𝅥𝅮
3/4	𝅘𝅥	3	𝅘𝅥𝅮 𝅘𝅥𝅮	𝅘𝅥𝅯 𝅘𝅥𝅯 𝅘𝅥𝅯 𝅘𝅥𝅯
3/8	𝅘𝅥𝅮	3	𝅘𝅥𝅯 𝅘𝅥𝅯	𝅘𝅥𝅰 𝅘𝅥𝅰 𝅘𝅥𝅰 𝅘𝅥𝅰
3/16	𝅘𝅥𝅯	3	𝅘𝅥𝅰 𝅘𝅥𝅰	𝅘𝅥𝅱 𝅘𝅥𝅱 𝅘𝅥𝅱 𝅘𝅥𝅱

TABLE I.6 *Simple meters*

CLASS DRILLS & HOME EXERCISES

The following exercises are designed to drill several common patterns found in the simple meters presented in Table I.6, while reviewing the scales that you encountered in Unit 1. Treat each excerpt as a complete piece of music; once you have begun, do not stop. Choose a tempo that will allow you to negotiate the syllables, letters, or numbers with which you choose to identify each pitch, without hesitation or errors. Work for complete accuracy as early in the process as possible. If you find that you have made a mistake, you are probably going too fast. Begin again at a slower tempo. Only after you have completed each line accurately should

you begin to increase the tempo gradually as you repeat each of the lines. In this manner you will perform securely and will solidify your familiarity with the various metrical patterns.

Conduct as you sing. This will give your mind physical reinforcement of where the beats in each measure lie. Begin now to train your eyes to see each beat of the measure, regardless of how the beat is divided or subdivided. Discipline yourself to keep the beat steady. (Conducting will also help to achieve this.) If you happen to make a mistake within one beat, move on without missing the next beat.

Learning to Hear Intervals

UNIT 3

Perfect Octaves, Unisons, Fifths, and Fourths

Intervals

The term **interval** refers to the relationship between two pitches, whether sounded melodically (one after the other) or harmonically (simultaneously). Regardless of whether two pitches are heard melodically or harmonically, the size of the interval separating the two sounds does not change. The interval separating any two pitches is traditionally given by the number of scale degrees spanned by the two notes, as shown in Table I.7.

PITCHES HEARD	INTERVAL
do–do (*do, re, mi, fa, so, la, ti, do*)	Octave
di–do (*di, ti, la, so, fa, mi, re, do*)	Octave
F–C (F, G, A, B, C)	5th
$\hat{7}$–$\hat{4}$ ($\hat{7}, \hat{1}, \hat{2}, \hat{3}, \hat{4}$)	5th

TABLE I.7 *Various sizes of octaves and fifths*

Interval Quality

Since the distances between successive scale degrees do not span the same number of half steps (as we saw in Unit 1), special adjectives are used to describe intervals with regard to the **quality**, or relative amount of tonal space (usually measured in the number of half steps), spanned by the two pitches heard. These adjectives, *perfect*, *major*, *minor*, *diminished*, and *augmented*, are used to describe intervallic content in both the major and minor scales.[1]

The term **perfect** (P) is reserved for describing the intervals of an octave, a fifth, and their inversions (discussed on pages 11–12) and derives from the pure sounds that were characteristic of these intervals in older tuning systems. The interval of a perfect octave (P8) sounds like the relationship between $\hat{1}$ and $\hat{8}$, which is twelve half steps higher than $\hat{1}$. When an octave is reduced by one half step, to a total of eleven, it is called a **diminished** octave (d8); when it is increased by one half step, to thirteen, it is called an **augmented** octave (A8). Likewise, a perfect fifth (P5) is defined as the interval that sounds like the relationship between $\hat{1}$ and $\hat{5}$, spanning seven half steps. If the 5th spans only six half steps, the interval is said to be a diminished fifth (d5). When a 5th spans eight half steps, the

---

1. We will begin to discuss major and minor intervals in Unit 6; diminished and augmented diatonic intervals will be discussed in Unit 14.

interval is called an augmented fifth (A5). Table I.8 lists these various qualities.

Pitches Heard	Interval	Number of Half Steps	Quality
do–do (*do, re, mi, fa, so, la, ti, do*)	Octave	12	Perfect
G–G♭ (G, A, B, C, D, E, F, G♭)	Octave	11	Diminished
di–do (*di, ti, la, so, fa, mi, re, do*)	Octave	13	Augmented
F–C (F, G, A, B, C)	5th	7	Perfect
$\hat{7}$–$\hat{4}$ ($\hat{7}, \hat{1}, \hat{2}, \hat{3}, \hat{4}$)	5th	6	Diminished
D–A♯ (D, E, F, G, A♯)	5th	8	Augmented

Table I.8 *Quality of various octaves and fifths*

Perfect Octaves and Perfect Fifths

Intervals of a perfect octave and a perfect 5th occur diatonically at positions other than between $\hat{1}$ and $\hat{8}$ and between $\hat{1}$ and $\hat{5}$ in both major and minor scales. All the possible diatonic locations of these intervals are summarized in Table I.9.

To facilitate your understanding of the structure of the most common scales and of the nature of the intervals between the pitches that constitute these scales,[2] we suggest that you memorize *all* of the intervallic relationships in Table I.9 as soon as possible. A knowledge of these relationships will greatly enhance your ability to advance to higher levels of functional hearing.

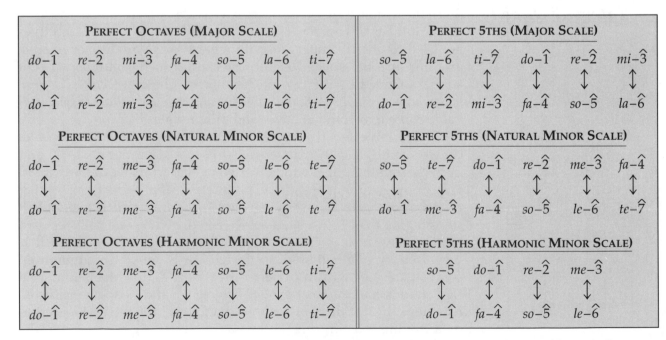

Table I.9 *Diatonic locations of perfect octaves and perfect fifths; double-headed arrows are placed between the syllables of each interval to indicate that the interval is of identical size and quality regardless of the direction sung.*

2. Unit 73 treats modes and less common scales.

CLASS DRILLS & HOME EXERCISES

1 Why do we usually use the half step to measure the size of an interval?

2 Your instructor will name two scale degrees, letter names, or solfège syllables, indicating which is the lower of the two. Identify the specified interval instantly as either a perfect octave or perfect 5th. Then quickly name each scale degree, letter, or syllable between the given two.

3 Given a pitch, match that pitch vocally, and then sing a perfect octave or perfect 5th on a neutral syllable above or below the given pitch, as instructed.

4 Given a pitch together with some form of diatonic identification, match the pitch vocally with its diatonic identity, and sing a perfect octave or perfect 5th above or below the given pitch, as instructed, using the diatonic identity of the second pitch.

5 After establishing a tonic, your instructor will play (melodically) two pitches that form a perfect octave or perfect 5th. Sing both pitches in the order heard, using their correct diatonic identities.

6 After establishing a tonic, your instructor will name two scale degrees, letter names, or solfège syllables that form a perfect octave or perfect 5th. Without first hearing those notes, sing the correct pitches in the order and direction requested, using their corresponding diatonic identities.

7 A single pitch (other than the tonic) will be played and given a diatonic identity. Two more pitches that form a perfect octave or perfect 5th will then be played melodically. State the interval formed by the last two pitches and sing all three pitches, indicating their diatonic identities.

8 In each of the following rows, sing the five pairs of pitches indicated by the solfège syllables and numbers. (Each pair is independent of the others in that row.) Translate from one system to the other: that is, given numbers, sing the corresponding solfège syllables, and, given solfège syllables, sing the corresponding numbers. With the tonic triad or the diatonic scale, establish a new tonic, as indicated, at the beginning of each row. You may need to reaffirm the tonic before the end of the row, but do so only as often as is really necessary. In each row, go as far as possible before reestablishing the tonic; this may not be necessary at all. However, you should be constantly singing the tonic and dominant pitches to yourself throughout this exercise.

F major	$do\uparrow do$	$fa\downarrow fa$	$\hat{5}\downarrow\hat{1}$	$\hat{3}\uparrow\hat{7}$	$la\uparrow la$
D♭ major	$re\uparrow re$	$\hat{5}\uparrow\hat{5}$	$la\downarrow re$	$\hat{1}\downarrow\hat{4}$	$la\uparrow mi$
A major	$mi\downarrow mi$	$\hat{3}\uparrow\hat{7}$	$la\uparrow mi$	$\hat{5}\uparrow\hat{2}$	$la\downarrow la$
G major	$so\downarrow so$	$ti\downarrow mi$	$\hat{6}\downarrow\hat{2}$	$\hat{1}\uparrow\hat{1}$	$\hat{6}\uparrow\hat{3}$
C minor *harmonic*	$\hat{6}\downarrow\hat{6}$	$\hat{5}\uparrow\hat{2}$	$\hat{4}\uparrow\hat{1}$	$me\downarrow le$	$do\uparrow so$
B minor *harmonic*	$\hat{2}\downarrow\hat{5}$	$\hat{3}\downarrow\hat{6}$	$do\uparrow so$	$ti\uparrow ti$	$fa\uparrow do$
F♯ minor *natural*	$te\uparrow fa$	$me\downarrow le$	$\hat{7}\downarrow\hat{3}$	$do\downarrow fa$	$\hat{2}\downarrow\hat{2}$
G minor *natural*	$\hat{7}\uparrow\hat{7}$	$\hat{2}\downarrow\hat{5}$	$me\uparrow te$	$so\downarrow do$	$fa\uparrow fa$

Inversions Two **simple intervals** are said to be **inversions** of each other if they combine to form an octave.[3] Numerically, the sum of an interval and its inversion is always 9. For example, the inversion of an octave (8) is a unison (1); here, 8 + 1 = 9. Similarly, the inversion of a 5th is a 4th (5 + 4 = 9). The phenomenon of intervallic inversion is independent of the order in which the intervals are combined. Thus, the inversion of a 4th is a 5th.

Inversions of perfect intervals are themselves perfect intervals. Thus, the inversion of a perfect octave (twelve half steps) is a perfect unison (0 half steps); the inversion of a perfect 5th (seven half steps)

---

3. A simple interval is one whose size is no larger than an octave.

Lower Octave	Reference Pitch	Upper Octave
E ← → A ← → E		
P4 · P5		
fa ← → *do* ← → *fa*		
P5 · P4		
le ← → *me* ← → *le*		
P5 · P4		
$\hat{6}$ ← → $\hat{6}$ ← → $\hat{6}$		
P1 · P8		

TABLE I.10 *Some interval inversions*

is a perfect 4th (five half steps). These examples illustrate another rather obvious feature of interval inversion, that the number of half steps in an interval added to the number in its inversion is always 12, which is the number of half steps spanned by an octave. Table I.10 illustrates some interval inversions. What do you think the inversion of an *augmented* octave is? What about that of a diminished 5th? Do you see why these are so?

Note: A unison (P1) may seem to be a somewhat abstract and theoretical interval. In fact, when two voices "sing" a unison on a keyboard instrument, it is impossible to discern this interval; but when the alto and tenor sections of a chorus or the oboe and flute of the orchestra come together on a unison, the expressive power of these sonorities is anything but abstract.

CLASS DRILLS HOME EXERCISES

1 Given a reference pitch, match that pitch vocally (using a neutral syllable), and then sing a perfect 5th above the reference pitch. Return to the reference pitch; sing a perfect 4th below it; then sing a perfect octave above the latter pitch (that is, a perfect 5th above the reference pitch).

2 Given a reference pitch, match that pitch vocally (using a neutral syllable), and then sing a perfect 4th above the reference pitch. Return to the reference pitch; sing a perfect 5th below it; then sing a perfect octave above the latter pitch (that is, a perfect 4th above the reference pitch).

3 Given a reference pitch, match that pitch vocally (using a neutral syllable), and then sing a perfect 5th below the reference pitch. Return to the reference pitch; sing a perfect 4th above it; then sing a perfect octave below the latter pitch (that is, a perfect 5th below the reference pitch).

4 Given a reference pitch, match that pitch vocally (using a neutral syllable), and then sing a perfect 4th below the reference pitch. Return to the reference pitch; sing a perfect 5th above it; then sing a perfect octave below the latter pitch (that is, a perfect 4th below the reference pitch).

5 Given a reference pitch, match that pitch vocally (using a neutral syllable), and then sing a perfect 5th above the reference pitch. From the resultant pitch, sing an ascending perfect 4th; from this latter point, sing a descending perfect 5th; finally, from this last pitch, sing a descending perfect 4th.

6 Given a reference pitch, match that pitch vocally (using a neutral syllable), and then sing a perfect 4th below the reference pitch. From the resultant pitch, sing a descending perfect 5th. From this latter pitch, sing an ascending perfect 4th; finally, from this last pitch, sing an ascending perfect 5th.

7 Repeat Exercises 1–6, but now using diatonic identities for all pitches sung.

8 Repeat Exercises 1–7, but now with small groups of students or with individuals singing every other note.

Perfect Unisons and Perfect Fourths

As with perfect octaves and 5ths, there are numerous possible perfect unison and perfect 4th relationships among the pitches of the diatonic major and minor scales. Perfect unisons can be heard on any diatonic pitch, and perfect 4ths occur between the pitches indicated in Table I.11.

TABLE I.11 *Diatonic locations of perfect fourths*

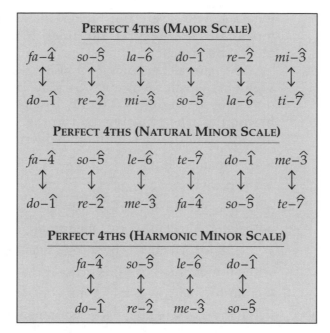

As a means of completely understanding the structure of the most common scales and the nature of the intervals that constitute them, memorize *all* of the intervallic relationships in these scales as soon as possible. Knowing these relationships will greatly facilitate your ability to advance to higher levels of functional hearing.

CLASS DRILLS & HOME EXERCISES

1 Your instructor will name two scale degrees, letter names, or solfège syllables, indicating which is the lower of the two. Identify the specified interval instantly as one of the following:

P4, P8, or P5

Then quickly name each scale degree, letter, or syllable between the given two.

2 Given a reference pitch, match that pitch vocally (using a neutral syllable), and then, as instructed, sing one of the intervals

P4, P8, or P5

above or below the given pitch.

3 Given a reference pitch together with some form of diatonic identification, match that pitch vocally with its diatonic identity, and then, as instructed, sing one of the intervals

P4, P8, or P5

above or below the given pitch, using the diatonic identity of the second pitch.

Intervals and the Overtone Series

All musical sound is created by the vibration of physical matter. When a string is set into motion by drawing a bow across it or when vocal cords vibrate as breath from the lungs passes through them, the actual sound we perceive is the result of both the physical properties and the pitch (or the frequency of the vibration, usually expressed as the number of oscillations per second) of the vibrating material. Although we experience each discrete pitch as a unified entity, a single pitch is actually the simultaneous sounding of a **fundamental** pitch together with a series of higher and weaker frequencies, which in most cases are integral multiples of the frequency of the fundamental pitch itself.

The natural tendency of vibrating bodies to divide into shorter segments which themselves oscillate at their own frequencies produces these **overtones** (literally, "tones over the fundamental"), or **harmonics**. The sensitive ear can discern these overtones in many musical contexts. The **(harmonic) overtone series** consists of:

◆ a fundamental pitch,
◆ the octave above it,
◆ the perfect 5th above that octave,
◆ the second octave above the fundamental,
◆ the major 3rd above the second octave,
◆ the minor 3rd above this major 3rd,
◆ a slightly narrower minor 3rd above the first minor 3rd,
◆ the third octave above the fundamental pitch,

and so on, until the limit of hearing is reached. Actually, the series continues ad infinitum! See Example I.3.

Consonance and Dissonance

It can now be seen that throughout this unit we are limiting ourselves to consideration of the intervals formed by the fundamental and the first three harmonics of any pitch. In an attempt to classify the character of these sounds and that of all other intervals, a tradition of separating the intervals into two principal groups according to their functional and acoustical properties has long been established. In addition to the perfect unison and perfect octave, the tradition has been to classify the intervals constituting the major and minor **triads** (and their inversions) as **consonant**, and all other intervals as **dissonant**. See Table I.12. All the consonant intervals are further classified as in Table I.13.

In an attempt to understand the basis for these categories and to learn how to hear these differences, let us consider the nature of consonance and dissonance.

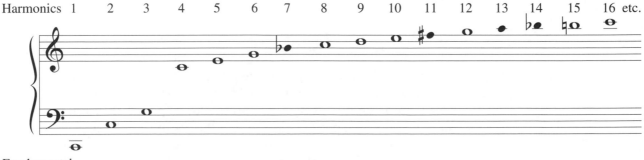

Harmonics 1   2   3   4   5   6   7   8   9   10   11   12   13   14   15   16 etc.

Fundamental

EXAMPLE I.3 *The overtone series*

CONSONANT INTERVALS	DISSONANT INTERVALS
P1	M2 and m2
P8	M7 and m7
P5	P4*
M3 and m3	All augmented and diminished intervals
M6 and m6	

* The perfect 4th is relatively unstable. Although it is the inversion of the perfect 5th, a consonant interval, in this book and in a variety of other musical contexts, perfect 4ths are classified as dissonant intervals.

TABLE I.12 *Consonant intervals and dissonant intervals*

PERFECT CONSONANCES	IMPERFECT CONSONANCES
P8 and P1	M3 and m3
P5	M6 and m6

TABLE I.13 *Types of consonant intervals*

Through our experiences with music from the time we were born, each of us has developed some level of intuitive or subconscious ability to differentiate subtle differences among the many kinds of sounds we hear. Have you ever thought of how you developed this ability? We would now like to explore briefly what provides the basis for the differences we perceive between different sounds and also how different sounds relate to one another. Stated less formally, we might ask, "What makes a perfect 5th a perfect 5th, and what makes it sound different from a perfect 4th?"

Between any two pitches there exist varying degrees of **stability**/instability or repose/activity that reflect the manner in which the two sounds relate, whether heard harmonically or melodically. When two pitches sound together, we often speak of a high or low level of **tension** between the two notes. When two sounds occur in succession, we can express the same phenomenon in terms of a greater or lesser **tendency** of the second to remain in that relationship with the first or to gravitate toward another note.

It is extremely important to understand that these are audible properties, not merely theoretical ones, which all of us can comprehend when listening to musical sounds; with a little effort, we can train our ears to perceive more clearly the character of interaction among sounds. The words *consonant* and *dissonant* are the traditional terms for expressing the tension or tendency between two notes. However, our cultural associations with these words usually do not allow them to connote the multitudinous gradations that actually exist in the realm of musical sound from the most consonant sound (sublime resonance) to the most dissonant one (excruciating cacophony). Therefore, in reality we often speak of *relative* consonance and *relative* dissonance.

Our perception of the character of particular intervals can be strongly influenced by the context in which we hear them. A truly dissonant interval, that is, one that has a strongly active character, can sound less active and more stable in certain situations, while the converse is also possible. Although the contexts can and do change, two pitches, even when heard by themselves, melodically or harmonically, are actually never "out of context" because our ears automatically relate one sound to the other when they occur at short temporal distances. We will first consider melodic intervals and learn to perceive the tendency of a single pitch to achieve a less active association with those sounds related to it during short periods of time.

CLASS DRILLS & HOME EXERCISES

Your instructor will play several melodic intervals for you. Listen to them carefully and answer the following questions *based on what your ears tell you.*

1 Of the two intervals, the perfect unison and the perfect octave, which is the more dissonant? Does the octave really sound dissonant? Can you hear that the twelve-half-step span of the perfect octave confers upon it a special sound that is more active than, and not as stable as, the perfect unison? Listen carefully to each of these sonorities several times. As you proceed through your study of aural skills, try to take the time and spend the energy to learn the character of each of these unique sonorities. On account of the wide variety of sounds (and noises) that our culture forces on us from day to day, it is easy to become insensitive to these subtle, but significant, differences; nevertheless, we *can* hear them.

2 Compare the relative consonance or dissonance of the perfect octave and the perfect 5th. Which one sounds more active? Which one sounds stabler? Why? What characteristics do these intervals have in common?

3 Compare the relative activities of the perfect 4th and the perfect 5th. Which pitch of the more active interval seems less stable?

4 In each of the following rows, sing the five pairs of pitches indicated by the solfège syllables and numbers. (Each pair is independent of the others in that row.) Translate from one system to the other; that is, given numbers, sing the corresponding solfège syllables, and, given solfège syllables, sing the corresponding numbers. With the tonic triad or the diatonic scale, establish a new tonic, as indicated, at the beginning of each row. You may need to reaffirm the tonic before the end of the row, but do so only as often as is really necessary. In each row, go as far as possible before reestablishing the tonic; this may not be necessary at all. However, you should be constantly singing the tonic and dominant pitches to yourself throughout this exercise.

F♯ major	so ↑ so	$\hat{2}$ ↓ $\hat{6}$	mi ↑ la	$\hat{5}$ ↑ $\hat{1}$	do ↓ fa
Eb major	$\hat{7}$ ↓ $\hat{3}$	la ↑ re	$\hat{3}$ ↑ $\hat{3}$	la ↓ mi	$\hat{2}$ ↑ $\hat{5}$
C♯ major	so ↓ re	$\hat{3}$ ↑ $\hat{6}$	ti ↑ mi	$\hat{2}$ ↓ $\hat{5}$	fa ↓ do
C major	$\hat{1}$ ↑ $\hat{4}$	la ↑ mi	$\hat{1}$ ↓ $\hat{5}$	re ↓ la	$\hat{3}$ ↓ $\hat{7}$

E minor *harmonic*	re ↑ so	$\hat{4}$ ↑ $\hat{1}$	do ↓ so	$\hat{3}$ ↓ $\hat{6}$	so ↓ do
Bb minor *harmonic*	$\hat{1}$ ↑ $\hat{4}$	le ↓ me	$\hat{4}$ ↑ $\hat{4}$	so ↑ do	$\hat{5}$ ↓ $\hat{2}$
C♯ minor *natural*	fa ↑ te	$\hat{1}$ ↑ $\hat{4}$	te ↑ me	$\hat{2}$ ↑ $\hat{5}$	le ↑ me
D minor *natural*	$\hat{3}$ ↑ $\hat{7}$	do ↓ fa	$\hat{7}$ ↓ $\hat{4}$	do ↓ so	$\hat{3}$ ↓ $\hat{7}$

5 After establishing a tonic, your instructor will play (melodically) two pitches that form a perfect 4th, perfect octave, or perfect 5th. Sing both pitches in the order heard, using their correct diatonic identities.

6 After establishing a tonic, your instructor will name two scale degrees, letter names, or solfège syllables that form a perfect 4th, perfect octave, or perfect 5th. Without hearing those notes first, sing the correct pitches in the order and direction requested, using their corresponding diatonic identities.

7 The following series of solfège patterns is in the major mode, and the range of each is limited to about one octave. Choose a starting pitch that enables you to sing in a comfortable register, and select a moderate tempo at which you can readily negotiate the given intervals without hesitating or stopping, giving the same duration to each syllable. In those patterns not ending on *do*, sing the tonic when you are through.

do	↓ so	↓ do	↑ fa	↑ do	↓ do
ti	↓ mi	↑ la	↓ la	↑ re	↑ so
do	↑ fa	↑ do	↓ so	↓ do	↑ do
do	↑ so	↑ do	↓ fa	↓ do	↑ do
do	↓ fa	↓ do	↑ so	↑ do	↓ do
so	↓ re	↑ la	↓ la	↑ mi	↑ ti

Practice increasing your fluency with the intervals and solfège syllables in these patterns while drilling different *rhythmic* patterns. Rather than singing each pitch with the same duration, vary the rhythmic patterns in various ways. Invent your own patterns. Be creative. No matter what your pattern is, your fluency with the material as well as your flexibility as a musician will improve.

Create your own solfège patterns and bring them to class so that your classmates can realize them. Discuss what makes some of these patterns easier to sing than others. What do the easier ones have in common?

8 Repeat Exercise 7, but with small groups of students or individuals singing every other note.

9 Analyze familiar classical, folk, and contemporary tunes to find examples of ascending and descending perfect octaves, perfect 5ths, and perfect 4ths within a specific diatonic context. Use the results of your analysis to remember the sound and character of these intervals. Usually, opening lines or refrains are the easiest to recall. In addition to the quality and size of an interval, you should be able to hear and identify where this interval lies in the diatonic scale. For instance, you should know with which perfect 4th in the major scale "Here Comes the Bride" begins.

Here are some suggested tunes to get you started:

P8: "Somewhere over the Rainbow"

P5: "Twinkle, Twinkle, Little Star"

P4: "Here Comes the Bride"
"I've Been Working on the Railroad"
Eine Kleine Nachtmusik

Dictation

UNIT
4

Guidelines for Melodic Dictation

*W*riting down music from dictation is a means to an end, not an end in itself! Certainly, you will almost never be asked to do this during an audition or a job interview. However, writing down the music that you hear is one of the few means you have to demonstrate accurately how well you hear what you listen to. One can also accomplish a great deal of ear training in the process of dictation, so there are multiple advantages. To ensure that you always do your best, we offer the following suggestions, techniques, and hints, which have been used by numerous students in the past.

If you already have experience in dictation and have developed your own system and techniques that work, that's great! There's no need to change what is already working for you. The goal is accuracy, no matter whose system you use. Perhaps you will be able to refine your ability to write down what you hear by applying some of the techniques that follow.

If you have little or no experience in this process, we recommend that you at first follow the guidelines we have assembled here; then, as you gain experience, you may wish to modify or replace certain methods with others that work better for you.

Step 1. Score Setup

Before your instructor begins a dictation, you will be given four essential pieces of information:

1. *The length of the dictation.* Mark your staff with bar lines to produce the exact number of measures you will need. Use as many lines as necessary to give yourself enough room in each measure.

2. *The clef for the dictation.* Sometimes the clef *indicated* will be different from that actually *heard*. Mark each staff line with the proper clef.

3. *The key for the dictation.* Sometimes the key *indicated* will be different from that actually *heard*. Mark each staff line with the proper key signature.

4. *The meter of the music.* Mark the first staff with the time signature. Unless it changes during the piece, the time signature is not customarily written on every staff.

The staff for a four-measure piece in $\frac{3}{4}$ meter, taken in B♭ major in the treble clef, will be prepared as follows: The clef, key, and meter of the music are traditionally placed in this order (which is alphabetical order) from left to right on the score, as in Example I.4.

We further recommend that before you begin, you add light vertical lines through each staff to represent the position of the principal beats in each measure. As will be explained, this preparation facilitates using a flexible shorthand method of quickly and accurately notating on the staff what you have heard. With these indications of the metrical framework, your staff should now appear as in Example I.5.

Step 2.   First Hearing: Establishing the Key

Your instructor will play the tonic triad, the diatonic scale, or the tonic and dominant pitches. This is your opportunity to establish *actively* the key of the music you are about to hear. As you may know, the best way to confirm any key is with repetition of the tonic and dominant. Silently sing the tonic and dominant pitches to yourself in succession several times. Sing the diatonic scale, ascending and descending. **Arpeggiate** the tonic and dominant triads, ascending and descending; that is, sing the members of the triad in succession. As you listen, relate everything you hear to the tonic and dominant scale degrees.

Step 3.   First Hearing: Setting the Tempo

Your instructor will give one or two complete measures "for nothing." During the preparatory measures, you must concentrate and *actively* internalize the tempo of the given beat. You must not only firmly

EXAMPLE I.4   *A staff with the four essentials prepared: number of measures, clef, key, and meter*

EXAMPLE I.5   *The prepared staff with all beats shown*

establish these parameters, but should try also to imagine what the division and subdivisions of the beat will sound and feel like, given the present tempo. It sounds like a lot to do in a brief period, but a bit of practice will show that this is easily done. Furthermore, this preparatory mental work should prove invaluable in recognizing the elements of what you are about to hear. Mentally, keep the beat going at the established tempo. Tap or clap silently, or conduct throughout the dictation as a means of relating what you hear to the metrical structure of the music.

Step 4. First Hearing: Listening without Writing

We strongly recommend listening without writing during the first complete hearing of the music. This approach will allow you to accomplish two important tasks most efficiently:

1. Begin to internalize the music by singing back to yourself what you hear. Even if you are initially uncertain about how to notate everything you hear, having the music firmly laid down in your mind's "tape recorder" will allow you to replay those segments repeatedly as you begin to represent the music on the staff you have prepared. Throughout the dictation, continue to internalize as many measures of the music as you can.

2. During this time, listen *actively* to very basic aspects of the music as it is being played. This means having a checklist, either written out or kept in mind, which can be consulted while listening. This procedure draws your attention to many details of the music that will ultimately help you to write accurately what you have heard. The main point is that you never want to get into the habit of listening passively. When you ask yourself questions as you listen, you find the answers to those questions in addition to many others. Here is a basic checklist of questions while listening. Can you add to this list other items for which you listen regularly?

    (a) How many rests are there? Do these rests occur on or off the principal beats of the measure?

    (b) What is the most common division of the beat? How many times do you hear durations that are longer than the beat?

    (c) Where are the highest and lowest pitches of the piece heard?

    (d) Is the melodic motion predominantly by step or by leaps? If there are leaps, are they relatively large or usually small?

    (e) How many different times is the tonic heard? the dominant?

    (f) How many instances are there when a single pitch is repeated? How many repetitions of that pitch occur? Do repeated notes occur in conjunction with other melodic/rhythmic events?

    (g) Are there repetitions of other melodic types or of rhythmic types?

    (h) Is the final pitch of the piece the same as the first pitch?

Step 5. Multiple Hearings: Writing Down What You Hear

As you begin to write on the staff, try to represent the rhythm first. This will give you a framework within which you can quickly represent the pitches. Example I.6 lists some convenient shorthand marks that will help you sketch in what you hear as you go along. Do not try to put stems on the marks yet. That is a finishing detail.

(a) A note of one beat's duration

(b) Two notes of equal duration within one beat

(c) Three notes of equal duration within one beat

(d) Four notes of equal duration within one beat

(e) Prolongation of a single note into the following beat

(f) A rest of one beat's duration

(g) A rest of half a beat followed by two notes of equal duration

(h) Two notes of equal duration followed by a rest of half a beat

(i) One short note followed by one long note within one beat

(j) One long note followed by one short note within one beat

EXAMPLE I.6 *Some suggested shorthand marks*

Example I.7 shows how a very simple dictation might look in shorthand form after a few hearings. (Remember that on the first hearing, we listen!)

EXAMPLE I.7 *Shorthand representation of a simple dictation*

Our staff would look like Example I.8 after we have listened for pitch:

EXAMPLE I.8 *Adding pitch to the shorthand representation*

After listening for the details of duration, Example I.8 would be translated into standard notation as illustrated in Example I.9:

EXAMPLE I.9 *Details of duration translated into standard notation*

Example I.10 shows a more challenging dictation in shorthand form:

EXAMPLE I.10 *Shorthand representation of a dictation*

How would you translate the dictation in Example I.10 into standard notation? Use the staff provided in Example I.11.

EXAMPLE I.11 *Translation into standard notation of the shorthand representation given in Example 1.10*

The goal of this shorthand procedure is to free your mind to concentrate on listening as much as possible. Once you have heard everything accurately and have written it down in shorthand form, you can quickly convert it into standard notation. Feel free to adapt this system so that it works best for you. Create new or modified shorthand symbols as necessary.

Melodic Constructs

UNIT 5

Incorporating Perfect Octaves, Unisons, Fifths, and Fourths

T he **melodic constructs** presented in this and in subsequent units of Area I have been created to drill the specific intervals encountered in the preceding units. These melodic constructs are not intended for sight-singing. They are designed to impart the skills of seeing, recognizing, and hearing intervals, in functional order and within a metrical context, as preparation for the practice of sight-singing more traditional melodic material, such as that presented in Unit 24.

Depending on your vocal capability, some of these melodic constructs will lie outside of a comfortable singing register for you. When this is the case, you may choose to sing a given melodic construct in a different clef or in a key that places the pitches to be sung in a more comfortable register. When the music is written beyond your vocal range, you also have the option of using the key and clef indicated, but singing those pitches that lie outside of your range in a more comfortable octave, either higher or lower than what is written. Your instructor will help you to make these adjustments.

For maximum benefit, these melodic constructs should be studied, analyzed, practiced, and performed both in class and at home. Used in this way, they will give you the technique and ability you need to sight-sing the music you regularly study, learn, and perform.

CLASS DRILLS & HOME EXERCISES

A. **Study, analyze, practice, and perform the following melodic constructs.**

© 1997 Ardsley House, Publishers, Inc.

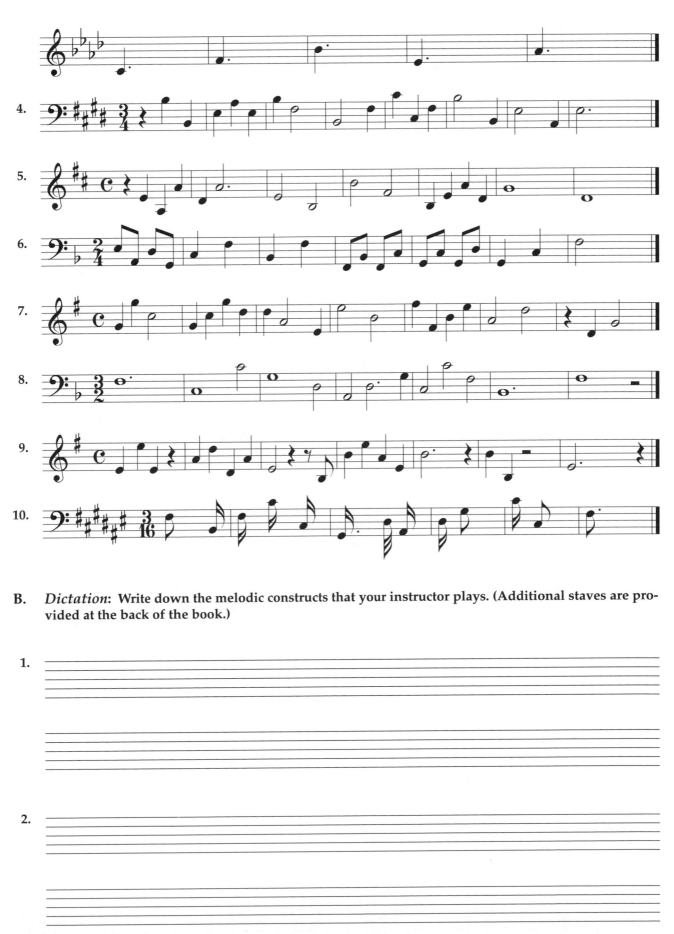

B. *Dictation*: **Write down the melodic constructs that your instructor plays. (Additional staves are provided at the back of the book.)**

1.

2.

3.

4.

5.

6.

7.

8.

Learning to Hear Intervals

UNIT 6

Major Thirds and Minor Sixths

Interval Quality

The interval of a major 3rd spans three scale degrees and four half steps. Given this information and the formulas that you learned in Unit 3, what is the inversion of a major 3rd, and how many half steps does this inversion span?

A **major interval** (M) that is reduced by a half step becomes a **minor interval** (m), and a minor interval that is reduced by a half step becomes a diminished interval. Conversely, a minor interval that is increased by a half step becomes major, and a major interval that has a half step added to it becomes augmented.

On the basis of this information, try to answer the following questions:

1. Which form of the interval of a 4th has the same number of half steps as an augmented 3rd?

2. What is the only real way we can distinguish between the sounds of these two intervals?

3. Which perfect interval has the same number of half steps as a diminished 6th?

4. By how many half steps do the minor 6th and the augmented 5th differ?

As we saw briefly in Unit 3, a major 3rd is classified as an imperfect consonance; that is, we hear the interval as being more active and less stable than any of the perfect consonances. Take time to listen to the unique character of a major 3rd, and compare its stability with that of an octave and a perfect 5th. Because the interval of a 3rd frequently serves as a quality-prescribing interval in triadic contexts (see Unit 25), you might guess that the 3rd has to have a more active sound than the other consonant intervals we have thus far encountered—and you would be correct.

Major Thirds and Minor Sixths

In this unit, we will concentrate on the sounds of the major 3rd and its inversion, the minor 6th. Your instructor will play both of these intervals for you several times. Which one sounds the most active? If you are having difficulty in making a decision, sing the two notes of the interval and then sing what your intuition and musical instinct tell you "should" be the next note. For which interval was singing the third note easier? Why? What does this tell you about the tendency of the major 3rd and minor 6th? Try to use your own words to describe what you hear as the differences between the two intervals and their relative stabilities.

Before checking Table I.14, develop your own list of all possible diatonic major 3rd and minor 6th relationships. Again, we strongly recommend that you commit these relationships to memory for the purpose of improving your fluency with this material.

TABLE I.14
Diatonic locations of major thirds and minor sixths

MAJOR 3RDS (MAJOR SCALE)			MINOR 6THS (MAJOR SCALE)		
$mi-\hat{3}$	$la-\hat{6}$	$ti-\hat{7}$	$do-\hat{1}$	$fa-\hat{4}$	$so-\hat{5}$
↕	↕	↕	↕	↕	↕
$do-\hat{1}$	$fa-\hat{4}$	$so-\hat{5}$	$mi-\hat{3}$	$la-\hat{6}$	$ti-\hat{7}$
MAJOR 3RDS (NATURAL MINOR SCALE)			**MINOR 6THS (NATURAL MINOR SCALE)**		
$so-\hat{5}$	$do-\hat{1}$	$re-\hat{2}$	$le-\hat{6}$	$te-\hat{7}$	$me-\hat{3}$
↕	↕	↕	↕	↕	↕
$me-\hat{3}$	$le-\hat{6}$	$te-\hat{7}$	$do-\hat{1}$	$re-\hat{2}$	$so-\hat{5}$
MAJOR 3RDS (HARMONIC MINOR SCALE)			**MINOR 6THS (HARMONIC MINOR SCALE)**		
$so-\hat{5}$	$ti-\hat{7}$	$do-\hat{1}$	$le-\hat{6}$	$me-\hat{3}$	$so-\hat{5}$
↕	↕	↕	↕	↕	↕
$me-\hat{3}$	$so-\hat{5}$	$le-\hat{6}$	$do-\hat{1}$	$so-\hat{5}$	$ti-\hat{7}$

CLASS DRILLS *&* HOME EXERCISES

1 The following procedure is recommended for solving *pitch puzzles*. Each line constitutes a different puzzle. The goal is to remain in the same key throughout the line. If the identity you choose for the *mystery pitch* (∗) causes you to go "out of key" anywhere along the given series of interval movements, that pitch cannot be a solution to the puzzle. Using the interval information given, determine the diatonic identity of the mystery pitch. Note that ∗ represents a pitch (the mystery pitch), not an interval. Without exception, all the intervals listed are diatonic, as is the mystery pitch. The mystery pitch is not necessarily *do*, and it is possible that more than one mystery pitch is diatonically consistent with the interval patterns presented. It is also possible that no such mystery pitch is diatonically possible for the given interval pattern.

Major	∗	↑P5	↓∗	↓P4	↑M3	↑P4
Major	∗	↑M3	↓∗	↓m6	↑∗	↑P4
Major	∗	↑m6	↓∗	↓P4	↑∗	↓M3
Major	∗	↓P4	↑m6	↑M3	↓P4	↑M3
Major	∗	↓m6	↑P4	↓M3	↑P8	↓∗

Once you have determined all possible identities for the mystery pitch in each puzzle, sing each line, in turn, using every possible diatonic identity of the mystery pitch.

2 Your instructor will name two scale degrees, letter names, or solfège syllables, indicating which is the lower of the two. Identify the specified interval instantly as one of the following intervals:

M3, m6, P8, P5, P4

Then quickly name each scale degree, letter, or syllable between the original two.

3 Given a reference pitch, match that pitch vocally (using a neutral syllable) and then, as instructed, sing one of the following intervals above or below the given pitch:

M3, m6, P8, P5, P4

4 Given a reference pitch together with some form of diatonic identification, match that pitch with its diatonic identity, and then, as instructed, sing one of the intervals

M3, m6, P8, P5, or P4

above or below the given pitch, using the diatonic identity of the second pitch.

5 Given a reference pitch, match that pitch vocally (using a neutral syllable), and then sing a major 3rd above it; return to the reference pitch; sing a minor 6th below it; finally, sing a perfect octave above the second pitch (that is, a major 3rd above the reference pitch).

6 Given a reference pitch, match that pitch vocally (using a neutral syllable), and then sing a minor 6th above it; return to the reference pitch; sing a major 3rd below it; finally, sing a perfect octave above the second pitch (that is, a minor 6th above the reference pitch).

7 Given a reference pitch, match that pitch vocally (using a neutral syllable), and then sing a major 3rd below it; return to the reference pitch; sing a minor 6th above it; finally, sing a perfect octave below the second pitch (that is, a major 3rd below the reference pitch).

8 Given a reference pitch, match that pitch vocally (using a neutral syllable), and then sing a minor 6th below it; return to the reference pitch; sing a major 3rd above it; finally, sing a perfect octave below the second pitch (that is, a minor 6th below the reference pitch).

9 Given a reference pitch, match that pitch vocally (using a neutral syllable), and sing a major 3rd above it; from the resultant pitch, sing an ascending minor 6th. From this point, sing a descending major 3rd; finally, from the resultant pitch, sing a descending minor 6th.

10 Given a reference pitch, match that pitch vocally (using a neutral syllable), and sing a minor 6th below it; from the resultant pitch, sing a descending major 3rd. From this point, sing an ascending minor 6th; finally, from the resultant pitch, sing an ascending major 3rd.

11 Repeat Exercises 5 through 10, but using diatonic identities for all pitches sung.

The Law of the Half Step

Now, in major scales, listen to the major 3rd between $\hat{1}$ and $\hat{3}$. Note that the upper note tends toward $\hat{4}$. Similarly, in the major 3rd between $\hat{5}$ and $\hat{7}$, the upper note tends toward $\hat{1}$. We call this the **Law of the Half Step**, wherein those notes of the scale that are a half step apart tend (or gravitate) toward each other. Indeed, we shall see that the **function** of these particular intervals is to progress or proceed to the next note (or chord) in question. It is extremely valuable to be able to identify the major 3rd between *do* and *mi* as the one that gravitates toward *fa*; similarly, the one between *so* and *ti* is the one tending toward *do*. But what about the major 3rd between $\hat{4}$ and $\hat{6}$? Note that, although we *can* hear a tendency on the part of $\hat{6}$ to proceed up by a half step, it is much more likely that we actually feel a certain tendency in *this* major 3rd for the bottom note to move *down* by a half step. Why might this be so? The tendencies of individual scale degrees play a much more important role than the tendencies of intervallic combinations. Thus, in inversion, the tendencies at the level of scale degree remain unaltered; for example, the minor 6th between $\hat{3}$ and $\hat{1}$ still shows a tendency for the bottom note, *mi*, to proceed up by a half step to $\hat{4}$. Examine Table I.15 at this time.

So, as you listen to all of the intervals played for identification in the following exercises, try to hear the tendencies that are governed by the Law of the Half Step (particularly in the case of major scales), and use this as an aid in the identification of both the quality of the interval and the scale degrees of which it is composed. In the case of the minor scale, there is an admitted amount of irregularity. Much of the tendency ascribed to scale degrees in the minor are inherited from the major, regardless of half-step relationships. For this reason,

M3 $\begin{array}{c}\hat{3}\\\hat{1}\rightarrow\hat{4}\end{array}$	M3 $\begin{array}{c}\hat{7}\rightarrow\hat{1}\\\hat{5}\end{array}$
M3 $\begin{array}{c}\hat{6}\\\hat{4}\rightarrow\hat{3}\end{array}$	m6 $\begin{array}{c}\hat{1}\\\hat{3}\rightarrow\hat{4}\end{array}$
m6 $\begin{array}{c}\hat{5}\\\hat{7}\rightarrow\hat{1}\end{array}$	m6 $\begin{array}{c}\hat{4}\rightarrow\hat{3}\\\hat{6}\end{array}$

TABLE I.15 *Major thirds and minor sixths in the major scale: intervals, scale degrees, and tendencies*

we use the harmonic form of the minor almost exclusively in functional contexts because this form, at the very least, preserves the important tendency of $\hat{7}$ to $\hat{1}$. However, $\hat{3}$ is expected to behave much as it did in a major scale, despite the fact that there is now a whole step between it and $\hat{4}$. And when the Law of the Half Step *is* applied to the minor mode, it usually sounds as if the music is actually in the relative major. Nonetheless, you have been exposed to so much music in this tradition that it is likely that this will pose no extra problem for you, as long as you remain aware of it.

CLASS DRILLS HOME EXERCISES

1 Set up a chart similar to Table I.15, wherein you list all the major 3rds and minor 6ths available in all three forms of the minor scale. Try to determine and show the characteristic tendencies of the scale degrees making up each interval. Check these by ear, and then with your instructor.

2 After establishing a tonic, your instructor will play melodically two pitches that form one of the following intervals:

M3, m6, P8, P5, or P4

Sing both pitches in the order heard, using their correct diatonic identities.

3 After establishing a tonic, your instructor will name two scale degrees, letter names, or solfège syllables that form one of the following intervals:

M3, m6, P8, P5, or P4

Without first hearing those notes, sing the correct pitches in the order and direction requested, using their corresponding diatonic identities.

4 A single pitch (other than the tonic) will be played and given a diatonic identity. Two more pitches will then be played melodically that form one of the following intervals:

M3, m6, P8, P5, or P4

State the interval formed by the last two pitches and sing all three pitches, using their diatonic identities.

5 In each of the following rows, sing the five pairs of pitches indicated by the solfège syllables and numbers. (Each pair is independent of the others in that row.) Translate from one system to the other: that is, given numbers, sing the corresponding solfège syllables, and, given solfège syllables, sing the corresponding numbers. With the tonic triad or the diatonic scale, establish a new tonic, as indicated, at the beginning of each row. You may need to reaffirm the tonic before the end of the row, but do so only as often as is really necessary. In each row, go as far as possible before reestablishing the tonic; this may not be necessary at all. However, you should be constantly singing the tonic and dominant pitches to yourself throughout this exercise.

E major	so ↑ re	$\hat{6}$ ↓ $\hat{4}$	mi ↑ do	$\hat{4}$ ↓ $\hat{1}$	la ↑ fa
A♭ major	$\hat{3}$ ↓ $\hat{1}$	ti ↑ so	$\hat{2}$ ↑ $\hat{5}$	ti ↓ ti	$\hat{5}$ ↑ $\hat{7}$
B major	do ↑ mi	$\hat{6}$ ↑ $\hat{4}$	la ↑ re	$\hat{4}$ ↑ $\hat{6}$	ti ↑ so
D major	$\hat{1}$ ↓ $\hat{3}$	la ↓ la	$\hat{4}$ ↓ $\hat{6}$	ti ↓ so	$\hat{3}$ ↑ $\hat{6}$
A♭ minor *harmonic*	so ↑ do	$\hat{5}$ ↓ $\hat{7}$	do ↓ le	$\hat{3}$ ↓ $\hat{5}$	le ↓ do
E♭ minor *harmonic*	$\hat{1}$ ↑ $\hat{6}$	ti ↑ so	$\hat{4}$ ↑ $\hat{1}$	le ↑ do	$\hat{7}$ ↓ $\hat{5}$
A minor *natural*	so ↑ me	$\hat{2}$ ↑ $\hat{7}$	le ↓ do	$\hat{4}$ ↓ $\hat{7}$	te ↑ re
F minor *natural*	$\hat{5}$ ↓ $\hat{3}$	le ↑ do	$\hat{7}$ ↓ $\hat{2}$	te ↓ me	$\hat{2}$ ↓ $\hat{7}$

6 The range of the following series of solfège patterns is limited to about one octave. Choose a starting pitch that enables you to sing in a comfortable register, and select a moderate tempo at which you can readily negotiate the given intervals without hesitating or stopping, giving the same duration to each syllable. In those patterns not ending on *do*, sing the tonic when you are through.

Minor	so	↓me	↑le	↑do	↓so	↓do
Minor	te	↑re	↑te	↓me	↑le	↓so	↓do
Major	fa	↓do	↑mi	↑do	↓so	↓ti	↑do
Major	so	↑ti	↓mi	↑la	↓fa	↓la	↑re
Minor	so	↓ti	↑do	↓so	↑me	↑so	↓do
Major	do	↑fa	↓la	↑re	↑so	↓ti	↑do

© 1997 Ardsley House, Publishers, Inc.

Practice increasing your fluency with the intervals and solfège syllables in these patterns while drilling different *rhythmic* patterns. Rather than singing each pitch with the same duration, vary the rhythmic patterns in various ways. Invent your own patterns. Be creative. No matter what your pattern is, your fluency with the material as well as your flexibility as a musician will improve.

Create your own solfège patterns and bring them to class so that your classmates can realize them. Discuss what makes some of these patterns easier to sing than others. What do the easier ones have in common?

7 Repeat Exercises 5 and 6, but with small groups of students or individuals, singing every other note in Exercises 5 and 6 and every other pair of notes in Exercise 5.

8 Analyze familiar classical, folk, and contemporary tunes to find examples of ascending and descending major 3rds and minor 6ths within a specific diatonic context. Use the results of your analysis to remember the sound and character of these intervals. Usually, opening lines or refrains are the easiest to recall. In addition to the quality and size of an interval, you should be able to hear and identify where this interval lies in the diatonic scale. For instance, you should know the specific major 3rd in the minor scale on which Beethoven's Fifth Symphony begins.

Here are some suggested tunes to get you started:

M3: 1st movement, Symphony no. 5,
    L. van Beethoven
  "Swing Low, Sweet Chariot"

m6: Theme from *Love Story*

Melodic Constructs

UNIT 7

Incorporating Major Thirds and Minor Sixths

*T*he melodic constructs presented in this and in other units of Area I have been created to drill the specific intervals encountered in the preceding units. These melodic constructs are not intended for sight-singing. They are designed to impart the skills of seeing, recognizing, and hearing intervals in functional order and within a metrical context, as preparation for the practice of sight-singing more traditional melodic material, such as that presented in Unit 24.

Depending on your vocal capability, some of these melodic constructs will lie outside of a comfortable singing register for you. When this is the case, you may choose to sing a given melodic construct in a different clef or in a key that places the pitches to be sung in a more comfortable register. When the music is written beyond your vocal range, you also have the option of using the key and clef indicated, but singing those pitches that lie outside of your range in a more comfortable octave, either higher or lower than what is written. Your instructor will help you to make these adjustments.

For maximum benefit, these melodic constructs should be studied, analyzed, practiced, and performed both in class and at home. Used in this way, they will give you the technique and ability you need to sight-sing the music you regularly study, learn, and perform.

CLASS DRILLS & HOME EXERCISES

A. Study, analyze, practice, and perform the following melodic constructs.

B. *Error detection*: Your instructor will play various melodic constructs for you. Compare what you hear with what is written on the corresponding staves that follow.

   i. Circle any pitch or rhythm that seems to be incorrect.

   ii. Correct any pitch or rhythm so that it matches what you hear.

7.

8.

C. *Dictation*: Write down the melodic constructs that your instructor plays. (Additional staves are provided at the back of the book.)

1.

2.

3.

4.

5.

6.

7.

8.

UNIT 8

Minor Thirds and Major Sixths

Diatonic Locations Before checking Table I.16, which follows, develop your own list of all possible diatonic minor 3rd and major 6th relationships. Again, you should memorize these intervallic relationships as a means of being as fluent as possible with this material. (Remember that an ascending melodic minor scale is identical with the corresponding major scale, with the single exception of the minor 3rd between $\hat{1}$ and $\hat{3}$; a descending melodic minor scale is identical with the natural form of that minor scale.)

Scale-Degree Function Having carefully studied the Law of the Half Step, listened to examples, and performed the exercises in the two preceding units, you are beginning to develop an awareness of the unique functional character of each scale degree. With the aural perception you now

MINOR 3RDS (MAJOR SCALE)				MAJOR 6THS (MAJOR SCALE)			
fa–$\hat{4}$	so–$\hat{5}$	do–$\hat{1}$	re–$\hat{2}$	la–$\hat{6}$	ti–$\hat{7}$	re–$\hat{2}$	mi–$\hat{3}$
$\updownarrow$	$\updownarrow$	$\updownarrow$	$\updownarrow$	$\updownarrow$	$\updownarrow$	$\updownarrow$	$\updownarrow$
re–$\hat{2}$	mi–$\hat{3}$	la–$\hat{6}$	ti–$\hat{7}$	do–$\hat{1}$	re–$\hat{2}$	fa–$\hat{4}$	so–$\hat{5}$
MINOR 3RDS (NATURAL MINOR SCALE)				MAJOR 6THS (NATURAL MINOR SCALE)			
me–$\hat{3}$	fa–$\hat{4}$	le–$\hat{6}$	te–$\hat{7}$	do–$\hat{1}$	re–$\hat{2}$	fa–$\hat{4}$	so–$\hat{5}$
$\updownarrow$	$\updownarrow$	$\updownarrow$	$\updownarrow$	$\updownarrow$	$\updownarrow$	$\updownarrow$	$\updownarrow$
do–$\hat{1}$	re–$\hat{2}$	fa–$\hat{4}$	so–$\hat{5}$	me–$\hat{3}$	fa–$\hat{4}$	le–$\hat{6}$	te–$\hat{7}$
MINOR 3RDS (HARMONIC MINOR SCALE)				MAJOR 6THS (HARMONIC MINOR SCALE)			
me–$\hat{3}$	fa–$\hat{4}$	le–$\hat{6}$	re–$\hat{2}$	do–$\hat{1}$	re–$\hat{2}$	fa–$\hat{4}$	ti–$\hat{7}$
$\updownarrow$	$\updownarrow$	$\updownarrow$	$\updownarrow$	$\updownarrow$	$\updownarrow$	$\updownarrow$	$\updownarrow$
do–$\hat{1}$	re–$\hat{2}$	fa–$\hat{4}$	ti–$\hat{7}$	me–$\hat{3}$	fa–$\hat{4}$	le–$\hat{6}$	re–$\hat{2}$

TABLE I.16
Diatonic locations of minor thirds and major sixths

have, you can probably predict the ways in which the minor 3rds and major 6ths function in various major or minor scales.

As we saw with major 3rds and minor 6ths in major scales, intervals of the same size and quality do not always function in the same way. Your challenge is to learn both to hear these variations in function and to recognize these differences. They can best be learned by repeated hearings, so as to establish familiarity.

Of the four minor 3rds in the major scale, we find that *ti* ↔ *re sounds* the most active. (Why?) Its structure with regard to the half step is identical with that of *mi* ↔ *so*: the lower pitch of each interval gravitates up by a half step. What accounts for the difference in sound and intensity between these two seemingly identical intervals? As always, it is the *context*. The pull of the tonic on *ti* is stronger than the pull of the subdominant on *mi*.

Listen to the relative stability and consonance of the intervals created by inverting the two minor 3rds that we have just been listening to. Which major 6th is more active, that is, more dissonant? Is your impression consistent with our characterization of the corresponding minor 3rds? Listen carefully to the other two pairs of minor 3rds and major 6ths in the major scale. How do they compare with those we have been considering? Be sure to listen to these intervals in several different keys.

What are your impressions of activity/stability when you hear the minor 3rds found among the pitches of the minor scale? In the natural form, $\hat{7}$ ↔ $\hat{2}$ does not form a minor 3rd because of the absence of the half step between the leading tone and the tonic. But what do the other minor 3rds sound like? Where do you hear that they lead and to which intervals do they have a tendency to go? Again, context and the Law of the Half Step can be our guides in explaining what we hear. In the absence of a leading tone to the tonic in the natural minor, we find that the minor 3rd, $\hat{2}$ ↔ $\hat{4}$, behaves as $\hat{7}$ ↔ $\hat{2}$ did in the major scale. Also, $\hat{2}$ ↔ $\hat{4}$ gravitates strongly to $\hat{3}$; this strong half-step pull from $\hat{2}$ to $\hat{3}$ has the effect of tonicizing the mediant scale degree. Continue to listen to the other minor 3rds and to all major 6ths to decide how they sound and what their tendencies are.

CLASS DRILLS & HOME EXERCISES

1 The following procedure is recommended for solving *pitch puzzles*. Each line constitutes a different puzzle. The goal is to remain in the same key throughout the line. If the identity you choose for the *mystery pitch* (∗) causes you to go "out of key" anywhere along the given series of interval movements, that pitch cannot be a solution to the puzzle. Using the interval information given, determine the diatonic identity of the mystery pitch. Note that ∗ represents a pitch (the mystery pitch), not an interval. Without exception, all the intervals listed are diatonic, as is the mystery pitch. The mystery pitch is not necessarily $\hat{1}$, and it is possible that more than one mystery pitch are diatonically consistent with the interval patterns presented. It is also possible that no such mystery pitch is diatonically possible for the given interval pattern.

Major	∗	↓m6	↑m3	↑P5	↓M6	↑∗
Major	∗	↓P4	↑M6	↓m3	↑m6	↑M3
Minor *natural*	∗	↓m3	↓M6	↑P8	↑m3	↑M3
Minor *harmonic*	∗	↑M6	↓M3	↑∗	↓m3	↑∗

Once you have determined all possible identities for the mystery pitch in each puzzle, sing each line, in turn, using every possible diatonic identity of the mystery pitch.

2 Your instructor will name two scale degrees, letter names, or solfège syllables, indicating which is the lower of the two. Identify the specified interval instantly as one of the following:

m3, M6, M3, m6, P8, P5, or P4

Then quickly name each scale degree, letter, or syllable between the original two.

3 Given a reference pitch, match that pitch vocally (using a neutral syllable) and then, as instructed, sing one of the following intervals above or below the given pitch:

m3, M6, M3, m6, P8, P5, or P4

4 Given a reference pitch together with some form of diatonic identification, match that pitch vocally with its diatonic identity, and then, as instructed, sing one of the following intervals above or below the given pitch, using the diatonic identity of the second pitch:

m3, M6, M3, m6, P8, P5, or P4

5 After establishing a tonic, your instructor will play melodically two pitches that form one of the following intervals:

m3, M6, M3, m6, P8, P5, or P4

Sing both pitches in the order heard, using their correct diatonic identities.

6 After establishing a tonic, your instructor will name two scale degrees, letter names, or solfège syllables that form one of the following intervals:

m3, M6, M3, m6, P8, P5, or P4

Without first hearing those notes, sing the correct pitches in the order and direction requested, using their corresponding diatonic identities.

7 A single pitch (other than the tonic) will be played and given a diatonic identity. Two more pitches that form one of the following intervals will then be played melodically:

m3, M6, M3, m6, P8, P5, or P4

State the interval formed by the last two pitches and sing all three pitches, using their diatonic identities.

8 In each of the following rows, sing the five pairs of pitches indicated by the solfège syllables and numbers. (Each pair is independent of the others in that row.) Translate from one system to the other: that is, given numbers, sing the corresponding solfège syllables, and, given solfège syllables, sing the corresponding numbers. With the tonic triad or the diatonic scale, establish a new tonic, as indicated, at the beginning of each row. You may need to reaffirm the tonic before the end of the row, but do so only as often as is really necessary. In each row, go as far as possible before reestablishing the tonic; this may not be necessary at all. However, you should be constantly singing the tonic and dominant pitches to yourself throughout this exercise.

F major	re ↑ fa		3̂ ↓ 5̂		mi ↑ so		3̂ ↓ 7̂		do ↑ la
D♭ major	6̂ ↑ 1̂		ti ↑ re		4̂ ↑ 2̂		so ↑ mi		7̂ ↓ 2̂
A major	re ↑ ti		4̂ ↓ 2̂		so ↑ mi		1̂ ↓ 6̂		re ↓ fa
G major	6̂ ↓ 1̂		fa ↓ re		2̂ ↑ 7̂		re ↓ fa		5̂ ↓ 3̂
C minor *harmonic*	2̂ ↓ 7̂		me ↓ do		2̂ ↑ 7̂		re ↓ fa		6̂ ↓ 4̂
B minor *harmonic*	fa ↑ le		7̂ ↓ 2̂		do ↓ me		2̂ ↑ 4̂		ti ↑ re
F♯ minor *natural*	5̂ ↑ 7̂		fa ↑ re		1̂ ↑ 3̂		so ↓ te		4̂ ↓ 6̂
G minor *natural*	le ↑ fa		7̂ ↑ 5̂		fa ↓ re		3̂ ↑ 1̂		te ↓ so

9 Given a reference pitch, match that pitch vocally (using a neutral syllable), and then sing a minor 3rd above it; return to the reference pitch; sing a major 6th below it; finally, sing a perfect octave above the last pitch (that is, a minor 3rd above the reference pitch).

10 Given a reference pitch, match that pitch vocally (using a neutral syllable), and then sing a major 6th above it; return to the reference pitch; sing a minor 3rd below it; finally, sing a perfect octave above the last pitch (that is, a major 6th above the reference pitch).

11 Given a reference pitch, match that pitch vocally (using a neutral syllable), and then sing a minor 3rd below it; return to the reference pitch; sing a major 6th above it; finally, sing a perfect octave below the last pitch (that is, a minor 3rd below the reference pitch).

12 Given a reference pitch, match that pitch vocally (using a neutral syllable), and then sing a major 6th below it; return to the reference pitch; sing a minor 3rd above it; finally, sing a perfect octave below the last pitch (that is, a major 6th below the reference pitch).

13 Given a reference pitch, match that pitch vocally (using a neutral syllable), and sing a minor 3rd above it; from the resultant pitch, sing an ascending major 6th. From that point, sing a descending minor 3rd; finally, from the resultant pitch, sing a descending major 6th.

14 Given a reference pitch, match that pitch vocally (using a neutral syllable), and sing a major 6th below it; from the resultant pitch, sing a descending minor 3rd. From that point, sing an ascending major 6th; from the resultant pitch, sing an ascending minor 3rd.

15 Repeat Exercises 9–14, but using diatonic identities for all pitches sung.

16 The range of the following series of solfège patterns is limited to about one octave. Choose a starting pitch that enables you to sing in a comfortable register, and select a moderate tempo at which you can readily negotiate the given intervals without hesitating or stopping, giving the same duration to each syllable. In those patterns not ending on *do*, sing the tonic when you are through.

Major	do	↓la	↑re	↓do	↓so	↓mi	↓do
Major	la	↓fa	↓re	↑ti	↑do	↓fa	↓do
Minor	do	↑me	↑do	↓so	↑re	↓te	↑do
Minor	me	↓do	↑fa	↑re	↓do	↓me	↓do
Major	la	↓do	↑fa	↓la	↑ti	↑do	
Minor	do	↓fa	↑le	↑fa	↓re	↓te	↑do

Practice increasing your fluency with the intervals and solfège syllables in these patterns while drilling different *rhythmic* patterns. Rather than singing each pitch with the same duration, vary the rhythmic patterns in various ways. Invent your own patterns. Be creative. No matter what your pattern is, your fluency with the material as well as your flexibility as a musician will improve.

Create your own solfège patterns and bring them to class so that your classmates can realize them. Discuss what makes some of these patterns easier to sing than others. What do the easier ones have in common?

17 Repeat Exercises 9–16, but with small groups of students or individuals singing every other pitch.

18 Analyze familiar classical, folk, and contemporary tunes to find examples of ascending and descending minor 3rds and major 6ths within a specific diatonic context. Use the results of your analysis to remember the sound and character of these intervals. Usually, opening lines or refrains are the easiest to recall. In addition to the quality and size of an interval, you should be able to hear and identify where this interval lies in the diatonic scale. For instance, you should know the minor 3rd in the major scale on which the "Star-Spangled Banner" begins.

Here are some suggested tunes to get you started:

m3: "The Star-Spangled Banner"
 Brahms's "Lullaby"

M6: "My Bonnie Lies over the Ocean"

Melodic Constructs

Incorporating Minor Thirds and Major Sixths

*T*he melodic constructs presented in this and in other units of Area I have been created to drill the specific intervals encountered in the preceding units. These melodic constructs are not intended for sight-singing. They are designed to impart the skills of seeing, recognizing, and hearing intervals, in functional order and within a metrical context, as preparation for the practice of sight-singing more traditional melodic material, such as that presented in Unit 24.

Depending on your vocal capability, some of these melodic constructs will lie outside of a comfortable singing register for you. When this is the case, you may choose to sing a given melodic construct in a different clef or in a key that places the pitches to be sung in a more comfortable register. When the music is written beyond your vocal range, you also have the option of using the key and clef indicated, but singing those pitches that lie outside of your range in a more comfortable octave, either higher or lower than what is written. Your instructor will help you to make these adjustments.

For maximum benefit, these melodic constructs should be studied, analyzed, practiced, and performed both in class and at home. Used in this way, they will give you the technique and ability you need to sight-sing the music you regularly study, learn, and perform.

CLASS DRILLS & HOME EXERCISES

Study, analyze, practice, and perform the given melodic constructs.

B. *Error detection*: Your instructor will play various melodic constructs for you. Compare what you hear with what is written on the corresponding staves that follow.

   i. Circle any pitch or rhythm that seems to be incorrect.

   ii. Correct any pitch or rhythm so that it matches what you hear.

7.

8.

C. *Dictation*: **Write down the melodic constructs that your instructor plays. (Additional staves are provided at the back of the book.)**

1.

2.

3.

4.

© 1997 Ardsley House, Publishers, Inc.

5.

6.

7.

8.

Learning to Hear Intervals

Major Seconds and Minor Sevenths

Diatonic Locations of Two Dissonant Intervals

We have already encountered the interval of a major 2nd informally in Unit 1 in the context of major and minor scales. The major 2nd, better known as the *whole step*, is one of the more familiar intervals because it is a defining element of both scales. The major 2nd and its inversion, the minor 7th, are both dissonant, active intervals. Table I.17 indicates the locations of major 2nds along with the corresponding minor 7ths.

Unique Functional Characteristics

Listen to the character of the interval between any two pitches played. Do any major 2nds sound more dissonant than the others? What about the minor 7ths? *Hint*: Play or sing "Chopsticks" with a classmate. What is the first interval? How do the two voices making up the first interval resolve? Does your ear expect this resolution? (What about the third and fourth intervals? Do the two voices follow the tendencies inherent in these **dyads** or are these tendencies frustrated?) By now you have realized, as we have discovered with other intervals in previous units, that not every major 2nd is as active as the next; likewise with minor 7ths.

Listen to the four diatonic minor 7ths in the major scale and determine which pair sounds the most dissonant.

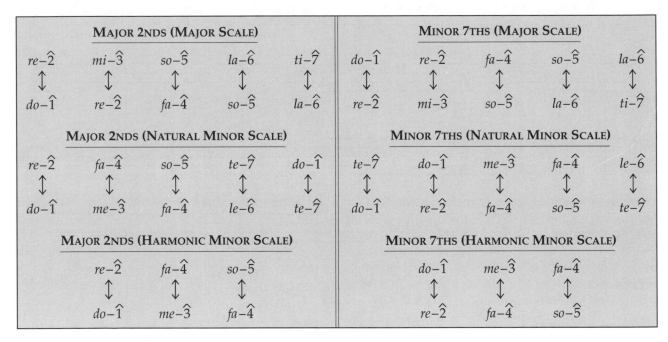

TABLE I.17 *Diatonic locations of major seconds and minor sevenths*

CLASS DRILLS *&* HOME EXERCISES

1 The following procedure is recommended for solving *pitch puzzles*. Each line constitutes a different puzzle. The goal is to remain in the same key throughout the line. If the identity you choose for the *mystery pitch* (∗) causes you to go "out of key" anywhere along the given series of interval movements, that pitch cannot be a solution to the puzzle. Using the interval information given, determine the diatonic identity of the mystery pitch. Note that ∗ represents a pitch (the mystery pitch), not an interval. Without exception, all the intervals listed are diatonic, as is the mystery pitch. The mystery pitch is not necessarily $\hat{1}$, and it is possible that more than one mystery pitch are diatonically consistent with the interval patterns presented. It is also possible that no such mystery pitch is diatonically possible for the given interval pattern.

Major	*	↓M2	↓M6	↑m7	↓M3	↓M2
Major	*	↑M2	↓M6	↑P8	↓m7	↑P4
Minor *natural*	*	↑P4	↑m3	↓m7	↓m3	↑*
Minor *harmonic*	*	↓m3	↑P5	↓M2	↓P5	↑m7

Once you have determined all possible identities for the mystery pitch in each puzzle, sing each line, in turn, using every possible diatonic identity of the mystery pitch.

2 Your instructor will name two scale degrees, letter names, or solfège syllables, indicating which is the lower of the two. Identify the specified interval instantly as one of the following:

M2, m7, m3, M6, M3, m6, P8, P5, or P4

Then quickly name each scale degree, letter, or syllable between the original two.

3 Given a reference pitch, match that pitch vocally (using a neutral syllable), as instructed, and then sing one of the intervals

M2, m7, m3, M6, M3, m6, P8, P5, or P4

above or below the given pitch.

4 Given a reference pitch together with some form of diatonic identification, match that pitch vocally with its diatonic identity, and then, as instructed, sing one of the intervals

M2, m7, m3, M6, M3, m6, P8, P5, or P4

above or below the given pitch, using the diatonic identity of the second pitch.

5 After establishing a tonic, your instructor will play melodically two pitches that form one of the following intervals:

M2, m7, m3, M6, M3, m6, P8, P5, or P4

Sing both pitches in the order heard, using their correct diatonic identities.

6 After establishing a tonic, your instructor will name two scale degrees, letter names, or solfège syllables that form one of the following intervals:

M2, m7, m3, M6, M3, m6, P8, P5, or P4

Without first hearing those notes, sing the correct pitches in the order and direction requested, using their corresponding diatonic identities.

7 A single pitch (other than the tonic) will be played and given a diatonic identity. Two more pitches that form one of the following intervals will then be played melodically:

M2, m7, m3, M6, M3, m6, P8, P5, or P4

State the interval formed by the last two pitches and sing all three pitches, using their diatonic identities.

8 In each of the following rows, sing the five pairs of pitches indicated by the solfège syllables and numbers. (Each pair is independent of the others in that row.) Translate from one system to the other: that is, given numbers, sing the corresponding solfège syllables, and, given solfège syllables, sing the corresponding numbers. With the tonic triad or the diatonic scale, establish a new tonic, as indicated, at the beginning of each row. You may need to reaffirm the tonic before the end of the row, but do so only as often as is really necessary. In each row, go as far as possible before reestablishing the tonic; this may not be necessary at all. However, you should be constantly singing the tonic and dominant pitches to yourself throughout this exercise.

F♯ major	*la* ↑ *ti*	$\hat{5}$ ↓ $\hat{4}$	*do* ↓ *re*	$\hat{6}$ ↓ $\hat{7}$	*mi* ↑ *re*
E♭ major	$\hat{7}$ ↓ $\hat{6}$	*re* ↑ *do*	$\hat{4}$ ↓ $\hat{5}$	*re* ↑ *mi*	$\hat{6}$ ↓ $\hat{5}$
C♯ major	*so* ↓ *la*	$\hat{7}$ ↑ $\hat{6}$	*so* ↑ *la*	$\hat{1}$ ↑ $\hat{2}$	*re* ↓ *mi*
C major	$\hat{2}$ ↓ $\hat{1}$	*so* ↑ *fa*	$\hat{6}$ ↑ $\hat{5}$	*re* ↑ *mi*	$\hat{4}$ ↑ $\hat{5}$
E minor *harmonic*	*do* ↓ *re*	$\hat{4}$ ↓ $\hat{3}$	*so* ↑ *fa*	$\hat{2}$ ↑ $\hat{1}$	*me* ↓ *fa*
B♭ minor *harmonic*	$\hat{4}$ ↑ $\hat{5}$	*fa* ↑ *me*	$\hat{2}$ ↓ $\hat{1}$	*fa* ↓ *so*	*me* ↑ *fa*
C♯ minor *natural*	*le* ↑ *te*	$\hat{2}$ ↑ $\hat{1}$	*te* ↑ *le*	$\hat{7}$ ↓ $\hat{1}$	*so* ↑ *fa*
D minor *natural*	$\hat{1}$ ↑ $\hat{7}$	*te* ↓ *le*	$\hat{3}$ ↓ $\hat{4}$	*do* ↓ *te*	$\hat{4}$ ↓ $\hat{3}$

9 〰 Given a reference pitch, match that pitch vocally (using a neutral syllable), and then sing a minor 7th above it; return to the reference pitch; sing a major 2nd below it; finally, sing a perfect octave above the last pitch (that is, a minor 7th above the reference pitch).

10 〰 Given a reference pitch, match that pitch vocally (using a neutral syllable), and then sing a major 2nd above it; return to the reference pitch; sing a minor 7th below it; finally, sing a perfect octave above the last pitch (that is, a major 2nd above the reference pitch).

11 〰 Given a reference pitch, match that pitch vocally (using a neutral syllable), and then sing a minor 7th below it; return to the reference pitch; sing a major 2nd above it; finally, sing a perfect octave below the last pitch (that is, a minor 7th below the reference pitch).

12 〰 Given a reference pitch, match that pitch vocally (using a neutral syllable), and then sing a major 2nd below it; return to the reference pitch; sing a minor 7th above it; finally, sing a perfect octave below the last pitch (that is, a major 2nd below the reference pitch).

13 〰 Given a reference pitch, match that pitch vocally (using a neutral syllable), and sing a major 2nd above it; from the resultant pitch, sing an ascending minor 7th. From that point, sing a descending major 2nd; finally, from the resultant pitch, sing a descending minor 7th.

14 〰 Given a reference pitch, match that pitch vocally (using a neutral syllable), and sing a minor 7th below it; from the resultant pitch, sing a descending major 2nd. From that point, sing an ascending minor 7th; finally, from the resultant pitch, sing an ascending major 2nd.

15 〰 Repeat Exercises 9–14, but using diatonic identities for all pitches sung.

16 〰 The range of the following series of solfège patterns is limited to about one octave. Choose a starting pitch that enables you to sing in a comfortable register, and select a moderate tempo at which you can readily negotiate the given intervals without hesitating or stopping, giving the same duration to each syllable. In those patterns not ending on *do*, sing the tonic when you are through.

Minor	do	↑te	↓le	↓me	↑so	↓te	↑do
Major	do	↓re	↑mi	↓so	↑re	↓la	↑do
Major	do	↓so	↑fa	↓mi	↓la	↑re	↓do
Minor	fa	↑me	↓re	↓te	↓le	↓fa	↑so
Major	fa	↓mi	↑re	↑mi	↑fa	↓so	↑do
Minor	so	↑me	↑fa	↑le	↓te	↑me	↓do

Practice increasing your fluency with the intervals and solfège syllables in these patterns while drilling different *rhythmic* patterns. Rather than singing each pitch with the same duration, vary the rhythmic patterns in various ways. Invent your own patterns. Be creative. No matter what your pattern is, your fluency with the material as well as your flexibility as a musician will improve.

Create your own solfège patterns and bring them to class so that your classmates can realize them. Discuss what makes some of these patterns easier to sing than others. What do the easier ones have in common?

17 〰 Repeat Exercises 9–16, but with small groups of students or individuals singing every other pitch.

18 〰 Analyze familiar classical, folk, and contemporary tunes to find examples of ascending and descending major 2nds and minor 7ths within a specific diatonic context. Use the results of your analysis to remember the sound and character of these intervals. Usually, opening lines or refrains are the easiest to recall. In addition to the quality and size of an interval, you should be able to hear and identify where this interval lies in the diatonic scale. For instance, you should know the specific major 2nd in the major scale on which the first four phrases of "Three Blind Mice" begin.

Here are some suggested tunes to get you started:

M2: "Three Blind Mice"

"Happy Birthday"

m7: "Somewhere" from *West Side Story*

Melodic Constructs

UNIT **11**

Incorporating Major Seconds and Minor Sevenths

T he melodic constructs presented in this and in other units of Area I have been created to drill the specific intervals encountered in the preceding units. These melodic constructs are not intended for sight-singing. They are designed to impart the skills of seeing, recognizing, and hearing intervals, in functional order and within a metrical context, as preparation for the practice of sight-singing more traditional melodic material, such as that presented in Unit 24.

Depending on your vocal capability, some of these melodic constructs will lie outside of a comfortable singing register for you. When this is the case, you may choose to sing a given melodic construct in a different clef or in a key that places the pitches to be sung in a more comfortable register. When the music is written beyond your vocal range, you also have the option of using the key and clef indicated, but singing those pitches that lie outside of your range in a more comfortable octave, either higher or lower than what is written. Your instructor will help you to make these adjustments.

For maximum benefit, these melodic constructs should be studied, analyzed, practiced, and performed both in class and at home. Used in this way, they will give you the technique and ability you need to sight-sing the music you regularly study, learn, and perform.

CLASS DRILLS & HOME EXERCISES

A. Study, analyze, practice, and perform the following melodic constructs.

B. *Error detection*: Your instructor will play various melodic constructs for you. Compare what you hear with what is written on the corresponding staves that follow.

   i. Circle any pitch or rhythm that seems to be incorrect.

   ii. Correct any pitch or rhythm so that it matches what you hear.

C. *Dictation*: Write down the melodic constructs that your instructor plays. (Additional staves are provided at the back of the book.)

1.

2.

3.

4.

5.

6.

7.

8.

Learning to Hear Intervals

UNIT **12**

Minor Seconds and Major Sevenths

● ●

Recognizing Interval Distances

We have already spent considerable time becoming familiar with the character and nature of the minor 2nd, or *half step*. Indeed, the Law of the Half Step exerts a considerable influence upon the character of various intervals according to their proximity to any diatonic half steps. Again, we realize that these are among the most dissonant intervals in the tonal system; therefore, their sound seems to require movement by one member of the pair to a less active pitch, relative to the other. Your ear has become well-accustomed by now to distinguishing between the size of intervals with similar levels of activity or dissonance. In this regard, no doubt, you will quickly be able to hear the difference between the distance separating the pitches constituting a minor 2nd and that for the major 7th. Remember, as you consider Table I.18, that it is not enough to know *intellectually* what the distance between two pitches is. You must also *hear* this characteristic in addition to the others inherent in each interval you encounter. Obviously, this will require much work and effort on your part, so be sure to listen carefully many times to each interval in the table. If you are having difficulty with some of these, take a break and try again.

Tendencies of Major Sevenths

As a means of refining our understanding of what we are hearing, let us examine more closely the character of the major 7ths found in the diatonic major and minor scales. As in previous units, we are interested in learning to hear not only the tendencies of various intervals, but also how these intervals function in different contexts. In this instance, we want to be able to detect by ear any differences, due to context, that exist between, for example, the two major 7ths

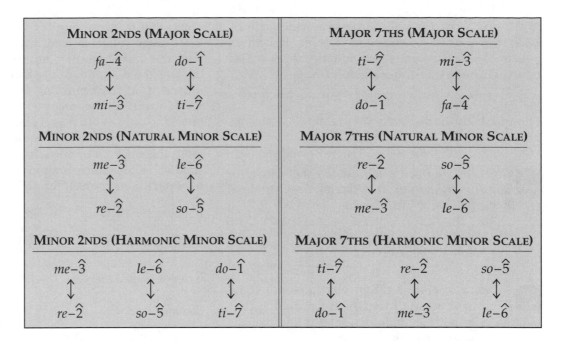

TABLE I.18
Diatonic locations of minor seconds and major sevenths

in the major scale. What is different between the two contexts of these seemingly identical intervals? Listen to them again carefully. Which one sounds like a stronger dissonance? Of course, within the diatonic major context, *do* ↔ *ti* is the stronger dissonance due to the presence of *ti*, the leading tone to the tonic.

In the natural minor, we also have two major 7ths present in the diatonic collection, but there is no leading tone to the tonic. Carefully listen to these two 7ths and decide which one sounds like a stronger dissonance. In the absence of the leading tone, which half step is the stronger and therefore can be said to simulate the $\hat{7}$ ↔ $\hat{1}$ half step?

CLASS DRILLS *&* HOME EXERCISES

1 ~ The following procedure is recommended for solving *pitch puzzles*. Each line constitutes a different puzzle. The goal is to remain in the same key throughout the line. If the identity you choose for the *mystery pitch* (∗) causes you to go "out of key" anywhere along the given series of interval movements, that pitch cannot be a solution to the puzzle. Using the interval information given, determine the diatonic identity of the mystery pitch. Note that ∗ represents a pitch (the mystery pitch), not an interval. Without exception, all the intervals listed are diatonic, as is the mystery pitch. The mystery pitch is not necessarily $\hat{1}$, and it is possible that more than one mystery pitch are diatonically consistent with the interval patterns presented. It is also possible

that no such mystery pitch is diatonically possible for the given interval pattern.

Major	∗	↑M7	↓P4	↑m2	↓m3	↓P5
Major	∗	↓M7	↑P5	↓m3	↓M2	↑∗
Minor *natural*	∗	↑m2	↓P4	↑M3	↓P5	↑m7
Minor *harmonic*	∗	↑M7	↑P4	↓m6	↑m2	↓P5

Once you have determined all possible identities for the mystery pitch in each puzzle, sing each line, in turn, using every possible diatonic identity of the mystery pitch.

2 Your instructor will name two scale degrees, letter names, or solfège syllables, indicating which is the lower of the two. Identify the specified interval instantly as one of the following:

m2, M7, M2, m7, m3, M6, M3, m6, P8, P5, or P4

Then quickly name each scale degree, letter, or syllable between the original two.

3 Given a reference pitch, match that pitch vocally (using a neutral syllable), as instructed, and then sing one of the intervals

m2, M7, M2, m7, m3, M6, M3, m6, P8, P5, or P4

above or below the given pitch.

4 Given a reference pitch together with some form of diatonic identification, match that pitch vocally with its diatonic identity, and then, as instructed, sing one of the intervals

m2, M7, M2, m7, m3, M6, M3, m6, P8, P5, or P4

above or below the given pitch, using the diatonic identity of the second pitch.

5 After establishing a tonic, your instructor will play melodically two pitches as one of the following intervals:

m2, M7, M2, m7, m3, M6, M3, m6, P8, P5, or P4

Sing both pitches in the order heard, using their correct diatonic identities.

6 After establishing a tonic, your instructor will name two scale degrees, letter names, or solfège syllables that form one of the following intervals:

m2, M7, M2, m7, m3, M6, M3, m6, P8, P5, or P4

Without first hearing those notes, sing the correct pitches in the order and direction requested, using their corresponding diatonic identities.

7 A single pitch (other than the tonic) will be played and given a diatonic identity. Two more pitches that form one of the intervals

m2, M7, M2, m7, m3, M6, M3, m6, P8, P5, or P4

will then be played melodically. State the interval formed by the last two pitches and sing all three pitches with their diatonic identities.

8 In each of the following rows, sing the five pairs of pitches indicated by the solfège syllables and numbers. (Each pair is independent of the others in that row.) Translate from one system to the other: that is, given numbers, sing the corresponding solfège syllables, and, given solfège syllables, sing the corresponding numbers. With the tonic triad or the diatonic scale, establish a new tonic, as indicated, at the beginning of each row. You may need to reaffirm the tonic before the end of the row, but do so only as often as is really necessary. In each row, go as far as possible before reestablishing the tonic; this may not be necessary at all. However, you should be constantly singing the tonic and dominant pitches to yourself throughout this exercise.

E major	*mi* ↓ *fa*	$\hat{7}$ ↑ $\hat{1}$	*mi* ↑ *fa*	$\hat{4}$ ↑ $\hat{3}$	*do* ↑ *ti*
A♭ major	$\hat{7}$ ↓ $\hat{1}$	*fa* ↑ *mi*	$\hat{4}$ ↓ $\hat{3}$	*do* ↑ *ti*	$\hat{1}$ ↓ $\hat{7}$
B major	*fa* ↓ *mi*	$\hat{7}$ ↓ $\hat{1}$	*ti* ↑ *do*	$\hat{3}$ ↓ $\hat{4}$	*do* ↑ *ti*
D major	$\hat{3}$ ↓ $\hat{4}$	*mi* ↑ *fa*	$\hat{1}$ ↑ $\hat{7}$	*fa* ↑ *mi*	$\hat{7}$ ↓ $\hat{1}$
A♭ minor *harmonic*	*ti* ↓ *do*	$\hat{5}$ ↑ $\hat{6}$	*re* ↓ *me*	$\hat{5}$ ↓ $\hat{6}$	*me* ↓ *re*
E♭ minor *harmonic*	$\hat{6}$ ↑ $\hat{5}$	*do* ↓ *ti*	$\hat{3}$ ↑ $\hat{2}$	*do* ↑ *ti*	*so* ↑ *le*
A minor *natural*	*so* ↓ *le*	$\hat{3}$ ↑ $\hat{2}$	*le* ↑ *so*	$\hat{3}$ ↓ $\hat{2}$	*re* ↓ *me*
F minor *natural*	$\hat{6}$ ↓ $\hat{5}$	*me* ↑ *re*	$\hat{7}$ ↑ $\hat{1}$	*so* ↓ *le*	$\hat{3}$ ↓ $\hat{2}$

9 Given a reference pitch, match that pitch vocally (using a neutral syllable), and then sing a minor 2nd above it; return to the reference pitch; sing a major 7th below it; finally, sing a perfect octave above the last pitch (that is, a minor 2nd above the reference pitch).

10 Given a reference pitch, match that pitch vocally (using a neutral syllable), and then sing a major 7th above it; return to the reference pitch; sing a minor 2nd below it; finally, sing a perfect octave above the last pitch (that is, a major 7th above the reference pitch).

11 Given a reference pitch, match that pitch vocally (using a neutral syllable), and then sing a minor 2nd below it; return to the reference pitch; sing a major 7th above it; finally, sing a perfect octave below the last pitch (that is, a minor 2nd below the reference pitch).

12 Given a reference pitch, match that pitch vocally (using a neutral syllable), and then sing a major 7th below it; return to the reference pitch; sing a minor 2nd above it; finally, sing a perfect octave below the last pitch (that is, a major 7th below the reference pitch).

3 Given a reference pitch, match that pitch vocally (using a neutral syllable), and sing a minor 2nd above it; from the resultant pitch, sing an ascending major 7th. From that point, sing a descending minor 2nd; finally, from the resultant pitch, sing a descending major 7th.

14 Given a reference pitch, match that pitch vocally (using a neutral syllable), and sing a major 7th below it; from the resultant pitch, sing a descending minor 2nd. From that point, sing an ascending major 7th; finally, from the resultant pitch, sing an ascending minor 2nd.

15 Repeat Exercises 9–14, but using diatonic identities for all pitches sung.

6 The range of the following series of solfège patterns is limited to about one octave. Choose a starting pitch that enables you to sing in a comfortable register, and select a moderate tempo at which you can readily negotiate the given intervals without hesitating or stopping, giving the same duration to each syllable. In those patterns not ending on *do*, sing the tonic when you are through.

Minor	re	↑fa	↑so	↓le	↓so	↑fa	↓me
Minor	so	↑re	↓me	↑le	↓te	↑te	↑do
Major	la	↓fa	↑mi	↑fa	↑re	↓so	↓do
Major	ti	↑re	↓do	↑fa	↓mi	↓fa	↑so
Minor	so	↓ti	↑do	↑re	↓me	↑le	↓so
Major	mi	↑la	↓do	↑ti	↓so	↑re	↓do

Practice increasing your fluency with the intervals and solfège syllables in these patterns while drilling different *rhythmic* patterns. Rather than singing each pitch with the same duration, vary the rhythmic patterns in various ways. Invent your own patterns. Be creative. No matter what your pattern is, your fluency with the material as well as your flexibility as a musician will improve.

Create your own solfège patterns and bring them to class so that your classmates can realize them. Discuss what makes some of these patterns easier to sing than others. What do the easier ones have in common?

17 Repeat Exercises 9–16, but with small groups of students or individuals singing every other pitch.

18 Analyze familiar classical, folk, and contemporary tunes to find examples of ascending and descending minor 2nds and major 7ths within a specific diatonic context. Use the results of your analysis to remember the sound and character of these intervals. Usually, opening lines or refrains are the easiest to recall. In addition to the quality and size of an interval, you should be able to hear and identify where this interval lies in the diatonic scale. For instance, you should know the specific minor 2nd in the major scale on which "Joy to the World" begins.

Here are some suggested tunes to get you started:

m2: "Joy to the World"

"I'm Dreaming of a White Christmas"

M7: "Somewhere over the Rainbow" (1st and 3rd pitches)

19 You now have had a great deal of practice in identifying the intervallic content in numerous familiar tunes, and our repertoire of intervals which we have studied and listened to at length is sizeable. Thus, you have the ability to sing many familiar melodies and tunes with the appropriate diatonic identity for each note of the tune. Here is an example:

mi, re, do; mi, re, do; so, fa, mi; so, fa, mi;

so, do, do, ti, la, ti, do, so, so; so, do, do, ti, la, ti, do, so, so;

so, do, do, ti, la, ti, do, so, so; fa, mi, re, do

By now, you undoubtedly know that we have given the syllables for "Three Blind Mice." (You can choose any system of diatonic identification.) While the rhythms of many familiar tunes vary from one geographical location to another, we can still represent the basic intervallic structure of many melodies. It is an enjoyable, challenging, and effective way to practice our intervals in a musical context. For the moment, we will avoid melodies with nondiatonic pitches, those that **modulate**, and those that outline a diminished 5th or augmented 4th.

Bring to class melodies or phrases of melodies for which you can sing the diatonic identities. Without looking at a score, be able to write these melodies on the bass or treble staff in any key requested, using only your knowledge of the intervallic content of the tune.

Here are some melodies you should use for practice:

◆ *Eine Kleine Nachtmusik*, measures 1–18

◆ "Here Comes the Bride," measures 1–8

◆ "My Bonnie Lies over the Ocean"

◆ "Somewhere over the Rainbow," measures 1–8

◆ "Happy Birthday"

Melodic Constructs

Incorporating Minor Seconds and Major Sevenths

The melodic constructs presented in this and in other units of Area I have been created to drill the specific intervals encountered in the preceding units. These melodic constructs are not intended for sight-singing. They are designed to impart the skills of seeing, recognizing, and hearing intervals, in functional order and within a metrical context, as preparation for the practice of sight-singing more traditional melodic material, such as that presented in Unit 24.

Depending on your vocal capability, some of these melodic constructs will lie outside of a comfortable singing register for you. When this is the case, you may choose to sing a given melodic construct in a different clef or in a key that places the pitches to be sung in a more comfortable register. When the music is written beyond your vocal range, you also have the option of using the key and clef indicated, but singing those pitches that lie outside of your range in a more comfortable octave, either higher or lower than what is written. Your instructor will help you to make these adjustments.

For maximum benefit, these melodic constructs should be studied, analyzed, practiced, and performed both in class and at home. Used in this way, they will give you the technique and ability you need to sight-sing the music you regularly study, learn, and perform.

CLASS DRILLS & HOME EXERCISES

A. Study, analyze, practice, and perform the following melodic constructs.

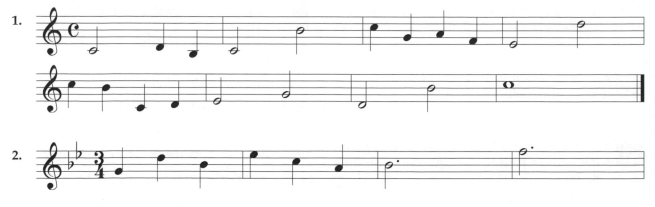

9.

10.

B. *Error detection*: Your instructor will play various melodic constructs for you. Compare what you hear with what is written on the corresponding staves that follow.

   i. Circle any pitch or rhythm that seems to be incorrect.

   ii. Correct any pitch or rhythm so that it matches what you hear.

© 1997 Ardsley House, Publishers, Inc.

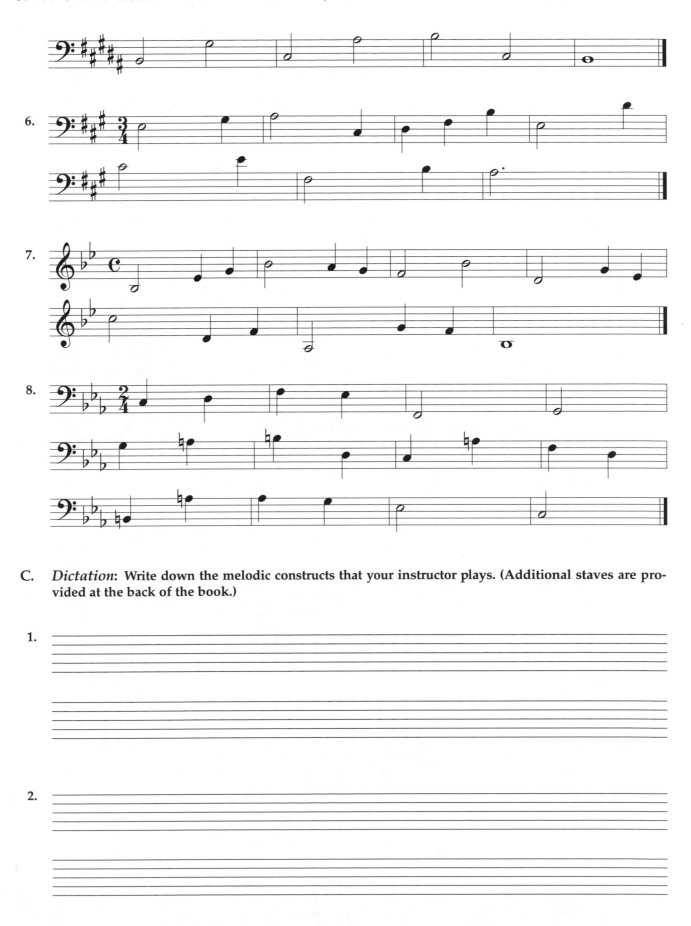

C. *Dictation*: Write down the melodic constructs that your instructor plays. (Additional staves are provided at the back of the book.)

1.

2.

3.

4.

5.

6.

7.

8.

Learning to Hear Intervals

UNIT 14

Diminished Fifths /Augmented Fourths and Diminished Sevenths / Augmented Seconds

*T*his unit introduces two pairs of intervals that are among the most active within the tonal system and that are therefore highly distinctive.

Diminished Fifths and Augmented Fourths

The diminished 5th and its inversion, the augmented 4th, are only heard between two members of any diatonic major scale: specifically, they are heard between $\hat{7}$ and $\hat{4}$ and $\hat{4}$ and $\hat{7}$ (that is, between *ti* ↔ *fa* and *fa* ↔ *ti*, as illustrated in Table I.19). These intervals, each known as a **tritone** because of the three whole steps that make up the interval, are symmetrical. That is, the inversion of a tritone (either the diminished 5th or augmented 4th) yields an interval of identical size. As we have come to appreciate, both $\hat{4}$ (*fa*) and $\hat{7}$ (*ti*) have a strong tendency to resolve by half step to the tonic triad degrees $\hat{1}$ (*ti* → *do*) and $\hat{3}$ (*fa* → *mi*). In the diatonic major scale, the tritone is unique in that it combines the strength of both tendency tones. No other interval suggests resolution to the tonic triad as strongly.

In the natural and harmonic forms of the diatonic minor scale, a tritone is heard between $\hat{6}$ and $\hat{2}$ and between $\hat{2}$ and $\hat{6}$. See Table I.20. While the strong tendency to resolve by half step is just as pronounced as that of the major-scale tritone, the resolution here is not to members of the tonic triad. Rather, these tritones lead to the **mediant triad**, which is the tonic chord of the **relative major**.

In the harmonic and ascending melodic forms of the minor scale, the raised $\hat{7}$ along with $\hat{4}$ creates the same tritone found in major scales, and just as in the major scale, this interval strongly suggests the identity of the tonic triad. Note, however, that in a minor scale, $\hat{4}$ tends to resolve downward by *whole* step to $\hat{3}$. In this context, therefore, the expectation that half-step motion will occur from either member of the tritone is inferred and recalled from the **parallel** major.

In the ascending melodic minor scale, an additional tritone is heard between $\hat{6}$ and $\hat{3}$ and $\hat{3}$ and $\hat{6}$. **Resolution** of this interval has no strong association with similar events in major scales, and the interval resolves to two scale degrees that do not carry such strong key-defining properties. For this reason, this tritone is not encountered frequently.

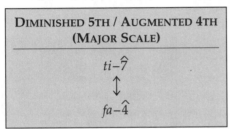

DIMINISHED 5TH / AUGMENTED 4TH (MAJOR SCALE)
ti–$\hat{7}$
↕
fa–$\hat{4}$

TABLE I.19 *Diatonic location of the diminished fifth and augmented fourth: major scale*

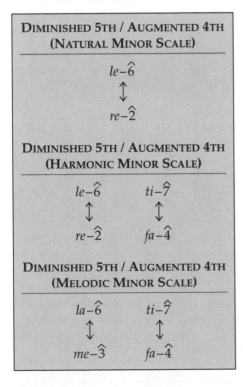

DIMINISHED 5TH / AUGMENTED 4TH (NATURAL MINOR SCALE)	
le–$\hat{6}$	
↕	
re–$\hat{2}$	

DIMINISHED 5TH / AUGMENTED 4TH (HARMONIC MINOR SCALE)	
le–$\hat{6}$	*ti*–$\hat{7}$
↕	↕
re–$\hat{2}$	*fa*–$\hat{4}$

DIMINISHED 5TH / AUGMENTED 4TH (MELODIC MINOR SCALE)	
la–$\hat{6}$	*ti*–$\hat{7}$
↕	↕
me–$\hat{3}$	*fa*–$\hat{4}$

TABLE I.20 *Diatonic locations of diminished fifths and augmented fourths: minor scale*

Diminished Sevenths and Augmented Seconds

Our second pair of distinctive intervals is found exclusively in the harmonic minor scale: the diminished 7th and its inversion, the augmented 2nd. See Tables I.21 and I.22.

The diminished 7th is the more active (dissonant) of the pair, as it has a key-defining potential similar to that of a tritone. The resolution of the diatonic diminished 7th ($\hat{7} \leftrightarrow \hat{6}$) strongly confirms the identity of the tonic and the dominant of the key since both elements of the interval lie within a half step of $\hat{1}$ and $\hat{5}$: $\hat{7}$ leads to $\hat{1}$ and $\hat{6}$ resolves down to $\hat{5}$. In contrast, the $\hat{7} \leftrightarrow \hat{4}$ and $\hat{2} \leftrightarrow \hat{6}$ tritones confirm not only the root but also the quality (minor or major) of the triad to which they customarily resolve.

The augmented 2nd, $\hat{6} \leftrightarrow \hat{7}$, produced by inversion of the diminished 7th, is a much weaker dissonance than its inversion. Both elements of this interval resolve by half step, but to elements of a mildly dissonant interval, the perfect 4th.

Again, we wish to emphasize here, as we have throughout the text, that these distinctive aural characteristics of intervals are only heard, recognized, and understood within a specific tonal context, that is, within a specific scale in which each member has a clear relationship and function with regard to the central or tonic pitch.

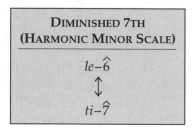

TABLE I.21 *Diatonic location of the diminished seventh*

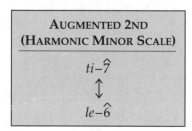

TABLE I.22 *Diatonic location of the augmented second*

CLASS DRILLS & HOME EXERCISES

1 The following procedure is recommended for solving *pitch puzzles*. Each line constitutes a different puzzle. The goal is to remain in the same key throughout the line. If the identity you choose for the *mystery pitch* (∗) causes you to go "out of key" anywhere along the given series of interval movements, that pitch cannot be a solution to the puzzle. Using the interval information given, determine the diatonic identity of the mystery pitch. Note that ∗ represents a pitch (the mystery pitch), not an interval. Without exception, all the intervals listed are diatonic, as is the mystery pitch. The mystery pitch is not necessarily $\hat{1}$, and it is possible that more than one mystery pitch are diatonically consistent with the interval patterns presented. It is also possible

that no such mystery pitch is diatonically possible for the given interval pattern.

Major	∗	↓m7	↑M3	↓A4	↓m2	↑m6
Minor *natural*	∗	↑P5	↓M6	↓P4	↑M2	↑A4
Minor *harmonic*	∗	↑d7	↓m3	↓d5	↑m6	↓m3
Minor *harmonic*	∗	↓d7	↑d5	↓M2	↑P4	↓d5

Once you have determined all possible identities for the mystery pitch in each puzzle, sing each line, in turn, using every possible diatonic identity of the mystery pitch.

2 Your instructor will name two scale degrees, letter names, or solfège syllables, indicating which is the lower of the two. Identify the specified interval instantly as one of the following:

> A4, d5, A2, d7, m2, M7, M2, m7,
> m3, M6, M3, m6, P8, P5, or P4

Then quickly name each scale degree, letter, or syllable between the original two.

3 Given a reference pitch, match that pitch vocally (using a neutral syllable), and then, as instructed, sing one of the intervals

> A4, d5, A2, d7, m2, M7, M2, m7,
> m3, M6, M3, m6, P8, P5, or P4

above or below the given pitch.

4 Given a reference pitch together with some form of diatonic identification, match that pitch vocally with its diatonic identity, and then, as instructed, sing one of the intervals

> A4, d5, A2, d7, m2, M7, M2, m7,
> m3, M6, M3, m6, P8, P5, or P4

above or below the given pitch, using the diatonic identity of the second pitch.

5 After establishing a tonic, your instructor will play melodically two pitches that form one of the following intervals:

> A4, d5, A2, d7, m2, M7, M2, m7,
> m3, M6, M3, m6, P8, P5, or P4

Sing both pitches in the order heard, using their correct diatonic identities.

6 After establishing a tonic, your instructor will name two scale degrees, letter names, or solfège syllables that form one of the following intervals:

> A4, d5, A2, d7, m2, M7, M2, m7,
> m3, M6, M3, m6, P8, P5, or P4

Without first hearing those notes, sing the correct pitches in the order and direction requested, using their corresponding diatonic identities.

7 A single pitch (other than the tonic) will be played and given a diatonic identity. Two more pitches that form one of the intervals

> A4, d5, A2, d7, m2, M7, M2, m7,
> m3, M6, M3, m6, P8, P5, or P4

will then be played melodically. State the interval formed by the last two pitches and sing all three pitches with their diatonic identities.

8 In each of the following rows, sing the five pairs of pitches indicated by the solfège syllables and numbers. (Each pair is independent of the others in that row.) Translate from one system to the other: that is, given numbers, sing the corresponding solfège syllables, and, given solfège syllables, sing the corresponding numbers. With the tonic triad or the diatonic scale, establish a new tonic, as indicated, at the beginning of each row. You may need to re-affirm the tonic before the end of the row, but do so only as often as is really necessary. In each row, go as far as possible before reestablishing the tonic; this may not be necessary at all. However, you should be constantly singing the tonic and dominant pitches to yourself throughout this exercise.

F major	*mi* ↑ *do*	$\hat{6}$ ↑ $\hat{4}$	*mi* ↓ *la*	$\hat{7}$ ↓ $\hat{4}$	*la* ↓ *do*
D♭ major	$\hat{7}$ ↑ $\hat{4}$	*ti* ↓ *la*	$\hat{3}$ ↓ $\hat{5}$	*fa* ↑ *mi*	$\hat{2}$ ↑ $\hat{7}$
A major	*re* ↓ *ti*	$\hat{5}$ ↓ $\hat{3}$	*re* ↓ *fa*	$\hat{1}$ ↓ $\hat{6}$	*fa* ↓ *ti*
G major	$\hat{2}$ ↓ $\hat{3}$	*fa* ↑ *ti*	$\hat{4}$ ↓ $\hat{6}$	*ti* ↑ *so*	$\hat{6}$ ↓ $\hat{2}$
C minor harmonic	*re* ↑ *le*	$\hat{7}$ ↑ $\hat{6}$	*ti* ↓ *le*	$\hat{7}$ ↑ $\hat{4}$	*le* ↑ *ti*
B minor harmonic	$\hat{7}$ ↑ $\hat{6}$	*fa* ↓ *ti*	$\hat{6}$ ↓ $\hat{2}$	*le* ↓ *ti*	$\hat{7}$ ↓ $\hat{6}$
F♯ minor natural	*re* ↑ *le*	$\hat{3}$ ↑ $\hat{2}$	*re* ↓ *le*	$\hat{7}$ ↑ $\hat{5}$	*le* ↓ *me*
G minor natural	$\hat{6}$ ↓ $\hat{2}$	*do* ↓ *me*	$\hat{7}$ ↓ $\hat{4}$	$\hat{6}$ ↑ $\hat{2}$	*so* ↑ *fa*

9 Given a reference pitch, match that pitch vocally (using a neutral syllable), and then sing an augmented 4th above it; return to the reference pitch; sing a diminished 5th below it; finally, sing a perfect octave above the last pitch (that is, an augmented 4th above the reference pitch).

10 Given a reference pitch, match that pitch vocally (using a neutral syllable), and then sing a diminished 5th above it; return to the reference pitch; sing an augmented 4th below it; finally, sing a perfect octave above the last pitch (that is, a diminished 5th above the reference pitch).

11 Given a reference pitch, match that pitch vocally (using a neutral syllable), and then sing an augmented 4th below it; return to the reference pitch; sing a diminished 5th above it; finally, sing a perfect octave below the last pitch (that is an augmented 4th below the reference pitch).

12 Given a reference pitch, match that pitch vocally (using a neutral syllable), and then sing a diminished 5th below it; return to the reference pitch; sing an augmented 4th above it; finally, sing a perfect octave below the last pitch (that is, a diminished 5th below the reference pitch).

13 〰 Given a reference pitch, match that pitch vocally (using a neutral syllable), and then sing an augmented 2nd above it; return to the reference pitch; sing a diminished 7th below it; finally, sing a perfect octave above the last pitch (that is, an augmented 2nd above the reference pitch).

14 〰 Given a reference pitch, match that pitch vocally (using a neutral syllable), and then sing a diminished 7th above it; return to the reference pitch; sing an augmented 2nd below it; finally, sing a perfect octave above the last pitch (that is, a diminished 7th above the reference pitch).

15 〰 Given a reference pitch, match that pitch vocally (using a neutral syllable), and then sing an augmented 2nd below it; return to the reference pitch; sing a diminished 7th above it; finally, sing a perfect octave below the last pitch (that is, an augmented 2nd below the reference pitch).

16 〰 Given a reference pitch, match that pitch vocally (using a neutral syllable), and then sing a diminished 7th below it; return to the reference pitch; sing an augmented 2nd above it; finally, sing a perfect octave below the last pitch (that is, a diminished 7th below the reference pitch).

17 〰 Given a reference pitch, match that pitch vocally (using a neutral syllable) and sing an augmented 2nd above it; from the resultant pitch, sing an ascending diminished 7th. From this point, sing a descending augmented 2nd; from the last pitch, sing a descending diminished 7th.

18 〰 Given a reference pitch, match that pitch vocally (using a neutral syllable) and sing a diminished 7th below it; from the resultant pitch, sing a descending augmented 2nd. From this point, sing an ascending diminished 7th; from the last pitch, sing an ascending augmented 2nd.

19 〰 Given a reference pitch, match that pitch vocally (using a neutral syllable) and sing a diminished 5th above it; from the resultant pitch, sing an ascending augmented 4th. From this point, sing a descending diminished 5th; from the last pitch, sing a descending augmented 4th.

20 〰 Given a reference pitch, match that pitch vocally (using a neutral syllable) and sing an augmented 4th below it; from the resultant pitch, sing a descending diminished 5th. From this point, sing an ascending augmented 4th; from the last pitch, sing an ascending diminished 5th.

21 〰 Repeat Exercises 9–20, but using diatonic identities for all pitches sung.

22 〰 The range of the following series of solfège patterns is limited to about one octave. Choose a starting pitch that enables you to sing in a comfortable register, and select a moderate tempo at which you can readily negotiate the given intervals without hesitating or stopping, giving the same duration to each syllable. In those patterns not ending on *do*, sing the tonic when you are through.

Major	*do*	↓*ti*	↓*fa*	↓*mi*	↑*la*	↓*so*	↓*do*	
Major	*mi*	↑*fa*	↑*ti*	↑*do*	↓*so*	↓*ti*	↑*fa*	↓*mi*
Minor	*so*	↑*le*	↓*ti*	↑*do*	↑*so*	↑*ti*	↑*re*	↓*do*
Minor	*do*	↑*re*	↑*fa*	↓*me*	↑*so*	↑*le*	↑*ti*	↑*do*
Minor	*re*	↓*ti*	↓*le*	↓*so*	↑*fa*	↓*me*	↓*do*	
Minor	*me*	↓*me*	↑*re*	↓*so*	↑*le*	↓*ti*	↑*do*	

Practice increasing your fluency with the intervals and solfège syllables in these patterns while drilling different *rhythmic* patterns. Rather than singing each pitch with the same duration, vary the rhythmic patterns in various ways. Invent your own patterns. Be creative. No matter what your pattern is, your fluency with the material as well as your flexibility as a musician will improve.

Create your own solfège patterns and bring them to class so that your classmates can realize them. Discuss what makes some of these patterns easier to sing than others. What do the easier ones have in common?

23 〰 Repeat Exercises 9–22, but with small groups of students or individuals singing every other pitch.

24 〰 Analyze familiar classical, folk, and contemporary tunes to find examples of ascending and descending augmented 4ths, diminished 5ths, augmented 2nds, and diminished 7ths within a specific diatonic context. Use the results of your analysis to remember the sound and character of these intervals. Usually, opening lines or refrains are the easiest to recall. In addition to the quality and size of an interval, you should be able to hear and identify where this interval lies in the diatonic scale.

Here are some suggestions to get you started: (Why does this particular set of intervals appear so infrequently in the most familiar music?)

A4/d5: "Maria" from *West Side Story*

A2:   "Hava Nagila" (third and fourth pitches)

d7:   "Irrevocable Law" leitmotif from *Das Rheingold*

25 You now have had a great deal of practice in identifying the intervallic content in numerous familiar tunes, and our repertoire of intervals which we have studied and listened to at length is sizeable. You therefore have the ability to sing many familiar melodies and tunes with the appropriate diatonic identity for each note of the tune.

Bring to class melodies or phrases of melodies for which you can sing all the diatonic identities.

Without looking at a score, be able to write these melodies on the bass or treble staff in any key requested, using only your knowledge of the intervallic content of the tune. Avoid melodies that appear to modulate or that contain nondiatonic pitches.

Here are some melodies you should use for practice:

◆ Brahms's "Lullaby"
◆ "Rudolph, the Red-Nosed Reindeer"
◆ "Over the River and through the Wood"
◆ "Jingle Bells"

Melodic Constructs

UNIT **15**

*Incorporating
Diminished Fifths / Augmented Fourths and
Diminished Sevenths / Augmented Seconds*

*T*he melodic constructs presented in this and in other units of Area I have been created to drill the specific intervals encountered in the preceding units. These melodic constructs are not intended for sight-singing. They are designed to impart the skills of seeing, recognizing, and hearing intervals, in functional order and within a metrical context, as preparation for the practice of sight-singing more traditional melodic material, such as that presented in Unit 24.

Depending on your vocal capability, some of these melodic constructs will lie outside of a comfortable singing register for you. When this is the case, you may choose to sing a given melodic construct in a different clef or in a key that places the pitches to be sung in a more comfortable register. When the music is written beyond your vocal range, you also have the option of using the key and clef indicated, but singing those pitches that lie outside of your range in a more comfortable octave, either higher or lower than what is written. Your instructor will help you to make these adjustments.

For maximum benefit, these melodic constructs should be studied, analyzed, practiced, and performed both in class and at home. Used in this way, they will give you the technique and ability you need to sight-sing the music you regularly study, learn, and perform.

CLASS DRILLS & HOME EXERCISES

A. Study, analyze, practice, and perform the following melodic constructs.

B. *Error detection*: Your instructor will play various melodic constructs for you. Compare what you hear with what is written on the corresponding staves that follow.

   i. Circle any pitch or rhythm that seems to be incorrect.

   ii. Correct any pitch or rhythm so that it matches what you hear.

C. *Dictation*: **Write down the melodic constructs that your instructor plays. (Additional staves are provided at the back of the book.)**

1.

2.

3.

4.

5.

6.

7.

8.

Rhythm

UNIT

16

*Compound Duple
and Triple Meters*

● ●

Division into Three   Up to this point, all the melodic constructs and melodies presented for practice and dictation have been in simple meters. That is, the first level of division of each beat has been into two, regardless of the number of beats per measure. In **compound meters**, the first level of division of each beat, regardless of the number of beats per measure, is into three, as indicated by Table I.23.

***The Numerator and
Beat Structure in
Compound Meters***   Unlike our experience with simple meters, the denominator of a time signature indicating compound meter does not specify the note value of the beat. For example, in $\frac{6}{8}$ meter, although the time signature does correctly inform us that we find the equivalent of six eighth-notes in each measure, the denominator does not tell us that the eighth notes are divisions of two dotted-quarter beats. In the case of compound meters, we should look to the numerator for an indication of the beat structure. Thus, if dividing the numerator by 3 produces a quotient other than 1, we have a compound meter. The resulting integer represents the number of beats in each measure. For example, for a compound meter in which the numerator is 6, there

© 1997 Ardsley House, Publishers, Inc.

TIME SIGNATURE	VALUE OF BEAT	BEATS PER MEASURE	DIVISION OF BEAT	SUBDIVISION OF BEAT
6/2	𝅝.	2		
6/4	𝅗𝅥.	2		
9/4	𝅗𝅥.	3		
12/4	𝅗𝅥.	4		
6/8	𝅘𝅥.	2		
9/8	𝅘𝅥.	3		
12/8	𝅘𝅥.	4		
6/16	𝅘𝅥𝅮.	2		
9/16	𝅘𝅥𝅮.	3		
12/16	𝅘𝅥𝅮.	4		

TABLE I.23 *Compound meters*

are 2 beats to the measure (6 ÷ 3 = 2); for a numerator of 9, there are 3 beats to the measure. In compound meters the note value of a beat is always a dotted note whose duration is equal to three times that of the note indicated by the denominator. What would the note value of the beat be in $\frac{9}{32}$?

When a composition in compound meter proceeds at a slow tempo, even though the division of the beat might be shown when conducting, the emphasis on the larger beats must be understood, felt, and projected in performance. We accomplish this, as we do in simple meters, by making sure that the regular pattern of strong beats in every measure is not disturbed by an emphasis on the divisions of each beat.

CLASS DRILLS & HOME EXERCISES

The following exercises are designed to drill several common patterns found in compound meters in Table I.23 while reviewing the scales that you encountered in Unit 1. As you have done throughout your study of functional hearing, treat each excerpt as a complete piece of music; once you have begun, do not stop. Conduct as you sing. For the syllables or numbers with which you choose to identify each scale degree, select a tempo that will allow you to negotiate them without hesitation or errors. If you find that you have made a mistake, begin again at a slower tempo. Work for complete accuracy as early in the process as possible. After you have completed each exercise accurately, increase the tempo gradually as you repeat each of the lines. In this manner you will achieve a secure performance and will solidify your familiarity with the various metrical patterns.

When practicing the exercises in the minor keys, be certain to make the correct alterations to the appropriate pitches, according to the form of minor scale indicated for each exercise.

A. Major Keys

B. Minor Keys

Natural

Harmonic

Learning to Hear Intervals

UNIT 17

Compound Intervals

*A*ny interval larger than an octave is said to be **compound**. Compound intervals are closely related to those **simple intervals** that have thus far been presented. By subtracting 7 from the size of the compound interval, one finds its equivalent simple interval, as is illustrated in Example I.12. There is no difference between any compound interval and its equivalent simple interval in their function and tendencies to resolve in predictable ways. However, there is a significant difference in **color** between compound and simple intervals attributable to the extra octave(s) found in compound intervals.

We study compound intervals as a means of further expanding our ability to distinguish between various characteristics of sounds and to develop an awareness of the register in which specific pitches sound.

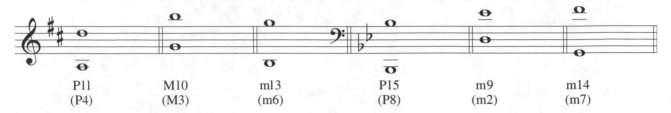

| P11 | M10 | ml3 | P15 | m9 | m14 |
| (P4) | (M3) | (m6) | (P8) | (m2) | (m7) |

EXAMPLE I.12 *Compound intervals with the corresponding simple intervals shown in parentheses*

CLASS DRILLS & HOME EXERCISES

1 Your instructor will name two scale degrees, letter names, or solfège syllables, indicating which is the lower of the two. Assume that an interval greater than an octave separates these two pitches. Identify the specified interval instantly as one of the following:

A11, d12, A9, d14, m9, M14, M9, m14, m10, M13, M10, m13, P15, P12, or P11

2 After establishing the tonic, your instructor will play melodically two pitches that form one of the following intervals:

A11, d12, A9, d14, m9, M14, M9, m14, m10, M13, M10, m13, P15, P12, or P11

Identify the quality and size of the interval and give the diatonic identities of the pitches heard. Sing both pitches, if possible. If your vocal range does not encompass these pitches, sing the simple-interval equivalent.

3 A single pitch (other than the tonic) will be played and given a diatonic identity. Two more pitches that form one of the intervals

A11, d12, A9, d14, m9, M14, M9, m14, m10, M13, M10, m13, P15, P12, or P11

will then be played melodically. State the quality and size of the interval formed by the last two pitches.

Melodic Constructs

UNIT **18**

Incorporating Compound Intervals

*I*n the exercises presented in this unit you will notice that there are no melodic constructs to be sung as written. This is an acknowledgment of the fact that unless you possess unusual vocal capability, most compound intervals will be difficult for you to sing accurately or comfortably, and most music that incorporates many such intervals spans an extremely wide range. Nevertheless, when given an excerpt that is written out of your vocal range or beyond your vocal capability, you will be asked to reduce the compound intervals to simple intervals at sight so that you can sing them in a comfortable register. (In fact, earlier in the text, you had performed a similar reduction when encountering large simple intervals that required singing in an extreme register.) This is an important skill which will ultimately help you to hear and comprehend music that is written in such a way that you can neither play it on your instrument nor sing it.

CLASS DRILLS & HOME EXERCISES

A. *Error detection*: **Your instructor will play various melodic constructs for you. Compare what you hear with what is written on the corresponding staves that follow.**

   i. **Circle any pitch or rhythm that seems to be incorrect.**

   ii. **Correct any pitch or rhythm so that it matches what you hear.**

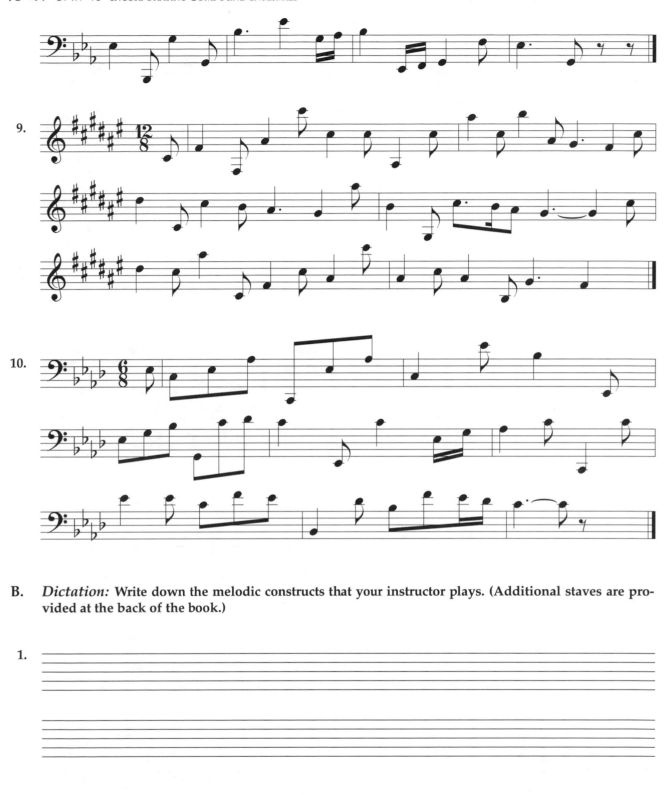

B. *Dictation:* **Write down the melodic constructs that your instructor plays. (Additional staves are provided at the back of the book.)**

1.

2.

3.

4.

5.

6.

7.

8.

Learning to Hear Intervals

UNIT **19**

Harmonic Intervals

*T*hroughout these past units we have spent considerable time and energy in hearing and learning the aural characteristics of the principal diatonic intervals of the major and minor scales. In the present unit and those that follow, we will again consider all of the common diatonic intervals, but with a different perspective from before. This time we will study these intervals *harmonically*, that is, with the constituent pitches of each interval sounding simultaneously.

In no way does this presentation alter the character and tendencies of the intervals as we have perceived them so far. The additional challenge for us in these units is to be able to hear the individual quality of the intervals when they are presented simultaneously. While each harmonic interval is truly the result of adding two diatonic pitches together, for a while you may still hear one pitch and then the other in any given interval; we encourage you to try to recognize the unique quality of each sonority *as a whole*. This skill will be developed throughout this text; what you do at this time will greatly enhance your ability to hear very quickly the quality and character of multiple-voice chords and to comprehend how they relate to one another.

Although there is nothing that we can do to speed up the information that travels along the neurosensory pathway from our ears to our brains, slow, regular, and frequent practice of this and every musical skill you develop will greatly increase your *familiarity* with what you are hearing. This undoubtedly takes a lot of time and effort. Those intervals that are the most familiar to you will be recognized more quickly than any others.

CLASS DRILLS & HOME EXERCISES

1 After establishing the tonic, your instructor will play harmonically two pitches that form one of the following intervals:

A4, d5, A2, d7, m2, M7, M2, m7,
m3, M6, M3, m6, P8, P5, or P4

First, state the quality and size of the interval, and then give the diatonic identities of the component pitches.

2 A single pitch (other than the tonic) will be played and given a diatonic identity. Two more pitches that form one of the intervals

A4, d5, A2, d7, m2, M7, M2, m7,
m3, M6, M3, m6, P8, P5, or P4

will then be played harmonically. First, state the quality and size of the harmonic interval, and then give the diatonic identities of the component pitches.

Dictation

UNIT 20

Harmonic Intervals

*I*n this unit you will be offered three separate methods of practicing and demonstrating your skill in perceiving scale-degree function and interval quality. In Exercise Set A, you will be relying solely on your aural perception of what you hear and then writing it down on a staff. In Exercise Sets B and C, you will need to combine your aural perception with your cognitive understanding of interval quality and diatonic location to determine whether what you have heard is, indeed, present on a given staff or is represented by syllables and scale-degree numbers. In Exercise Set A, the choice of possible intervals is unrestricted; in Exercise Sets B and C, where the choices are more narrowly prescribed, you will have to evaluate each interval separately to see if it matches what you have heard.

CLASS DRILLS & HOME EXERCISES

A. *Interval identification*: Using the following blank staves, for each exercise prepare a staff with either the treble or the bass clef and with a key signature designated by your instructor. After the tonic has been established by your instructor, you will hear a series of harmonic intervals played in that key. First, write each interval that you hear on the staff that you have prepared; then, underneath the staff, below the interval, write the quality and size of that interval.

B. *Interval detection*: Your instructor will establish the tonic in the given key and play one harmonic interval for each measure in this exercise set. Mark a check (✓) on an appropriate line below the interval you hear in each measure. If the interval is not present, do not mark the lines below that measure. You can use each exercise for up to three separate dictations. Simply mark your answers on the first, second, or third set of lines underneath the measures, corresponding to the dictation you are taking.

For example, in Exercise 1, measure 1, when the instructor plays and the student hears:

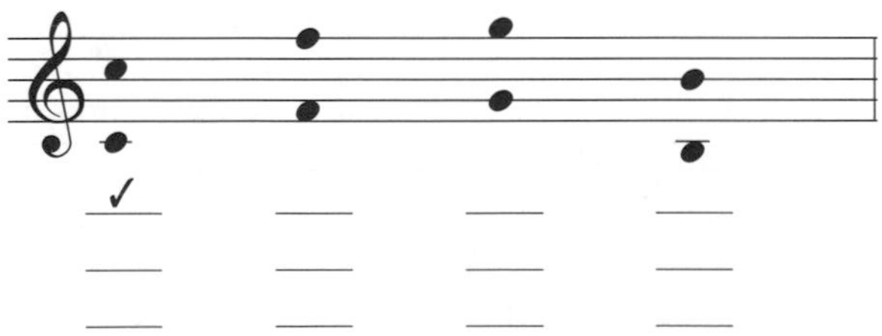

And when the instructor plays and the student hears:

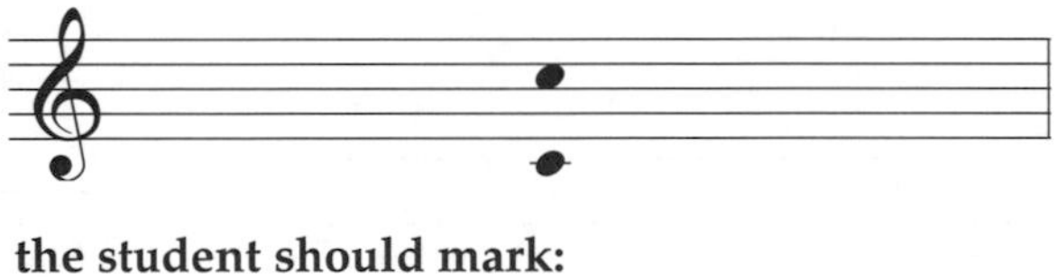

the student should mark:

the student should make no mark:

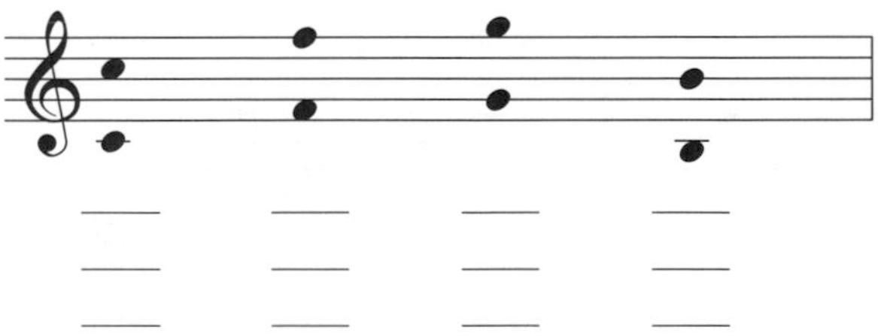

1.

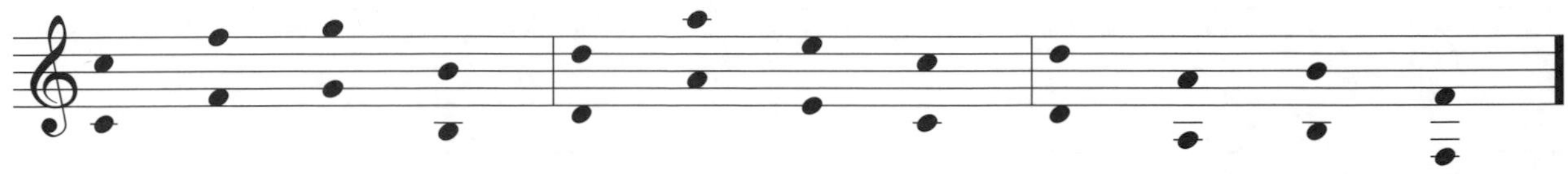

Dictation 1: ____

Dictation 2: ____

Dictation 3: ____

2.

Dictation 1: _____ _____ _____ _____ _____ _____ _____ _____ _____
Dictation 2: _____ _____ _____ _____ _____ _____ _____ _____ _____
Dictation 3: _____ _____ _____ _____ _____ _____ _____ _____ _____

3.

Dictation 1: _____ _____ _____ _____ _____ _____ _____ _____ _____
Dictation 2: _____ _____ _____ _____ _____ _____ _____ _____ _____
Dictation 3: _____ _____ _____ _____ _____ _____ _____ _____ _____

4.

Dictation 1: _____ _____ _____ _____ _____ _____ _____ _____ _____
Dictation 2: _____ _____ _____ _____ _____ _____ _____ _____ _____
Dictation 3: _____ _____ _____ _____ _____ _____ _____ _____ _____

5.

Dictation 1: _____ _____ _____ _____ _____ _____ _____ _____ _____
Dictation 2: _____ _____ _____ _____ _____ _____ _____ _____ _____
Dictation 3: _____ _____ _____ _____ _____ _____ _____ _____ _____

6.

Dictation 1: _____ _____ _____ _____ _____ _____ _____ _____ _____
Dictation 2: _____ _____ _____ _____ _____ _____ _____ _____ _____
Dictation 3: _____ _____ _____ _____ _____ _____ _____ _____ _____

7.

Dictation 1: _____ _____ _____ _____ _____ _____ _____ _____ _____
Dictation 2: _____ _____ _____ _____ _____ _____ _____ _____ _____
Dictation 3: _____ _____ _____ _____ _____ _____ _____ _____ _____

8.

Dictation 1: ___ ___ ___ ___ ___ ___ ___ ___ ___ ___ ___ ___

Dictation 2: ___ ___ ___ ___ ___ ___ ___ ___ ___ ___ ___ ___

Dictation 3: ___ ___ ___ ___ ___ ___ ___ ___ ___ ___ ___ ___

9.

Dictation 1: ___ ___ ___ ___ ___ ___ ___ ___ ___ ___ ___ ___

Dictation 2: ___ ___ ___ ___ ___ ___ ___ ___ ___ ___ ___ ___

Dictation 3: ___ ___ ___ ___ ___ ___ ___ ___ ___ ___ ___ ___

10.

Dictation 1: ___ ___ ___ ___ ___ ___ ___ ___ ___ ___ ___ ___

Dictation 2: ___ ___ ___ ___ ___ ___ ___ ___ ___ ___ ___ ___

Dictation 3: ___ ___ ___ ___ ___ ___ ___ ___ ___ ___ ___ ___

11.

Dictation 1: ___ ___ ___ ___ ___ ___ ___ ___ ___ ___ ___ ___

Dictation 2: ___ ___ ___ ___ ___ ___ ___ ___ ___ ___ ___ ___

Dictation 3: ___ ___ ___ ___ ___ ___ ___ ___ ___ ___ ___ ___

12.

Dictation 1: ___ ___ ___ ___ ___ ___ ___ ___ ___ ___ ___ ___

Dictation 2: ___ ___ ___ ___ ___ ___ ___ ___ ___ ___ ___ ___

Dictation 3: ___ ___ ___ ___ ___ ___ ___ ___ ___ ___ ___ ___

13.

Dictation 1: ___ ___ ___ ___ ___ ___ ___ ___ ___ ___ ___ ___

Dictation 2: ___ ___ ___ ___ ___ ___ ___ ___ ___ ___ ___ ___

Dictation 3: ___ ___ ___ ___ ___ ___ ___ ___ ___ ___ ___ ___

14.

Dictation 1: _____ _____ _____ _____
Dictation 2: _____ _____ _____ _____
Dictation 3: _____ _____ _____ _____

15.

Dictation 1: ____ ____ ____ ____ ____ ____
Dictation 2: ____ ____ ____ ____ ____ ____
Dictation 3: ____ ____ ____ ____ ____ ____

C. *Error detection*: Your instructor will establish the tonic in a given key. You will then hear a series of five harmonic intervals in that key. For each interval, compare what you hear with the diatonic identities listed for each interval. If the interval you hear is correctly represented by the diatonic identities given, mark a check (✓) on the first line below the interval; if not, mark a cross (✗). You can then place the correct diatonic identities to the right of those printed. If you hear a compound interval, circle the diatonic identities of the two pitches involved.

You can use the chart for three separate dictations. Simply mark your answer on the appropriate line underneath the diatonic identities of the interval in question, corresponding to the dictation you are taking. For example, when the instructor plays and the student hears:

A major:

the student marks:

Higher pitch: *la*	$\widehat{2}$	*do* **re**	$\widehat{\widehat{4}}$ **re**	*re*
Lower pitch: *la*	$\widehat{7}$	*mi* **fa**	$\widehat{7}$ **la**	*la*

Dictation 1:	✓	✓	✗ M6	✗ P11	✓
Dictation 2:	_____	_____	_____	_____	_____
Dictation 3:	_____	_____	_____	_____	_____

Major Keys

1.

Higher pitch: *la*	$\widehat{2}$	*do*	$\widehat{4}$	*re*
Lower pitch: *la*	$\widehat{7}$	*mi*	$\widehat{7}$	*la*

Dictation 1:	_____	_____	_____	_____	_____
Dictation 2:	_____	_____	_____	_____	_____
Dictation 3:	_____	_____	_____	_____	_____

2. Higher pitch: $\hat{5}$ do $\hat{7}$ fa $\hat{1}$
   Lower pitch: $\hat{4}$ re $\hat{3}$ ti $\hat{6}$

   Dictation 1: _____ _____ _____ _____ _____
   Dictation 2: _____ _____ _____ _____ _____
   Dictation 3: _____ _____ _____ _____ _____

3. Higher pitch: so $\hat{6}$ fa $\hat{3}$ so
   Lower pitch: ti $\hat{1}$ re $\hat{3}$ la

   Dictation 1: _____ _____ _____ _____ _____
   Dictation 2: _____ _____ _____ _____ _____
   Dictation 3: _____ _____ _____ _____ _____

4. Higher pitch: $\hat{6}$ re $\hat{7}$ mi $\hat{6}$
   Lower pitch: $\hat{7}$ so $\hat{1}$ re $\hat{4}$

   Dictation 1: _____ _____ _____ _____ _____
   Dictation 2: _____ _____ _____ _____ _____
   Dictation 3: _____ _____ _____ _____ _____

5. Higher pitch: ti $\hat{3}$ re $\hat{3}$ do
   Lower pitch: re $\hat{5}$ fa $\hat{6}$ ti

   Dictation 1: _____ _____ _____ _____ _____
   Dictation 2: _____ _____ _____ _____ _____
   Dictation 3: _____ _____ _____ _____ _____

6. Higher pitch: $\hat{7}$ la $\hat{5}$ fa $\hat{2}$
   Lower pitch: $\hat{4}$ mi $\hat{1}$ la $\hat{3}$

   Dictation 1: _____ _____ _____ _____ _____
   Dictation 2: _____ _____ _____ _____ _____
   Dictation 3: _____ _____ _____ _____ _____

7. Higher pitch: fa $\hat{7}$ do $\hat{3}$ ti
   Lower pitch: do $\hat{6}$ so $\hat{4}$ so

   Dictation 1: _____ _____ _____ _____ _____
   Dictation 2: _____ _____ _____ _____ _____
   Dictation 3: _____ _____ _____ _____ _____

Natural Minor Keys

8. Higher pitch: *re*   *le*   *re*   *me*   *te*
Lower pitch: *te*   *do*   *so*   *do*   *fa*

Dictation 1: ____ ____ ____ ____ ____
Dictation 2: ____ ____ ____ ____ ____
Dictation 3: ____ ____ ____ ____ ____

9. Higher pitch: $\hat{5}$ $\hat{4}$ *me*   *le*   *te*
Lower pitch: $\hat{2}$ $\hat{7}$ *fa*   *le*   *do*

Dictation 1: ____ ____ ____ ____ ____
Dictation 2: ____ ____ ____ ____ ____
Dictation 3: ____ ____ ____ ____ ____

10. Higher pitch: *fa*   *do*   *te* $\hat{5}$ $\hat{4}$
Lower pitch: *le*   *so*   *me* $\hat{6}$ $\hat{1}$

Dictation 1: ____ ____ ____ ____ ____
Dictation 2: ____ ____ ____ ____ ____
Dictation 3: ____ ____ ____ ____ ____

11. Higher pitch: $\hat{1}$ *le* $\hat{1}$ *me* $\hat{2}$
Lower pitch: $\hat{4}$ *te* $\hat{6}$ *me* $\hat{4}$

Dictation 1: ____ ____ ____ ____ ____
Dictation 2: ____ ____ ____ ____ ____
Dictation 3: ____ ____ ____ ____ ____

12. Higher pitch: *te* $\hat{2}$ *me* $\hat{6}$ *so*
Lower pitch: *re* $\hat{3}$ *le* $\hat{5}$ *me*

Dictation 1: ____ ____ ____ ____ ____
Dictation 2: ____ ____ ____ ____ ____
Dictation 3: ____ ____ ____ ____ ____

13. Higher pitch: $\hat{6}$ *so* $\hat{4}$ *le* $\hat{3}$
Lower pitch: $\hat{3}$ *te* $\hat{4}$ *re* $\hat{7}$

Dictation 1: ____ ____ ____ ____ ____
Dictation 2: ____ ____ ____ ____ ____
Dictation 3: ____ ____ ____ ____ ____

14. Higher pitch: *so* $\hat{6}$ *do* $\hat{3}$ *te*

      Lower pitch: *do* $\hat{4}$ *me* $\hat{5}$ *le*

Dictation 1: _____ _____ _____ _____ _____

Dictation 2: _____ _____ _____ _____ _____

Dictation 3: _____ _____ _____ _____ _____

Harmonic Minor Keys

15. Higher pitch: $\hat{1}$ *re* $\hat{6}$ *do* $\hat{4}$

      Lower pitch: $\hat{4}$ *me* $\hat{7}$ *so* $\hat{6}$

Dictation 1: _____ _____ _____ _____ _____

Dictation 2: _____ _____ _____ _____ _____

Dictation 3: _____ _____ _____ _____ _____

16. Higher pitch: *me* $\hat{5}$ *me* $\hat{1}$ *ti*

      Lower pitch: *do* $\hat{2}$ *fa* $\hat{6}$ *so*

Dictation 1: _____ _____ _____ _____ _____

Dictation 2: _____ _____ _____ _____ _____

Dictation 3: _____ _____ _____ _____ _____

17. Higher pitch: $\hat{4}$ *me* $\hat{7}$ *re* $\hat{6}$

      Lower pitch: $\hat{5}$ *le* $\hat{1}$ *le* $\hat{3}$

Dictation 1: _____ _____ _____ _____ _____

Dictation 2: _____ _____ _____ _____ _____

Dictation 3: _____ _____ _____ _____ _____

18. Higher pitch: *fa* $\hat{2}$ *le* $\hat{7}$ *me*

      Lower pitch: *me* $\hat{5}$ *do* $\hat{7}$ *re*

Dictation 1: _____ _____ _____ _____ _____

Dictation 2: _____ _____ _____ _____ _____

Dictation 3: _____ _____ _____ _____ _____

19. Higher pitch: *do* $\hat{7}$ *le* $\hat{4}$ *do*

      Lower pitch: *re* $\hat{6}$ *fa* $\hat{7}$ *me*

Dictation 1: _____ _____ _____ _____ _____

Dictation 2: _____ _____ _____ _____ _____

Dictation 3: _____ _____ _____ _____ _____

20. Higher pitch: $\hat{5}$ *ti* $\hat{3}$ *le* $\hat{1}$

Lower pitch: $\hat{6}$ *fa* $\hat{5}$ *re* $\hat{7}$

Dictation 1: _____   _____   _____   _____   _____

Dictation 2: _____   _____   _____   _____   _____

Dictation 3: _____   _____   _____   _____   _____

Dictation

UNIT 21

Guidelines for Two-Part Rhythmic Dictation

Two-Part Dictation

In preparation for our study of multiple-part textures in Area II, we need some preliminary practice in listening to and notating more than one part at a time.

In order to familiarize you with this process, we will present all of our rhythmic material in the context of the harmonic intervals which you have been studying. Our aim is to introduce you to the practice of hearing and writing two parts and to reinforce your familiarity with the harmonic form of the diatonic intervals. We will present an increasingly varied set of rhythmic patterns for practice.

The techniques for writing down a two-part dictation are essentially the same as for writing down a single-part line. The score setup and your work in establishing the key and tempo will be the same. There is no need to change the shorthand symbols we use to write down what we hear. As before, the challenge will be to analyze the melodic/intervallic content accurately and to place it in the appropriate metrical context. Remember that you are asked to represent each beat of every measure during the score setup as an aid to maintaining your place in the measure at all times.

Hearing the Composite Rhythm

When the dictation is completed, the result we hope to produce is a representation of two independent rhythms playing simultaneously, as shown in Example I.13. But this is not the actual rhythm presented

EXAMPLE I.13   *Two simultaneous rhythms*

to our ears. We hear the combination or sum of these two patterns, the **composite rhythm**. As its name suggests, the composite rhythm represents the totality of what we hear when the rhythms of the two independent lines actually coincide and sound together. Therefore, in two-part dictation, we ask that you *first* write the composite rhythm as illustrated in Example I.14.

This is the most successful and accurate way of hearing and representing the complete rhythmic activity. Writing down the composite rhythm first helps us to describe what we are hearing more completely. Were we first to isolate the parts and hear them separately, we might become confused and write what is being performed incorrectly.

Completing the Dictation

Once the composite rhythm is comprehended and written down, the following steps should be taken to complete the dictation. (Of course, in this instance we know the answer is Example I.13, and we are working backward to illustrate how to proceed.)

1. During the next few hearings, determine where the two parts sound in each measure, and indicate this with short vertical dashes above and below the staff. (This is the step with which we are frequently tempted to start, as we are anxious to get to the heart of the matter. However, this step will be easier, quicker, and more accurate if we have the composite rhythm to work from.) See Example I.15.

2. During the next several hearings, we concern ourselves with durations, especially those of the longer notes. We can add rests where we are certain, as in Example I.16.

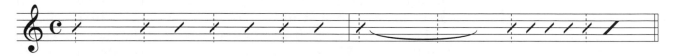

EXAMPLE I.14 *The resulting composite rhythm heard in Example I.13*

EXAMPLE I.15 *Indicating where each part sounds in each measure*

EXAMPLE I.16 *Indicating rests and duration*

3. In the final hearings, we can make ultimate decisions about subtle differences in durations. See Example I.17.

Example I.18 presents another completed two-part dictation. What would the composite rhythm of these two patterns be? Use the staff provided in Example I.19.

Now let's try the reverse process. Example I.20 presents a composite rhythm.

Using the blank staff lines that follow in Example I.21, create three possible two-part solutions for this composite rhythm. There are many possibilities. Be creative!

EXAMPLE I.17 *Adding more details of duration*

EXAMPLE I.18 *A completed two-part dictation*

EXAMPLE I.19 *The composite rhythm of the two patterns presented in Example I.18*

EXAMPLE I.20 *A composite rhythm*

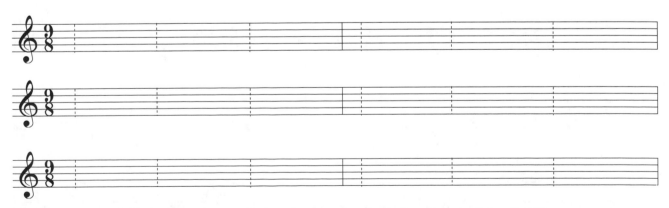

EXAMPLE I.21 *Three possible two-part solutions for the composite rhythm given in Example I.20*

Rhythm

UNIT

22

Two-Part Rhythms in Simple Meters

*I*n the exercises that follow, regardless of the meter in which you are performing, you should make every attempt to project the principal beats clearly in each measure and to de-emphasize their divisions and subdivisions. Likewise, try to see where the natural phrases occur in each line, and use the expressive capabilities of your voice to show how you think the measures are grouped into phrases and what the contour of those phrases might be. In addition to the techniques given in the following Class Drills and Home Exercises, your instructor may suggest other methods of performing these patterns. Can you think of different ways to perform this music that will challenge, and thereby improve, your sense of rhythm? Be certain to analyze, practice, and perform the rhythms that you hear and write down from dictation.

CLASS DRILLS & HOME EXERCISES

A. Study, analyze, practice, and perform the following rhythmic patterns.

  i. Perform each voice part as a solo.

  ii. With a classmate or in ensemble, perform the duets by vocalizing both voice parts with the proper diatonic identity. Conduct as you sing.

  iii. Perform the duets by yourself, vocalizing the upper voice with the proper diatonic identity and tapping the rhythm of the lower voice.

  iv. Perform the duets by yourself, vocalizing the lower voice with the proper diatonic identity and tapping the rhythm of the upper voice.

© 1997 Ardsley House, Publishers, Inc.

17.

B.   *Dictation*: Write down the rhythmic patterns that your instructor presents. Use the procedures outlined in Unit 21, on pages 87–89. (Additional staves are provided at the back of the book.)

1.

2.

3.

4.

5.

6.

7.

8.

9.

10.

Rhythm

UNIT

23

*Two-Part Rhythms
in Compound Meters*

I n the exercises that follow, regardless of the meter in which you are performing, you should make every attempt to project the principal beats clearly in each measure and to de-emphasize their divisions and subdivisions. Likewise, try to see where the natural phrases occur in each line, and use the expressive capabilities of your voice to show how you think the measures are grouped into phrases and what the contour of those phrases might be. In addition to the techniques given in the following Class Drills and Home Exercises, your instructor may suggest other methods of performing these patterns. Can you think of different ways to perform this music that will challenge, and thereby improve, your sense of rhythm? Be certain to analyze, practice, and perform the rhythms that you hear and write down from dictation, in Section B.

Whether you are performing or writing down a rhythm in compound meter, make sure that you understand the relationship between the time signature and the value of the beat before you begin. You should also clearly understand how each note value relates to the beat.

CLASS DRILLS & HOME EXERCISES

A. Study, analyze, practice, and perform the following rhythmic patterns.

 i. Perform each voice part as a solo.

 ii. With a classmate or in ensemble, perform the duets by vocalizing both voice parts with the proper diatonic identity. Conduct as you sing.

 iii. Perform the duets by yourself, vocalizing the upper voice with the proper diatonic identity and tapping the rhythm of the lower voice.

 iv. Perform the duets by yourself, vocalizing the lower voice with the proper diatonic identity and tapping the rhythm of the upper voice.

B. *Dictation:* **Write down the rhythmic patterns that your instructor presents. Use the procedures outlined in Unit 21, on pages 87–89. (Additional staves are provided at the back of the book.)**

1.

2.

3.

4.

5.

6.

7.

8.

Melody

UNIT 24

Sight-Singing

S ight-singing and sight-reading are invaluable skills for you as an aspiring musician. You must train your eye to extract the essential information quickly and accurately from any score and to train your voice to translate this information into an effective realization.

Many students misconstrue the purpose of learning to sight-sing: we are not attempting to train your voice *per se*, although good vocal production will enhance many aspects of your sight-singing. Rather, we are calling upon your voice to demonstrate the ability you possess to read music effectively, without practicing beforehand. The use of one's voice as an essential tool in teaching, learning, comprehending, and communicating about music is an ancient tradition that is just as relevant and valuable in our modern era as it has been for centuries.

Throughout Area I, you have been asked to learn to hear the unique functional character of all diatonic scale degrees and intervals in a variety of forms and contexts. The melodies assembled in Unit 24 will help you to practice and solidify your ability to recognize many of these intervals in a traditional melodic context.

Successful sight-singing of these melodies requires a strategy and a method, in addition to your knowledge and aural perception of intervals within the context of major and minor scales.

The first step in attempting to sight-sing or sight-read any music should be to gain an understanding of the general characteristics of the music you are about to read. In this step, you should consider range, key, clef, meter, and rhythmic vocabulary, and you should also look for any unusual melodic or rhythmic events.

Once you have determined the parameters and the atypical aspects of the music, you should turn your attention to establishing the tempo at which you will first attempt to sight-sing. This may be slower than the tempo at which the music will be ultimately performed. Experience and practice with sight-singing will help to close the gap between these two tempos. Choose a realistic tempo, based on your assessment of the difficulty of the music, that is likely to yield a high degree of accuracy. On subsequent readings, you can choose a faster tempo, if necessary, but in your first time through, your main goal should be complete accuracy, regardless of the tempo you choose.

After choosing your tempo, internalize the beat for at least two complete measures, and let this become your constant guide throughout. Conduct (or tap) as you prepare and as you sing. It is essential that nothing disturb the regularity of beats in each measure, not even a mistake in pitch or rhythm. Conducting will help you to achieve this solidity.

When sight-singing, you must proceed as if you are giving a public performance, in that you must not stop to correct errors of any kind. If, when sight-singing, you make a habit of stopping when the unintentional or unexpected occurs, you will quickly learn this reaction as a performance technique. You must discipline yourself to commit to a chosen tempo and to maintain it throughout the piece. If mistakes occur, improvise until you can recover and proceed according to what is written, or simply mark the time for the measures you are unable to sing.

Firmly establish the tonic and dominant in your mind with a scale or tonic triad, and relate everything you hear and see while sight-singing to these tonal guideposts.

Using your knowledge of intervals and function along with the aural perception you have developed in your mind's ear, sing the music that is before you. Make every effort to read ahead of the note you are singing at the moment. Try to see, think, and sing in phrases.

If a particular melody seems unusually challenging, silently realize the rhythm and/or the diatonic identities of each pitch before you sight-sing.

CLASS DRILLS & HOME EXERCISES

Study, analyze, and sight-sing each of the following (45) melodies.

"Lauda Sion Salvatorem"

12th century plainsong

"Veni Redemptor gentium"

12th century plainsong

"Jesu, nostra redemptio"

13th century plainsong

"Victimae Paschali laudes"

11th century plainsong

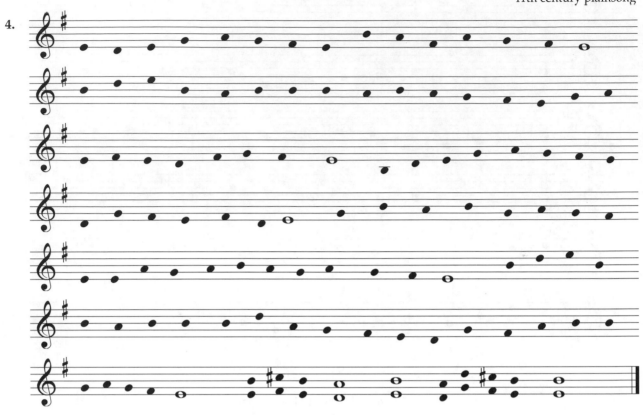

J. Crüger

W. Boyce

"Hatikvah"

Folk song

"La Marseillaise"

C. J. Rouget de l'Isle

8.

Canadian folk song

9.

Spanish folk song

10.

German folk song

11.

German folk song

12.

German folk song

13.

German folk song

14.

German folk song

15.

German folk song

16.

German folk song

17.

Austrian folk song

18.

Traditional Latin canon

19.

The Southern Harmony

20.

Hebrew folk song

21.

Rabbi M. Rothblum

22.

Chassidic melody

23.

Supplement to Kentucky Harmony

24.

H. Wilson

25.

H. H. Parry

26.

W. H. Monk

The Southern Harmony

H. J. Gauntlett

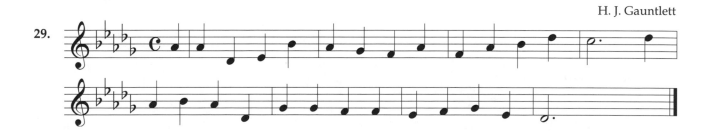

R. Courtville

F. Lewis

R. Redhead

M. Praetorius

J. Stainer

F. Lewis

The Southern Harmony

C. Goudimel

Then Swenska Psalmboken

41.

English melody

42.

att. E. K. Dare

43.

Antiphoner, 1681

44.

Folk song

45.

Hearing
Quality,
Function,
and
Inversion
in
Triads

Learning to Hear Chords

UNIT 25

Root-Position Triads in the Major Mode

Triads in Root Position

A **triad** is simply a collection of three different pitches, often played simultaneously. For our purposes, and in its most common usage, the term *triad* can be more specifically defined as a three-note **chord** formed by alternate notes of a scale. For example, the triad C–E–G, that is,

C (D) E (F) G

is built on $\hat{1}$ in the *key* of C major. (Here, the notes D and F are skipped.) Examining the triad's intervallic content, we quickly see that this type of triad will always consist of a 3rd on top of another 3rd, where the distance from the bottom to the top note is some form of 5th (usually a perfect 5th). When we construct a triad in this fashion, that is, by *stacking* 3rds, the triad is said to be in **root position**. The bottom note of the triad is known as the **root**, the middle note as the 3rd, and the top note as the 5th. (If either the 3rd or the 5th of the chord is the lowest sounding note, then the triad is no longer in root position, but rather is in an **inversion**.)

Applying this construction technique to all the notes of the diatonic major scale, that is, building a triad on each note of the major scale, we end up with the chords shown in Table II.1.

Note that we use uppercase Roman numerals to denote **major triads** and lowercase Roman numerals for **minor** and **diminished triads**. Uppercase is used for **augmented triads** as well, but Table II.1 indicates that there are none in the diatonic major scale. We add a superscript ° to indicate a diminished triad and we will use a superscript + for an augmented triad. Remember that major triads are those consisting of a major 3rd on the bottom and a minor 3rd on the top (spanning a perfect 5th); minor triads are those consisting of a minor 3rd on the bottom and a major 3rd on the top (again, spanning a perfect 5th). Diminished triads are those consisting of two minor 3rds stacked one above the other, spanning a diminished 5th. This is the characteristic interval from which the diminished triad takes its name.

A diminished triad is usually encountered in **first inversion**, for reasons we will explain later. That is to say, we generally find the 3rd of the diminished triad as the lowest sounding note (the bass). For the sake of consistency, we elect to present the vii° chord in the first inversion (vii°6) and all the others in root position.

Notice that in the major diatonic collection of triads there are three major triads (I, IV, and V), three minor triads (ii, iii, and vi), and one diminished triad (vii°, usually encountered in first inversion, vii°6). As a first step toward hearing the function of triads, let's

Scale Degrees	Roman Numeral
$\hat{1} - \hat{3} - \hat{5}$	I
$\hat{2} - \hat{4} - \hat{6}$	ii
$\hat{3} - \hat{5} - \hat{7}$	iii
$\hat{4} - \hat{6} - \hat{1}$	IV
$\hat{5} - \hat{7} - \hat{2}$	V
$\hat{6} - \hat{1} - \hat{3}$	vi
$\hat{7} - \hat{2} - \hat{4}$	vii°

TABLE II.1 *Triads on each major scale degree*

© 1997 Ardsley House, Publishers, Inc.

practice identifying the scale degree that constitutes the lowest note, the **bass** of each triad in our collection. For now, all triads, with the exception of the vii°⁶, will be played in root position; we will therefore be identifying the root of each triad. Note, then, that both the ii *and* the vii°⁶ will consequently have $\hat{2}$ in the bass. How will you be able to differentiate between the two?

CLASS DRILLS

A.   Identify the scale degree or syllable in the bass of each triad that you hear. This task should be relatively easy. It requires matching the pitch of the bottom note (as with the harmonically presented dyads in Area I) and relating it to the tonic to determine its scale degree.

1.	2.	3.	4.	5.	6.	7.	8.
9.	10.	11.	12.	13.	14.	15.	

B.   Just for practice, let's try a similar exercise in another key. Identify the scale degree or syllable in the bass of each triad that you hear.

1.	2.	3.	4.	5.	6.	7.	8.
9.	10.	11.	12.	13.	14.	15.	

Chord Quality   Of course, differentiating between the ii and the vii°⁶, despite their both having $\hat{2}$ on the bottom, was merely a matter of hearing the difference in chord **quality**. In fact, they are easily distinguished from one another: the ii has a minor quality and the vii°⁶, a diminished quality. Hearing the quality of a triad is an extremely useful tool and will be important in later steps of functional hearing. After all, the process of determining the root of a chord and the ability to discern the quality of a chord reinforce each other. If you are not sure whether the bottom pitch of the triad is $\hat{2}$ or $\hat{4}$, but you *are* sure that the triad is major, then the chances are that the triad you are hearing is IV, since IV is the only major triad with $\hat{4}$ in the bass or, indeed, that contains $\hat{4}$. So, knowing the scalar content of each triad *and* its quality makes the task of triad identification much easier because you have a number of aural clues to assist you. Let's try focusing on just the quality of some triads.

CLASS DRILLS

Identify the quality of each triad that you hear.

1.	2.	3.	4.	5.	6.	7.	8.
9.	10.	11.	12.	13.	14.	15.	

These exercises shouldn't really be difficult. As a matter of fact, you are most likely hearing the quality of the triad *and* its origin (root) at the same time. This is because you are listening to the quality of triads common to the same diatonic major scale. However, try to divorce the triads from a diatonic reference and concentrate exclusively on the subject of chord quality, as in the following exercises.

CLASS DRILLS

Identify the quality of each triad that you hear.

1.	2.	3.	4.	5.	6.	7.	8.
9.	10.	11.	12.	13.	14.	15.	

Since the idea is to hear *functionally*, that is, *within a harmonic context*, it makes more sense to listen to triads with reference to a specific key, as encountered in tonal music. So let's go ahead and identify triads by their true identities, as functional harmonies. Diatonic triads are identified by names (the same names as the scale degrees upon which they are built) as well as by Roman numerals. Because both Roman numerals (for example, IV) and Arabic numerals (for example, 4) sound alike when spoken, let's try using the names indicated in Table II.2 for our triads. Use these names, for now, when identifying diatonic triads, as in the exercises that follow.

Scale Degrees	Roman Numeral	Name
$\hat{1}-\hat{3}-\hat{5}$	I	Tonic
$\hat{2}-\hat{4}-\hat{6}$	ii	Supertonic
$\hat{3}-\hat{5}-\hat{7}$	iii	Mediant
$\hat{4}-\hat{6}-\hat{1}$	IV	Subdominant
$\hat{5}-\hat{7}-\hat{2}$	V	Dominant
$\hat{6}-\hat{1}-\hat{3}$	vi	Submediant
$\hat{7}-\hat{2}-\hat{4}$	vii°	Leading tone

TABLE II.2 *Names of diatonic triads*

CLASS DRILLS

Identify, by name, each of the triads that you hear.

1.	2.	3.	4.	5.
6.	7.	8.	9.	10.
11.	12.	13.	14.	15.

Not so hard? Still a bit puzzling? Remember to use both chord quality and scalar content as your aids. Suppose you hear a minor triad, but are not quite sure if it's ii, iii, or vi. If you hear $\hat{6}$ as a chord member, which of your three choices is automatically eliminated? Suppose you hear $\hat{1}$, but it sounds like a minor triad. Which chord must it be? Try again in the following exercise.

CLASS DRILLS

Identify, by name, each of the triads that you hear.

1.	**2.**	**3.**	**4.**	**5.**
6.	**7.**	**8.**	**9.**	**10.**
11.	**12.**	**13.**	**14.**	**15.**

By now, you should be able to answer the following questions:

1. Which triad is the easiest for you to identify?
2. Which triads are the most confusing?

Regardless of your answers, don't despair. There are perfectly valid reasons for both your certainty and your possible uncertainty. The tonic (I) is usually the most readily identifiable in context because functionally it is the most important, that is, the most *structural*, and is at the harmonic center of any specific diatonic collection. As we've seen earlier, retaining the tonic pitch is a crucial skill in developing functional hearing. If the I chord is ever misidentified, it is usually confused with IV. And which scale degree do these major triads (I and IV) share? Frequently, ii and IV are confused, but after all, they share *two* scale degrees (which ones?) and are about equally important in the chordal hierarchy. Because of its unique quality, vii°6 usually stands out; but some students may confuse it with V. This is due to their shared scalar content and a shared tendency (about which, more later). A little more practice should enhance your ability and build your confidence.

Triads as Arpeggios   Let's listen to a similar set of triads; rather than hear them as chords, let's listen to them as **arpeggios**. Recognizing the melodic outline of triads is just as important; it creates an awareness of scalar and intervallic content, and should present no additional difficulties. If need be, your instructor can use the *sostenuto* pedal on the piano, and you will have both the melodic presentation (the arpeggio) and the harmonic residue (the chord).

CLASS DRILLS

A.   **Identify, by name, each of the triads that you hear. They are presented as arpeggios, and may take the form of root, 3rd, and 5th, from bottom to top, or of 5th, 3rd, and root, from top to bottom. Remember that the vii°6 chord would be 3rd, 5th, root—or root, 5th, 3rd!**

1.	**2.**	**3.**	**4.**	**5.**

| 6. | 7. | 8. | 9. | 10. |
| 11. | 12. | 13. | 14. | 15. |

B. **Identify, by name, each of the triads that you hear. The arpeggios will go from top to bottom followed by bottom to top, or vice versa.**

1.	2.	3.	4.	5.
6.	7.	8.	9.	10.
11.	12.	13.	14.	15.

Function   The identification of any particular triad in a diatonic collection is an invaluable skill, and it is well worth the practice. It is helpful to realize that there are even more clues to identification than those furnished by scalar content and chord quality alone. There is also the consideration of *function*, that particular property of each triad which governs its relation to the others in the same key. By utilizing an understanding and appreciation of harmonic function (as we did with tendency tones in Area I), and combining these with the skills just reviewed, you can identify not only individual triads, but also successions of triads, or harmonic **progressions**, as we will see in the next unit.

HOME EXERCISES

1 Play or sing your scales as triadic outlines, using the following pattern (or one of your own devising):

$\hat{1}$–$\hat{3}$–$\hat{5}$–$\hat{3}$–$\hat{1}$, $\hat{2}$–$\hat{4}$–$\hat{6}$–$\hat{4}$–$\hat{2}$, $\hat{3}$–$\hat{5}$–$\hat{7}$–$\hat{5}$–$\hat{3}$,
$\hat{4}$–$\hat{6}$–$\hat{1}$–$\hat{6}$–$\hat{4}$, $\hat{5}$–$\hat{7}$–$\hat{2}$–$\hat{7}$–$\hat{5}$, $\hat{6}$–$\hat{1}$–$\hat{3}$–$\hat{1}$–$\hat{6}$,
$\hat{7}$–$\hat{2}$–$\hat{4}$–$\hat{2}$–$\hat{7}$, $\hat{1}$–$\hat{3}$–$\hat{5}$–$\hat{3}$–$\hat{1}$

2 Repeat Exercise 1, but in reverse order and direction.

3 In any major key, arpeggiate the following triads by singing and/or playing your instrument:

I, iii, IV, vi, ii, V, vii°, I

Move through a succession of keys whose roots are each related by ascending perfect 5ths (the **circle of fifths** taken clockwise), and repeat this exercise in each new key until you've returned to your original key (that is, until you have completed the circle of fifths). Note that we ask you to use the vii° in root position since this is a progression of roots.

4 Choose any note. Assuming the chosen note is the root, then the 3rd, and finally, the 5th of the triad, arpeggiate three versions of a major triad. Repeat the process for minor triads and for diminished triads. Let your ear tell you whether or not you "got it."

5 It is a fact that any major triad can exist in three different major keys; the same is true for any minor triad. In which major keys might you find F♯M? Cm? E♭M? Gm? Dm? BM? What about F♯°? What are their functions in these various keys?

Fundamentals

UNIT 26

Functional Harmony

Harmonic Function

Triads, as well as other aspects of pitch, are not truly functional outside of a specific harmonic context. There are certain laws governing their relationship with one another, determined in tonal music through observation of music of the **common-practice period**. We call this process of observation and analysis **theory**, and the behavior exhibited by triads and other chords in relation to one another is known as **function**.

There are various types of **harmonic functions**. Indeed, a chord may be used purely for its sound value, with little or no regard to its relationship with its neighbors; this is a **function of color**. But there are, nonetheless, three basic **structural functions**, or **functions of hierarchy**, that usually apply to the chords in a tonal system: namely, the **tonic**, **dominant**, and **pre-dominant functions**.

The tonic function is structurally the most important; but this does not necessarily mean that the tonic *chord* is the most prevalent. The sound of the tonic, once established and in root position, is so closely associated with harmonic **closure** that using it too often might make the music sound like a series of one-word sentences. The effect would be a stop/start kind of sound, which might occasionally be useful in some contexts, perhaps. Similarly, the dominant function, the next most important one in the hierarchy, if used too frequently in root position, would create the effect of a sentence filled with too many colons, semicolons, or dashes. So in most tonal music, the pre-dominant function is the most prevalent; we find the majority of diatonic triads carrying that function as well. To avoid confusion, note that a subdominant triad has a pre-dominant function, but not every triad with a pre-dominant function is a subdominant.

These functions can best be described in terms of their relative freedom of motion. A chord with a tonic function, in addition to serving as the ultimate goal, may also move to any other chord. Thus, the tonic chord (I in the diatonic major) may move to ii, iii, IV, V, vi, or vii° (more about iii later). A dominant function implies the most restricted direction of movement; a chord with this function must resolve to a tonic-function chord. Chords with a pre-dominant function may precede a dominant-function chord (hence, the name *pre-dominant*) or another pre-dominant-function chord.

Chord Progressions

Of course, many exceptions to these rules can be found in the literature; but for the most part, these rules govern the majority of harmonic movements, or **chord progressions**. Table II.3 categorizes triads in the major mode at their primary level of function.

Note that iii is parenthesized in Table II.3. It is an unusual triad in that it contains two notes of the tonic triad (I), namely, $\hat{3}$ and $\hat{5}$, and two notes of the dominant triad (V), namely, $\hat{5}$ and $\hat{7}$, the latter of which is the leading tone. It is, as you can see, the only triad containing the leading tone that is *not* a dominant-function chord. This somewhat ambiguous character makes the iii chord difficult to categorize, yet its minor quality definitely places it among the pre-dominants. Its main function is as a pre-dominant that is closely allied to the pre-dominant-function vi chord, with which it has a root/fifth relationship. Specifically, the iii descends a perfect 5th to the root of the vi; moreover, the roots of these two chords are adjacent to one another on the circle of fifths.

Inversion *does* affect function in many cases. However, even when restricting ourselves to root-position triads, we find a few chords whose functions vary, depending upon context. Most notably, vi can sometimes substitute for I when vi follows V, resulting in a **deceptive cadence** and giving vi a temporary tonic function. The IV occasionally substitutes for V, as in a **plagal cadence**, temporarily lending to it a dominant function. Thus, the information in Table II.4 is an extension of that in Table II.3.

These three harmonic functions operate together to create **harmonic periods**, involving successions of chords of varying length. However, there are basically three types of harmonic periods: **circular**, **open**, and **closed** progressions. A **circular progression** is a chord sequence that begins on one chord (generally, the tonic) and ends on the same chord. A typical circular progression might take the form I–V–I. An **open progression** is one that begins on a chord (again, typically the tonic) but does not return to it. A common example of this is I–IV–V. A **closed progression** starts on a chord other than the tonic but ends on the tonic, as in ii–V–I.

An open progression ending on any chord with the dominant function is often called a **half cadence**, whereas a closed progression ending with V–I is called an **authentic cadence**. We've already discussed plagal and deceptive cadences; in what type of progression might these be encountered?

TONIC	PRE-DOMINANT	DOMINANT
I	ii	V
	IV	vii°
	vi	
	(iii)	

TABLE II.3 *The primary function of each triad in the diatonic major mode*

TONIC	PRE-DOMINANT	DOMINANT
I	ii	V
vi	IV	vii°
	vi	**IV**
	(iii)	

TABLE II.4 *Modified list of functions*

Let's listen to the following **miniprogressions**. These three-chord progressions, which exhibit properties of larger progressions, will use only vii°⁶ root-position triads from the major mode. For now, determine only if they are open, closed, or circular.

CLASS DRILLS

Listen and determine whether each of the progressions that you hear is open, closed, or circular.

1.	2.	3.	4.	5.
6.	7.	8.	9.	10.
11.	12.	13.	14.	15.

Root Relationships

Notice that some of these progressions sound more satisfactory than others do. This is because the concept of **root relationship** is essential to the integrity of harmonic progressions. This concept concerns the intervallic relation between the roots of several chords, regardless of the actual notes in the bass. In general, progressions that follow root relationships up a perfect 4th or down a perfect 5th are the strongest. Root movement by step can also be relatively strong. Moving triads by 3rds (or 6ths) is much weaker, as the chords involved will share two notes apiece, again leading to the ambiguity of feeling and direction discussed in connection with the iii chord. Moving up a perfect 5th or down a perfect 4th may sound weak or strong, depending upon the context; but since this forces a clockwise (functionally *backward*) rotation around the circle of fifths, it is often weak and, moreover, harmonically confusing. After all, I–IV–I can easily *sound* like V–I–V in the key of IV! (Why?)

Now let's listen again to miniprogressions to determine their exact triadic content. Remember two things:

1. If you hear a circular progression, the first and last chords must be the same.

2. If the miniprogression sounds like *strong* closure in a closed progression, the last two chords are likely V–I (the authentic cadence).

Reasoning that uses your knowledge of these fundamental laws governing harmonic progression aids you in limiting your choices and thus leaves you free to hear context and function.

CLASS DRILLS

Listen and identify each of the triads that you hear in the three-chord progressions.

1.	2.	3.	4.	5.	6.	7.
8.	9.	10.	11.	12.	13.	14.
15.	16.	17.	18.	19.	20.	21.

Chord Patterns Hopefully, patterns are already beginning to emerge and to become aurally recognizable. Many of them are time-honored (if not time-worn), such as the ii–V–I and I–IV–V progressions. The number of available three-chord patterns is, of course, limited; these patterns are easily discernable by the motion of the bass and by the succession of chord qualities and functions. Where a similar function is shared by two chords, their quality becomes a determining factor in distinguishing between them. Compare the progressions ii–V–I and IV–V–I. (When using only root-position triads, the motion of the bass provides a strong aural clue, as well.) Considering our three strongest pre-dominants, we recognize again that ii and IV share two scale degrees, as do IV and vi; all three share $\hat{6}$. The strongest individual characteristic of the IV chord is obviously *not* its function, which is shared by three others, but its quality of being the only major pre-dominant. This is the reason that it "works" in a plagal cadence as a dominant substitute. It is the only major chord beside V that does not have the tonic function. Why do you think that vi can step in so nicely for the I chord in the deceptive cadence?

Let's review all this aurally, within the same limits. As you hear the progressions, first determine the *type* of progression (open, closed, or circular) and then the *content* (the actual triads involved).

CLASS DRILLS

For each three-chord progression that you hear, listen for and identify the type of progression represented and the actual triads involved.

1.   2.   3.   4.   5.
6.   7.   8.   9.   10.
11.   12.   13.   14.   15.
16.   17.   18.   19.   20.
21.

HOME EXERCISES

1 Starting with the tonic chord, write all the three-chord open progressions that are available with the chords found in the diatonic major. How many are there? Which ones sound the most familiar to you? Which ones sound the least satisfactory?

2 Write all the P–D–T (**P**re-dominant, **D**ominant, **T**onic) closed progressions available with the chords found in the diatonic major. How many are

there? Which ones sound the most familiar to you? Which sound the most conclusive?

3 Write a T–D–T deceptive cadence, a P–D–T deceptive cadence, a T–D–T plagal cadence, and a P–D–T plagal cadence. Write a T–P–D half cadence and a P–D–T authentic cadence. Bring them to class for dictation practice.

Learning to Hear Function

UNIT 27

Root-Position Triads in Harmonic Progressions

Three-Chord Progressions

This unit is designed to provide you with additional practice in hearing the harmonic structure of chordal progressions before we continue any further down the path toward functional hearing. We will start with short three-chord progressions, as in the preceding unit, and then begin our first attempts at longer ones.

CLASS DRILLS

Identify the triads that you hear in each of the following progressions.

First key

1.	2.	3.	4.	5.
6.	7.	8.	9.	

New key

10.	11.	12.	13.	14.
15.	16.	17.	18.	

New key

19.	20.	21.	22.	23.
24.	25.	26.	27.	

New key

28.	29.	30.	31.	32.
33.	34.	35.	36.	

New key

37.	38.	39.	40.	41.
42.	43.	44.	45.	

Longer Progressions

Again, some of these miniprogressions are probably beginning to sound quite familiar. Many of them may be instantaneously recognizable (hopefully, like old friends), for they are on the order of harmonic clichés. At this point, we should be able to tackle longer progressions. The good news is that longer harmonic progressions are merely collections of these shorter modules. Consider the following circular progression:

$$\text{I–vii}^{\circ 6}\text{–I–vi–ii–V–I}$$

We can break this down into a small circular progression, I–vii$^{\circ 6}$–I, followed by an open progression, I–vi–ii, and then by a closed progression, ii–V–I. Indeed, many extended harmonic progressions follow this type of pattern—in fact, entire pieces do! The initial module, the small circular progression, is used to establish the key, or tonic. The second module, the open progression, is used to go somewhere (makes the trip more interesting), and the last module, the closed progression, is used to return to the tonic, lending a feeling of closure and completeness to the longer circular progression as a whole. We could extend the phrase by substituting vi for I at the end (deceptive cadence), giving the first seven chords the feeling of an **antecedent**, and then add an additional closed progression for a **consequent** feeling, as follows:

$$\text{I–vii}^{\circ 6}\text{–I–vi–ii–V–vi–ii–V–I}$$

It helps to hear longer progressions as a series of short modules; this enhances your ability to hear functionally. Tonic and dominant chords often act as "road signs" to help you keep on track. For example, if you hear a six-chord circular progression, on the tonic, the first and last chords are likely I. The penultimate chord is likely V, or perhaps vii$^{\circ 6}$. Therefore, our hypothetical six-chord progression, upon first hearing, could be described as follows:

$$\text{I–\_\_\_–\_\_\_–\_\_\_–(V or vii}^{\circ 6}\text{)–I}$$

Since it's relatively easy to distinguish between V and vii$^{\circ 6}$, it's even more likely that we heard

$$\text{I–\_\_\_–\_\_\_–\_\_\_–V–I}$$

Thus, this six-chord progression rapidly reduces to a three-chord exercise. One more hearing, and you can probably get the missing harmonies!

$$\text{I–IV–I–ii–V–I}$$

Let's try some longer progressions and see how it goes. Here are some pointers:

1. Don't lose the tonic.
2. Make sure that you count the number of chords played.
3. Fill in the obvious (road-sign) chords immediately.

CLASS DRILLS

Identify the triads that you hear in each of the following progressions.

First key

1.   2.

3.   4.

5.   6.

7.   8.

New key

9.   10.

11.   12.

13.   14.

15.   16.

New key

17.   18.

19.   20.

21.   22.

23.   24.

Cadence   Once again, cadence is a consideration. With these longer progressions, one should concentrate on the nature of the phrase and its cadence. As was pointed out previously, circular progressions and closed progressions end with some kind of dominant-to-tonic motion, usually vii°⁶–I or V–I. Of the two, V–I, the authentic cadence, is the stronger. Occasionally, the last two chords may be IV–I, the plagal cadence. In most tonal music a plagal cadence sounds as if it has been tagged on because a plagal cadence usually works best when it follows an authentic cadence. An open progression is *almost* always in the style of a half cadence, ending on V (more rarely, on vii°⁶), or in the style of a deceptive cadence, ending on vi. However, an antecedent phrase *might* end on another pre-dominant harmony, such as ii. It might help to think of these as "dangling" phrases, with no real cadence.

CLASS DRILLS

Listen and determine the type of progression (open, closed, circular) and the type of cadence (authentic, plagal, deceptive, half) that you hear.

1.	2.	3.
4.	5.	6.
7.	8.	9.

Progressions of Root-Position Triads

Since triadic function governs the harmonic movement, and since we are limited to only the root-position triads found in the diatonic major collection (in addition to vii°^{6}), the progressions probably sound very formulaic. If so, that's good. We are rather limited not only in harmonic vocabulary but also in our direction of motion. And yet, much wonderful music has been written within these limitations. A good proportion of popular music goes no farther: we can often find a certain profundity within this simplicity. Now, remind yourself that a problem, no matter how large, can usually be solved by breaking it down into smaller component tasks—in our case, by hearing the smaller harmonic modules. Let's have some more practice.

CLASS DRILLS

Listen and then use Roman numerals to describe each of the progressions that you hear.

First key

1.	2.
3.	4.
5.	6.
7.	8.

New key

9.	10.
11.	12.
13.	14.
15.	16.

New key

17.	18.
19.	20.
21.	22.
23.	24.

As you have discovered, determining the harmonic content of longer progressions is not particularly difficult when approached with an understanding of function and structure. This is especially true when so many options are limited. We have limited our options intentionally in order to make the task easier and progressive. It would be good if at this point a certain dissatisfaction with the musicality of the exercises has set in. The question might be asked, "How can we alleviate the predictability and the sameness of sound of such limited harmonic movements?" Our answer would be to explore triadic inversions and the impact they have upon a progression. Inversions are used for many purposes: to vary the colors of chords subtly, to allow for chordal repetition without concomitant redundancy, to enhance triadic function, and to create smoother, more effective bass lines. We'll explore these uses in the next unit, just before we begin to focus more on the **bass line**.

HOME EXERCISES

1 Use only root-position triads from one diatonic major collection to write a nine-chord progression consisting of a circular three-chord progression, followed by a three-chord open progression, and ending with a three-chord closed progression. Triadic repetition will be allowed only between the third and fourth chords, if necessary or desired. Bring your efforts to class for discussion and for use as additional dictation material.

2 Beginning in C major, play or sing the following progression by arpeggiating in the order of root–3rd–5th–3rd–root:

I–IV–vii°–iii–vi–ii–V–I

(How could you describe this type of progression?) Repeat the progression as you continue counterclockwise through the circle of fifths, until you return to C major.

3 In the following progressions, analyze the component modules (open, closed, circular miniprogressions). Play and sing them, if possible, in various keys.

(a) I–vi–ii–V–vi–ii–vii°6–I

(b) I–ii–V–vi–ii–V–I–IV–I

(c) vi–vii°6–vi–V–I–IV–ii–V–I

(d) I–vi–IV–V–vi–ii–V–I

Fundamentals

UNIT 28

Triads in Inversion

*I*nversion can enhance the natural function of a triad or change it to a certain extent. Up to now, we've only examined and listened to triads in root position, with the single exception of the vii°⁶ chord. Placing the third of a chord on the bottom in the bass creates a first-inversion chord; placing the fifth in the bass creates a second-inversion chord. In each case the interval content is affected, although the pitch content is not. Regardless of its appearance in any of the three possible positions, the identity of a C major chord is unchanged; that is, although the root of the chord changed position, it still retains its identity as the root. Listen to the following chords:

$$\text{C} \qquad \text{C}^6 \qquad \text{C}^6_4$$

First Inversion

Let's systematically examine the effect of inversion. When we place a major chord in first inversion, the pitches above the bass note together with the bass form a minor 3rd and a minor 6th. The interval between the top two notes could be a perfect 4th or a perfect 5th, depending on the vertical distribution (or **voicing**, as it is often called). The overall effect is still consonant and still major. However, close listening reveals an interesting difference. The triad now sounds somewhat *less stable*. Indeed, it seems as if the triad, particularly the bass note (the 3rd of the triad), should move (or progress) *upward*. There is good reason for this. Examine the V⁶ chord. The leading tone is in the bass, so a motion of V⁶ to I is expected—or at least there is an expectation that the bass note, $\hat{7}$, should move (resolve) upward to $\hat{1}$. Now consider the I⁶ chord. It creates the expectation of motion to IV for similar reasons (I⁶–IV = V⁶–I in the key of IV). Because of this, even though the I⁶ has a tonic function, it does not have a strong, conclusive sound, and would never make a particularly satisfying resolution at a final cadence, in contrast to the much more stable-sounding I in root position. Listen:

$$\text{IV–V–I}^6 \qquad \text{IV–V–I} \qquad \text{V}^6\text{–I} \qquad \text{I}^6\text{–IV}$$

In the diatonic major collection there is, of course, another major triad, the IV chord. Its 3rd is $\hat{6}$; here there is no half step above or below, and there is less tendency for the bass of the IV⁶ to move upward or downward. Nonetheless, the IV⁶ sounds less stable than the root-position IV. The IV is a pre-dominant chord, of course, so under ordinary circumstances it enjoys freedom of progression to any other triad (including to I in a plagal cadence). Placing the IV in first inversion somewhat restricts its movement. The bass note of the IV⁶ wants to move, and move by step, as did those of the V⁶ and I⁶, except that here, the bass note sounds as likely to move *downward* as upward. The following possibilities result:

$$\text{IV}^6\text{–V}^6 \qquad \text{IV}^6\text{–V} \qquad \text{IV}^6\text{–I}^6_4$$

Less likely, the sound will be:

$$\text{IV}^6\text{–iii}^6 \qquad \text{IV}^6\text{–iii}^6_4 \qquad \text{IV}^6\text{–vii}°$$

Looking at the first-inversion *minor* chords, we can hear and see that they follow the example set by the IV⁶; that is, they are less stable forms of their corresponding root-position triads. In each case there is a whole step above the bass (the 3rd of the chord); in the case of the vi⁶ and the ii⁶ there is a half step below the bass. Taking function and tendency of scale degree into account (all minor chords in the major mode are pre-dominant), we hear an instability in the ii^6, iii^6, and vi^6 that suggests the following possible motions:

probable: ii^6–V   ii^6–I$^6_4$ *less likely*: ii^6–iii   ii^6–iii^6

probable: iii^6–vi   *less likely*: iii^6–IV^6 iii^6–IV   iii^6–ii$^6_4$ iii^6–IV^6

probable: vi^6–ii   vi^6–V^6 vi^6–V$^6_4$ *less likely*: vi^6–iii$^6_4$

We have already dealt with the diminished triad. The first inversion is the only position in which the bass note is not part of the tritone. For the purposes of this method, we will use diminished chords only in first inversion, without apology.

Second Inversion

Now, second-inversion triads introduce something new. Placing the 5th of a chord in the bass creates the intervals of a 6th and of a 4th above the bass. If the triad is major, this will result in a major 6th; if the triad is minor, the result is a minor 6th. In both cases there will be a perfect 4th above the bass. The pitch content of the second-inversion chord will be identical with that of the corresponding root-position triad; the interval content will be markedly different. Since one of the intervals, the perfect 4th, is classified as a dissonance (though an admittedly mild one), there will be an even more marked change in stability. Second-inversion triads are the least stable.

Consider the classic case, the I$^6_4$. The interval of the perfect 4th sounds as if the top note wants to resolve down by step, thus compressing the interval with the bass to that of a 3rd. The 6th above the bass in the I$^6_4$ often participates similarly:

I$^6_4$–V   *less likely*: I$^6_4$–iii^6

The I$^6_4$ chord is often used in cadential formulae for that reason (it resolves so convincingly to V), and its sound has become almost synonymous with cadence. In a concerto, the **cadenza** is often introduced with a I$^6_4$ and ends with a V. Leopold Mozart is reputed to have awakened his young son by playing an unresolved I$^6_4$ on the piano (forcing the boy to leap from his bed, rush to the piano, and provide the requisite resolution). Thus, second-inversion chords are used cadentially, as in the following progression:

ii^6–I$^6_4$–V–I

They are also used as part of an arpeggiated series in the bass, as in the following progression:

I–I^6–I$^6_4$–I

Or they can retain the function of the root-position triad and move as a **passing chord**; that is, they can connect two chords whose bass notes lie a 3rd apart:

I–V$^6_4$–I^6 I–iii$^6_4$–vi

By itself and out of context, a second-inversion chord always sounds very unstable and suggests an imminent cadence, whether the $^6_4$ chord is major or minor, making a second-inversion chord easy to identify aurally. Since the root-position triad, due to its strong stability, is also relatively easy to identify, determining a triad's

Tonic	Pre-dominant	Dominant
I, I^6	ii, ii^6, ii^6_4	V, V^6, V^6_4
vi, vi^6	IV, IV^6, IV^6_4	$vii^{\circ 6}$
IV^6_4	vi, vi^6, vi^6_4	IV
	(iii, iii^6, iii^6_4)	I^6_4

TABLE II.5 *An update of the list of functions*

inversion out of a field of three possibilities should not prove to be a daunting task.

Table II.5 adds the available triadic inversions to our list of functions.

Note the unusual placement of the IV^6_4 and the I^6_4. The IV^6_4 occasionally acts as a "tonic auxiliary," as in "Silent Night":

$$I–IV^6_4–I–I$$

We've just discussed the cadential implication of the I^6_4, which is so strong that most theorists (as well as other musicians) analyze the cadential I^6_4 as a V chord with the 6th and 4th suspended above the bass, resolving, in turn, to the 5th and 3rd respectively:

$$V^{6-5}_{4-3} \qquad I^6_4–V$$

Notice that the IV^6 and IV^6_4 are not present in the *Dominant* column of Table II.5; the plagal function of the IV chord is removed through the use of inversion.

Summary

In summary, we can state the following:

1. First-inversion I and V chords sound as if they should resolve upward in the bass, as in $I^6–IV$ and $V^6–I$.

2. First-inversion IV, ii, iii, and vi chords sound as if they should move either up by a whole step, as in $IV^6–V^6$, $ii^6–V$, or $vi^6–ii$, or down by step (either a half or whole step) as in $IV^6–V$ or $vi^6–V^6$. The iii^6 chord sounds as if it will move to a vi, by a whole step in the bass.

3. Second-inversion chords are the least stable, due to the dissonance of a perfect 4th above their bass; this can occasionally affect how they function, as in the auxiliary IV^6_4 or the cadential I^6_4.

4. Second-inversion chords are usually used as part of an arpeggiated bass series, such as $V–V^6–V^6_4–V$, as passing chords, such as $IV–I^6_4–IV^6$, or as a cadential antecedent, such as $I^6_4–V–I$.

HOME EXERCISES

In the space provided, determine whether each of the following two-chord progressions is strong, weak, or is unlikely to occur. Explain your choices. These exercises do not have to be presented aurally; but listening to them after you make your analysis is recommended, as this may help reinforce your decisions or cause you to rethink them.

1. $V–I^6_4$

2. $I^6–IV$

3. $iii^6_4–vi$

4. $IV^6_4–I$

5. $V^6–I$

6. $ii^6–I^6$

7. $IV–iii^6$

8. $vi–V^6$

9. $V^6_4–I^6$

10. $V–IV^6$

11. IV^6–V

12. ii^6–V

13. vi^6–IV$^6_4$

14. ii–I^6

15. I$^6_4$–IV

16. ii$^6_4$–V^6

17. V$^6_4$–IV$^6_4$

18. iii–ii^6

19. ii^6–I$^6_4$

20. iii$^6_4$–I

21. IV–I$^6_4$

22. vi$^6_4$–ii

23. I–ii^6

24. vi–ii^6

25. iii^6–V

26. V–ii^6

27. vii^{o6}–I^6

28. vii^{o6}–iii

Learning to Hear Chords

UNIT 29

Triads in Inversion

• •

Triadic Possibilities   Listen carefully to the lowest note of any triad, and identify its scale degree. Once this scale degree has been identified, the number of triadic possibilities is limited to three; that is, the note in the bass could be the root, third, or fifth of the triad.

CLASS DRILLS

Quickly name all the triadic possibilities in the major scale, assuming that each diatonic pitch, in turn, appears in the bass of a chord. For example, $\hat{1}$: I, vi^6, IV$^6_4$.

Inversions of Triads   Listen carefully to the sound, tendency, and stability of a triad. A major or minor triad in root position sounds quite stable, the first inversion sounds less so, and the second inversion sounds the least stable. You can also arpeggiate the triad, out loud or in your mind's ear, starting on the lowest note. If you arpeggiate up from the bass and hear consecutive 3rds (major or minor), the triad is in root position. If you arpeggiate up from the bass and hear a 3rd (major or minor) and then a perfect 4th, the triad is in first inversion. If you arpeggiate up from the bass and first hear a perfect 4th, the triad is in second inversion.

CLASS DRILLS

Without a specific tonal context, identify the inversion of each of the triads that you hear. Use the method of arpeggiation suggested in the text. Remember that for now, if you hear a diminished triad, you can safely assume that it is in first inversion.

1.	2.	3.	4.	5.
6.	7.	8.	9.	10.
11.	12.	13.	14.	15.
16.	17.	18.	19.	20.
21.	22.	23.	24.	25.
26.	27.	28.	29.	30.

The Identification of Function

Now you have three important clues with which you can play "harmonic detective," because the chord *quality*, as well as the scale degree of the bass and the inversion, also helps limit the number of possibilities. Consider the following scenario: You believe that you've identified $\hat{2}$ in the bass, and the inversion sounds like $^6_4$. Listening carefully, you decide that the chord quality is minor. What's the problem? What could you do to rectify these discrepancies? Now suppose that you've identified $\hat{6}$ in the bass, and the chord quality is major. You can *automatically* assume that you're listening to a IV^6 chord. Why?

So each of these three factors—scale degree in the bass, inversion, and chord quality—serves as a check on one another when attempting to identify the function (Roman numeral) and the inversion (Arabic numeral). There's no time like the present to jump right in and try this! Be methodical at first, and apply each of the three tests to every triad that you hear. They will be presented four times each, once for each factor and once more to confirm your aural analysis.

CLASS DRILLS

A. Using Roman and Arabic numerals, identify the function and inversion of each chord that you hear.

C major

1.	2.	3.	4.	5.	6.
7.	8.	9.	10.	11.	12.
13.	14.	15.	16.	17.	18.

E♭ major

19.	20.	21.	22.	23.	24.
25.	26.	27.	28.	29.	30.
31.	32.	33.	34.	35.	36.

B.   **Using Roman and Arabic numerals, identify the function and inversion of each chord that you hear.**

1.	2.	3.	4.	5.	6.
7.	8.	9.	10.	11.	12.
13.	14.	15.	16.		

Notice how important it is to identify the scale degree in the bass; it is certainly *more* than half of the battle. (It is four-sevenths, to be precise. Why?) Perhaps we should review and concentrate on making a quick and accurate identity of the bass.

CLASS DRILLS

A.   **Identify the scale degree of each bass note that you hear.**

D major

1.	2.	3.	4.	5.	6.
7.	8.	9.	10.	11.	12.
13.	14.	15.	16.	17.	18.

F major

19.	20.	21.	22.	23.	24.
25.	26.	27.	28.	29.	30.
31.	32.	33.	34.	35.	36.

B.   **Now in addition to determining quickly and accurately the scale degree in the bass, also identify the quality of each triad that you hear.**

1.	2.	3.	4.	5.	6.
7.	8.	9.	10.	11.	12.
13.	14.	15.	16.		

In one of the exercises in the preceding Class Drills, we heard $\hat{1}$ in the bass in conjunction with a minor quality. What are the possibilities of this combination with regard to function and inversion? We continue with such analyses.

CLASS DRILLS

Determine the triadic possibilities, given the following indications of bass scale degree and chord quality.

1. $\hat{7}$, m	2. $\hat{2}$, °	3. $\hat{2}$, m	4. $\hat{6}$, M	$\hat{2}$, M
6. $\hat{6}$, m	7. $\hat{3}$, M	8. $\hat{5}$, M	9. $\hat{4}$, m	10. $\hat{3}$, m
11. $\hat{1}$, M	12. $\hat{1}$, m	13. $\hat{7}$, M	14. $\hat{4}$, M	15. $\hat{5}$, m

These are *all* of the possible combinations, given our present limitations. Note that in every case, the number of triadic possibilities (three) has been reduced by at least one; in those cases where the possibilities have been reduced by two, identity is *certain*.

The Role of Inversions

How, then, can we distinguish, for instance, between a I$_4^6$ and a V, both of which are "$\hat{5}$, M"? With our third clue, of course—the perception of tendency and stability that comes with inversion. The I$_4^6$ sounds less stable than the V, *and* it has a perfect 4th as the first interval heard when arpeggiated upward from the bass.

At any rate, this type of discernment and perception will keep you "in the ballpark," and prevent you from helplessly floundering around, hoping to *guess* the function and inversion of a triad. And the good news is, as more and more triads are added to a progression, the *easier* the task becomes because additional cues and clues are provided as the variety of functions in a progression increases. This is as it should be since we do not generally listen to sounds like those we've been practicing when they are removed from a musical context. Providing such a context through harmonic progression restores a certain familiarity to the material.

Let's put it all together again, and see if you notice the improvement.

CLASS DRILLS

A. Identify the function and inversion of each triad that you hear.

E major

1.	2.	3.	4.	5.	6.
7.	8.	9.	10.	11.	12.
13.	14.	15.	16.	17.	18.

G major

19.	20.	21.	22.	23.	24.
25.	26.	27.	28.	29.	30.
31.	32.	33.	34.	35.	36.

B. Using Roman and Arabic numerals, identify the function and inversion of each chord that you hear. Each chord will be played in a different key.

1.	2.	3.	4.	5.	6.
7.	8.	9.	10.	11.	12.
13.	14.	15.	16.	17.	18.
19.	20.	21.	22.	23.	24.
25.	26.	27.	28.	29.	30.
31.	32.				

HOME EXERCISES

Practice singing triads (major, minor, or diminished) in root position, first inversion, and second inversion using the following model:

$$\hat{1}-\hat{3}-\hat{5}, \quad \hat{3}-\hat{5}-\hat{1}, \quad \hat{5}-\hat{1}-\hat{3};$$

$$\hat{2}-\hat{4}-\hat{6}, \quad \hat{4}-\hat{6}-\hat{2}, \quad \hat{6}-\hat{2}-\hat{4}; \quad \text{etc.}$$

Drop to a lower octave where necessary. Try this exercise on your instrument or on a keyboard, rapidly and in succession, in all major keys, following the circle of fifths.

Fundamentals

UNIT 30

Figured Bass

When the tonal system of functional harmony was evolving, late in the sixteenth century, the practice of "figuring" basses was established as a means of indicating the general harmonic progressions to be followed by **continuo players**, musicians who perform from **figured bass** parts. By placing Arabic numerals beneath the bass notes of a composition, specifying which pitches, relative to the bass, were to be played simultaneously, the harmony desired by the composer was prescribed. Matters of voicing, doubling, texture, and style were left to the skill and creativity of the continuo players. This system of indicating harmony without writing out every note above the bass is still used by musicians in various disciplines in our own era.

A few conventions of the figured bass system will be useful to us and are presented here.

A chord in root position is figured $\frac{8}{5}$, as shown in Example II.1.

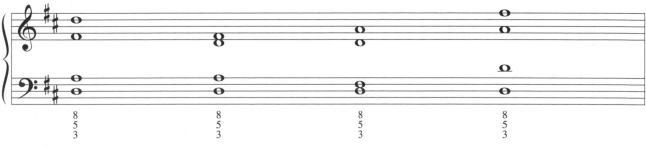

EXAMPLE II.1   *A chord in root position*

A chord in first inversion is figured $\begin{smallmatrix}8\\6\\3\end{smallmatrix}$, as shown in Example II.2.

A chord in second inversion is figured $\begin{smallmatrix}8\\6\\4\end{smallmatrix}$, as shown in Example II.3.

Notice that the same figures under a fixed bass note can indicate various voicings of a given harmony. As was mentioned, continuo players make these choices from among the many possible voicings as they perform. We are presently interested in the figures and in what they tell us about inverted harmonies.

The three figures illustrated in Examples II.1–3, $\begin{smallmatrix}8\\5\\3\end{smallmatrix}$, $\begin{smallmatrix}8\\6\\3\end{smallmatrix}$, and $\begin{smallmatrix}8\\6\\4\end{smallmatrix}$, are seldom written out completely. In practice they are commonly abbreviated as follows:

no figure = root position

^{6} = first inversion

$\begin{smallmatrix}6\\4\end{smallmatrix}$ = second inversion

These are the only figures one encounters in describing triads. See Example II.4.

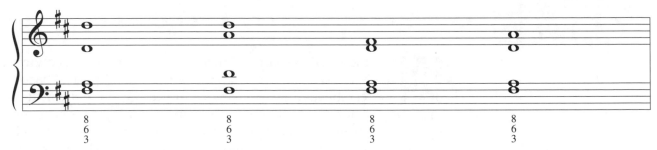

EXAMPLE II.2 *A chord in first inversion*

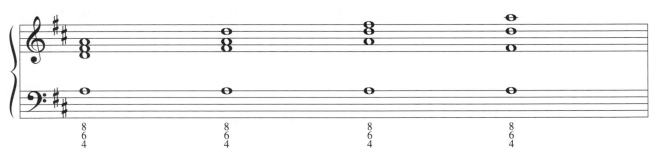

EXAMPLE II.3 *A chord in second inversion*

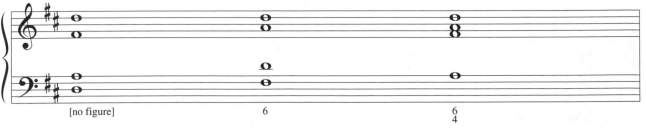

EXAMPLE II.4 *Abbreviations used in common practice*

This is why a triad's function and inversion require both Roman and Arabic numerals in most cases; you are probably all too familiar with these conventions at this stage in your musical education and development.

Analyzing and Figuring Bass Lines

You are also acquainted with the creation of a bass line when triads of various functions and inversions are combined to form a progression. In our previous harmonic progressions, there was little we could do in the way of a smooth, linear, and effective bass line, since we had restricted ourselves to root-position triads. Now, with the addition of two inversions, we can use many more musically compelling bass lines.

Here are a few hints for determining bass lines. Bass lines tend to move by step, or by leap of a 5th or 4th. The leaps are most common in cadential areas. Movement by 3rds (and, even more so, by 6ths) is generally considered weak, unless the bass is involved in some sort of arpeggiation, or unless the bass is in descending 3rds, as in certain stylistic procedures. If the bass moves by leap of a 4th or 5th, root-position triads are generally involved. Stepwise motion generally involves the use of inversions. It is rare to find consecutive root-position triads separated by step, except when the IV and vi pre-dominant triads move to the dominant V and when V moves to vi in a deceptive cadence.

If you keep in mind chord function (**Tonic**, **Pre-dominant**, **Dominant**), diatonic pitch content, and the few guidelines just given regarding bass-line motion, one can predict with considerable success the harmonic implications of any given diatonic bass line, as illustrated in Example II.5.

Assuming this is the bass line of a circular progression, one would predict that the Cs framing this line are the roots of tonic triads in the key of C major. It is also probable that the penultimate G supports a V chord in root position. Working backward from the cadence (a time-honored technique, by the way), we determine that the third chord from the end *could* be another V in root position. However, it's more likely a I_4^6, given the previous discussion of the cadential implications of the I_4^6. Then we are confronted with three bass notes, D, E, and F, of whose harmony we are at first less sure. The D could be ii, vii°⁶, or V_4^6; the E could be iii, I^6, or vi_4^6; and the F could be IV, ii^6, or $vii°_4^6$. We can discard the notion of $vii°_4^6$, as we've made a commitment to use only first-inversion diminished triads. Either IV or ii^6 would make an acceptable pre-dominant harmony to precede the cadential I_4^6. To choose iii from the options for the bass note E is not satisfactory. It progresses neither to the IV nor to the ii^6 successfully. We should discard this possibility as very unlikely. For the D, the ii chord is a possible choice, unless the E is the bass of a I^6. Why?

EXAMPLE II.5 *A diatonic bass line*

EXAMPLE II.6 *Harmonic reasoning*

We like to call this type of harmonic reasoning the "board game of harmony." If you "land" on a pre-dominant, you must proceed to another pre-dominant or to a dominant, unless the pre-dominant you have landed on has temporarily assumed another function. If you make your moves correctly, you will eventually be rewarded by achieving final authentic cadence on tonic, etc. So, returning to Example II.5, we have a pretty good idea of what the harmonic progression is without ever having listened to anything but the bass line. This is illustrated in Example II.6.

After listening to this progression, it becomes apparent that we should concentrate our listening attention and aural analysis on the second, third, and fourth chords. And in each case, chord *quality* will be the factor that will allow us to make an accurate determination. Let's try some simple exercises to test your understanding and to strengthen your grasp of the material. Look at and listen to these bass lines, and locate any errors in their construction (there are some). Explain your findings.

CLASS DRILLS

A. In the space provided, locate and explain errors in the construction of each of the following C-major bass lines.

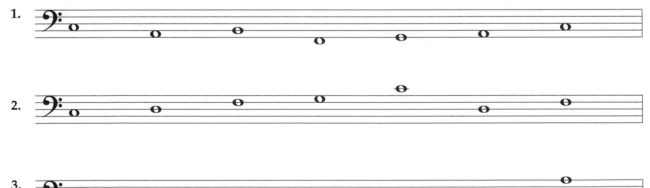

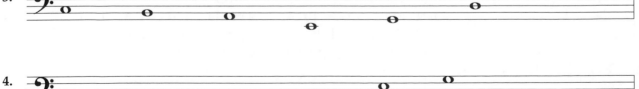

B. Examine these bass lines for their harmonic implications, and in the space provided, write the possible progressions. Assume for now that we are in the key of C major.

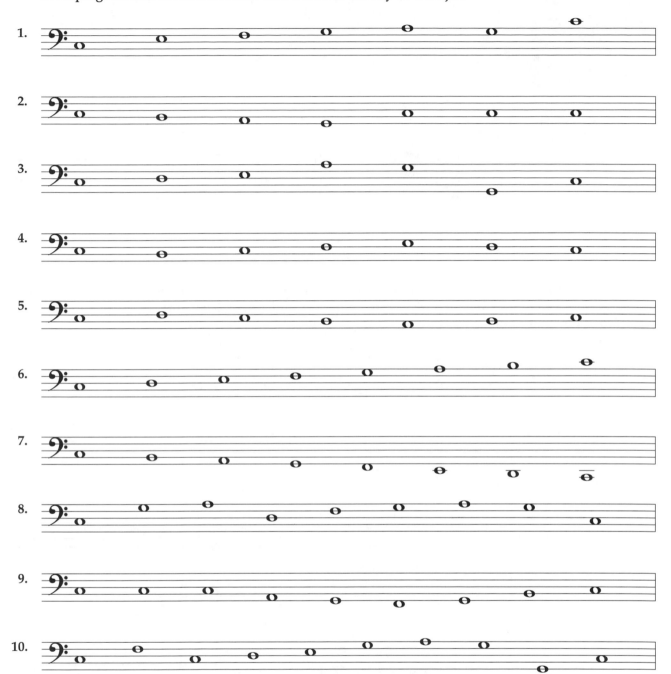

HOME EXERCISES

List as many ways as possible to harmonize the following bass-line fragments in the key of C major, given all of our current limitations.

1. C–D–E   **2.** C–B–A   **3.** C–E–F   **4.** F–G–C   **5.** A–B–C   **6.** A–G–C   **7.** C–E–G   **8.** D–G–C

Learning to Hear Function

UNIT 31

Major-mode Progressions Incorporating Inverted Triads

*U*sing some three-chord miniprogressions, let's try to combine our understanding of harmonic functions with our ability to determine chord inversions in a diatonic context.

CLASS DRILLS

Dictation: Write down the bass line of each three-chord progression that you hear, and provide a complete harmonic analysis (Roman and Arabic numerals) under each bass note. (Additional staves are provided at the back of the book.)

1.

2.

3.

4.

5.

6.

7.

8.

9.

10.

11.

12.

13.

14.

15.

16.

17.

18.

19.

20.

21.

22.

23.

24.

25.

26.

27.

28.

29.

30.

31.

32.

Now, let's try longer, more complete harmonic statements. Remember that most extended progressions can be reduced to a series of smaller open, closed, and circular progressions, as in the following progression:

$$\text{I} - \text{V}^6_4 - \text{I}^6 - \text{IV} - \text{iii}^6 - \text{vi} - \text{I}^6_4 - \text{V} - \text{I}$$

⌞circular⌟ ⌞open⌟ ⌞closed⌟

CLASS DRILLS

Dictation: **Write down the bass line of each progression that you hear, and provide a complete harmonic analysis (Roman and Arabic numerals) under each bass note.**

A. C major

1.

2.

3.

4.

B. A major

1.

2.

3.

4.

C. F major

1.

2.

3.

At first, try to approach these dictations systematically.

1. Write the bass line.

2. Identify the chord qualities.

3. Analyze the possibilities.

4. Listen for the inversions.

5. Check your work.

Once you have completed this five-step process, you will be able to "name that progression."

CLASS DRILLS

Dictation: **Write down the bass line of each progression that you hear, and provide a complete harmonic analysis (Roman and Arabic numerals) under each bass note.**

1.

2.

3.

4.

5.

6.

7.

8.

Take these next exercises as "**air dictations**." Your instructor will play the bass line alone on the first hearing and will then pause long enough for you to come up with the most likely harmonic progression. Following this, all the parts will be played twice—once to correct your assumptions (if necessary), and once more to check your work.

CLASS DRILLS

Dictation: Write down the bass line of each progression that you hear, and provide a complete harmonic analysis (Roman and Arabic numerals) under each bass note.

1.

2.

3.

4.

5.

6.

7.

8.

HOME EXERCISES

Provide harmonies for each of the following bass lines by placing the appropriate figures below the bass notes.

1.
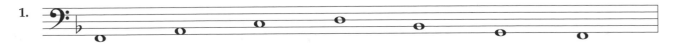

2.

3.
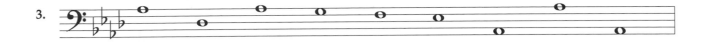

4.

Melody

UNIT
32

Soprano and Bass Lines in the Major Mode

*I*n the music that follows, be certain to listen and sing analytically. With some adjustments in register, every part for each voice can be sung by everyone. Don't limit yourself just to the part you customarily sing, but rather, sing all of the music in both the treble and bass clefs, changing octaves when necessary. When the parts are inverted and the upper voice sings below the lower voice, what happens to the harmonies implied by the two parts?

Experiment with various tempos and dynamics. Attempt to identify those rhythmic, harmonic, and melodic components of the music that suggest a faster or slower tempo and those that suggest a particular phrasing to you. Trust your ears to tell you what makes musical sense.

CLASS DRILLS & HOME EXERCISES

A. *Sight-singing*: Study, analyze, sight-sing, practice, and perform each of the following melodies with their bass lines.

B. *Dictation*: **Write down the soprano and bass lines that your instructor presents.**

3.

4.

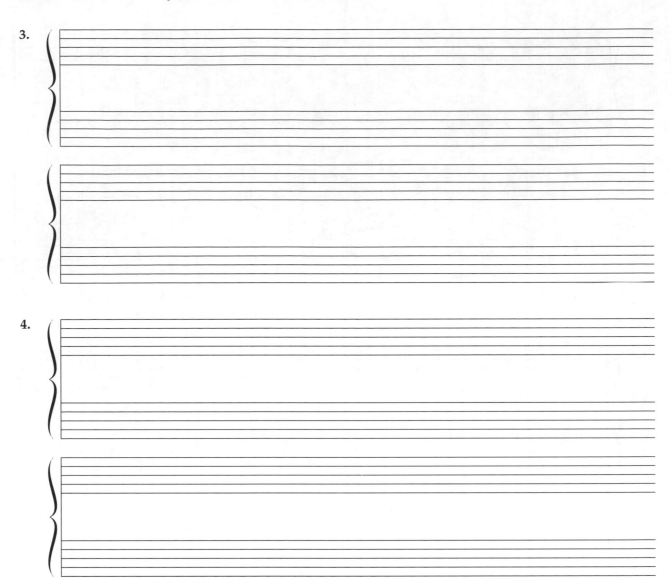

C. *Error detection*: Your instructor will play several examples for you. Compare what you hear with what is written on the corresponding staves that follow.

   i. Circle any pitch or rhythm which seems to be incorrect.

   ii. Correct any pitch or rhythm so that it matches what you hear.

1.

2.

3.

Rhythm

UNIT 33

Dual-Identity Divisions

● ●

**Dual
Metric Identity**

What are the differences among the following tempo/time signature combinations?

1. 1/4 note = 90, time signature = $\frac{3}{4}$
2. dotted 1/4 = 60, time signature = $\frac{6}{8}$
3. 1/4 note = 60, time signature = $\frac{2}{4}$

In combination 1, the **metric accent** (**pulse**) is on the first note of every eighth-note pair; in combination 2, it is on the first and fourth eighth notes of the measure. Combination 3 places metric stress on every beat, so that to the ear it sounds identical with combination 2, given the indicated tempo. If we remove every accent from the notes in these examples (to obtain **neutral metrics**), then to the ear the three combinations are indistinguishable from one another. This idea of dual metric identity has allowed composers to find a certain elasticity in rhythm and meter, which can be heard in works such as the first movement of Hector Berlioz's *Symphonie Fantastique*, Paul Dukas's *The Sorcerer's Apprentice*, and Gustav Holst's "Mercury," from the suite *The Planets*. It has also led to the notion of "metric modulation," a device that, perhaps, finds its ultimate expression in many of the works of Elliott Carter (for example, "Canaries" from *Eight Pieces for Four Tympani*).

Duple and Triple Divisions

Such a simple device as alternating duple and triple divisions can lead to rather complex and profound music. Performing alternating duple and triple divisions requires of us an ability to prepare each alternate division mentally, in advance of its actual performance. If you are to play or sing a passage such as the one in Example II.7 accurately, it is necessary to anticipate the quarter-note triplet by beginning mentally to change the division of the beat in the second measure.

On beat 2 of measure 2, think in terms of eighth-note triplets. Then perform the quarter-note triplets as a series of duple groupings of the eighth-note triplets, as shown in Example II.8.

Just guessing, hoping, and trying to squeeze three "quarter" notes into one $\frac{2}{4}$ bar often leads to results such as those shown in Example II.9 because duple thinking continues to prevail into measure 3 and (belated) triple thinking likewise continues into measure 5.

EXAMPLE II.7   *Rhythm with double and triple divisions of the beat*

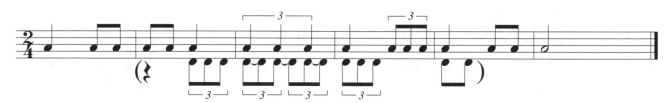

EXAMPLE II.8   *Dividing the beat mentally*

EXAMPLE II.9   *A typical instance of a sloppy performance of Example II.7*

EXAMPLE II.10   *Wagner's message*

This kind of performance practice drives conductors *mad*. Legend has it that Richard Wagner had painted on the wall of the rehearsal room at Bayreuth the two rhythms shown in Example II.10.

Lest we bring the wrath of the ghost of Wagner down upon ourselves, it is fitting that we put in some practice with duple and triple divisions and with combinations thereof in opposition.

CLASS DRILLS

Study and analyze the following rhythms and then perform them. Use the syllable *ta* so that attacks *and* releases are absolutely accurate. Don't forget to hold all notes for their full duration. In Exercises 13–23, be aware of the metric and notated accents and of any cross-accents.

© 1997 Ardsley House, Publishers, Inc.

© 1997 Ardsley House, Publishers, Inc.

23.

24.

Rhythmic Dictation   Now we will reverse the process and write down the rhythms that we hear. Several hints are in order.

1. Listen at first for **rhythmic vocabulary**; that is, determine whether the rhythm is primarily quarter notes and eighth notes; quarters, eighths, and sixteenths; eighths and eighth-note triplets; eighths and sixteenths; or any other combination.

2. Listen for anomalies, those rhythmic events that stand out from the prevailing rhythmic vocabulary that you have identified. Locate these anomalies in musical time by determining on which beats and in which measures they occur.

3. Listen for repetition on any level. Most music has structure and form, and repetition is the key to form and structure. Small rhythmic units (**cells**) may occur more than once; if so, identify them and place them metrically.

You can end up with a fairly accurate and complete "map" or sketch of the rhythm by taking these steps. After a first listening, for example, you may have determined that the vocabulary consists primarily of eighth-note duplets and triplets. You then identify some anomalies—for example, sixteenth notes; locate them on your next hearing, as shown in Example II.11.

You also heard **agogic accents** (rhythmic events longer in duration than their surroundings) at the end and in measure 2. See

$\frac{3}{4}$ ___ ___ ___ | ___ ___ ___ | ___ X ___ | X ___ ___ | ___ ___ ‖

EXAMPLE II.11   X = *anomaly*

Example II.12. You then identified the agogics and anomalies as shown in Example II.13.

Since you know that the remainder consists primarily of eighth-note duplets and triplets, locate them accordingly. See Example II.14.

Finally, concentrate on filling in the actual details. See Example II.15. Try this method and see if it helps.

EXAMPLE II.12 A = *agogic accent,* X = *anomaly*

EXAMPLE II.13 *Identifying the agogics and anomalies*

EXAMPLE II.14 *Locating the eighth-note duplets and triplets*

EXAMPLE II.15 *Filling in the details*

CLASS DRILLS

Dictation: **Write down the rhythms that your instructor presents.**

1.

2.

3.

4.

5.

6.

HOME EXERCISES

Convert the following rhythm in $\frac{6}{8}$ meter to exactly the same rhythm in $\frac{2}{4}$ meter using the same tempo (that is, dotted quarter = quarter).

(Dotted quarter = 90)

(Quarter = 90)

Dictation

UNIT 34

Bass Lines

• •

*U*ntil now, most of our linear exercises have been of a melodic nature, with the exception of those constructs used in Area I, which were created to improve interval recognition. This unit will present lines in the bass that were designed to *be* basses of

EXAMPLE II.16 *A diatonic bass line*

functional harmonic progressions, such as those studied in Unit 31. Though we will treat them as melodies, that is, sing them at sight and write them down from dictation, we shall also concern ourselves with analyzing their harmonic implication and potential. Keep in mind all that we have covered thus far regarding harmonic function and chord inversion. For example, sing the bass line given in Example II.16.

Analyzing Harmonic Possibilities

Now analyze the bass line of Example II.16 for its harmonic potential. It is a safe assumption that this bass line represents a circular progression; therefore, the first and eleventh notes are roots of I chords. The tenth note is the root of a V (why?), so the preceding note, also $\hat{5}$, is quite likely the 5th of a I (I$_4^6$). The eighth needs to carry a pre-dominant function, and so $\hat{4}$ could be the root of a IV or the 3rd of a ii (ii^6). Since it, in turn, is preceded by $\hat{2}$, we must eliminate the possibility of the $\hat{2}$ being a part of a V (V$_4^6$) or vii° (vii^{o6}). Why? Therefore, ii is the only triad available for the seventh note. Do you see the value of working backward from the cadence? Now, from the sixth note to the seventh we find the interval of a descending perfect 5th, suggesting root-position-to-root-position (circle of fifths) motion; thus, the sixth note is likely the root of a vi chord. Hence, the fifth note could be a V or iii^6; but since $\hat{4}$ (which, again, could only be a IV or ii^6) precedes it, we can all but discard the notion that the fifth note, in this case, supports a iii^6 (again, why?). The second and third notes are $\hat{2}$ and $\hat{3}$, respectively; coming from the opening of a circular progression, where the tonic chord is generally established, it is extremely likely that they represent either a V$_4^6$ or vii^{o6} moving to a I^6. Our preliminary analysis is indicated in Example II.17.

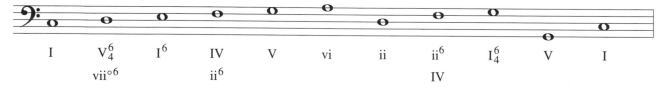

I	V$_4^6$	I^6	IV	V	vi	ii	ii^6	I$_4^6$	V	I
	vii^{o6}		ii^6				IV			

EXAMPLE II.17 *A preliminary analysis of the bass line shown in Example II.16*

CLASS DRILLS

A. **Sing the following bass lines at sight, and then analyze them for their harmonic potential.**

1.

© 1997 Ardsley House, Publishers, Inc.

B. *Dictation*: Write down the bass lines that your instructor presents. Study them and provide all reasonable harmonic analyses (Roman and Arabic numerals) for each note.

1.

2.

3.

4.

5.

HOME EXERCISES

Most popular music contains simple diatonic bass lines (the obvious exception being the reliance on the device known as **pedal**, wherein the bass maintains a note while the chords change above it, so that the bass is occasionally nonharmonic). For this reason, popular music makes excellent practice for bass-line dictation and analysis. Try this using your favorite pop music. Be aware that "funky" bass lines are often quite **contrapuntal**, projecting multiple lines. If you prefer, try this technique using the popular music of other eras, such as the early Baroque and the Classical. You'll find that they have much in common with current popular music and much that is even *more* banal!

Learning to Hear Chords

UNIT 35

Triads in the Minor Mode

*I*n the minor mode, there are more triads available than in the major mode. If we construct a "source set" of all pitches available through all three forms of the minor (natural, melodic, and harmonic), we obtain the following:

$$\hat{1}, \hat{2}, \flat\hat{3}, \hat{4}, \hat{5}, \flat\hat{6}, \hat{6}, \flat\hat{7}, \hat{7}$$

—a nine-note set or scale. Note the use of flats preceding scale degrees 3, 6, and 7. Of course, not all minor keys use all of these particular alterations. For an explanation, see *Notational Convention for the Minor Mode* on page 163. Constructing triads with these resources yields the following combinations:

i, ii°, ii, ♭III, III⁺, iv, IV, v, V, ♭VI, vi°, ♭VII, vii°

—thirteen different (and even some exotic) triads! Luckily for the tasks at hand, many of these are either of little importance or are actually nondiatonic in function. We use the harmonic form of the minor scale to generate all of the triads we will use—hence the term

© 1997 Ardsley House, Publishers, Inc.

harmonic minor—except for one chord, which requires a single note from the natural minor. Here is the resultant collection:

$$\text{i, ii}°, ♭\text{III, iv, V, }♭\text{VI, vii}°$$

The V chord *must* be major and its root *must* be a perfect 4th below the tonic in order to retain its dominant function. Similarly, the vii° *must* be built on the leading tone to the tonic and *must* be diminished. Tonic and subdominant chords become minor, reflecting the mode. They exchange modalities, so to speak, with ♭III and ♭VI, reflecting the pitch content brought about by the modal shift. The ♭III uses a pitch that is not taken from the harmonic form of the scale; it uses ♭$\hat{7}$ from the natural form so that ♭III can be a major triad, not an augmented triad. (If augmented, it could not function effectively as a **relative major**, the major key whose tonic lies a minor 3rd above i.) The ii° chord presents an additional challenge. We now have *two* diminished triads, and they both contain $\hat{2}$ and $\hat{4}$. Because of its quality and leading-tone function with respect to $\hat{3}$, ii° will sound most often like vii°/♭III, and, indeed, it functions this way when used in conjunction with ♭III. Despite its diminished quality, however, the ii° still retains its pre-dominant function because of its root relation to $\hat{5}$. And because ii° is diminished, we shall use it only in first inversion (ii°⁶).

Note that the minor mode contains three major chords and two diminished ones, but only two minor chords. Many minor pieces spend a good deal of their time in areas closely related to the relative major. What would happen if we analyzed the preceding triads in the *key* of the relative major? Consider the following:

$$♭\text{III:}\quad \text{vi, vii}°, \text{I, ii, V/vi, IV, vii}°/\text{vi}$$

This is pretty close to the collection formed in the major mode. Keep this in mind when listening to pieces and progressions in the minor mode; the availability of the two diminished triads makes it just as easy to slip into the relative major as it is to remain in the minor.

Notational Convention for the Minor Mode

For the reason just given, we shall now adopt the following convention: if a chord is built on a note chromatically *lowered* from its diatonic version, we shall precede its Roman numeral designation with a flat sign (♭), regardless of whether or not a *flat* was actually used to lower that scale degree. Hence, a major chord built on a lowered $\hat{2}$ in C♯ minor will be shown as ♭II, despite the fact that its root is D natural. Conversely, if a chord is built on a note chromatically *raised* from its diatonic version, we shall precede its Roman numeral designation with a sharp sign (♯), regardless of whether or not a *sharp* was actually used to raise that scale degree. Hence, a diminished chord built on a raised $\hat{6}$ in D minor will be shown as ♯vi°, even though its root is B natural. And because the raised $\hat{7}$ is critical to the determination of the tonic in the minor mode and is more prevalent than the lowered $\hat{7}$ found in the key signature, we need to state clearly our convention for notating these two forms. Because we are always referring to the harmonic form of the minor scale, unless otherwise indicated, the unaltered $\hat{7}$ signifies the diatonic form of that scale degree; ♭$\hat{7}$ constitutes the nondiatonic version.

Diatonic Triads in Root Position

Let's try to identify root-position triads from the diatonic minor collection, as well as the ii°6 and vii°6. As with the major mode, identifying the scale degree in the bass and determining the quality of the triad are all that you will really need to do to accomplish this task.

CLASS DRILLS

A. Identify the triad that you hear.

A minor

1.	2.	3.	4.	5.	6.	7.	8.
9.	10.	11.	12.	13.	14.	15.	16.
17.	18.	19.	20.				

C minor

21.	22.	23.	24.	25.	26.	27.	28.
29.	30.	31.	32.	33.	34.	35.	36.
37.	38.	39.	40.				

B. Using Roman and Arabic numerals, identify the function and inversion of each chord that you hear. Each chord will be played in a different key.

1.	2.	3.	4.	5.	6.	7.	8.
9.	10.	11.	12.	13.	14.	15.	16.

These triads function similarly to their diatonic equivalents in the major mode, as shown in Table II.6.

Inversion of Minor-mode Triads

The use of inversion affects the triads in much the same way that inversion affects the triads of the major diatonic collection: first inversions are less stable (and thus have a greater tendency to "progress"), and second inversions are quite unstable. The function of these inverted minor-mode triads follows similarly, as shown in Table II.7.

Of course, you have one fewer triad to worry about when it comes to discerning inversion. Since the ii° is diminished in the

TONIC	PRE-DOMINANT	DOMINANT
i	iv	V
VI (deceptive)	VI	vii°6
	ii°6	iv (plagal)
	(III)	

TABLE II.6 *The primary function of each triad in the harmonic minor mode*

TONIC	PRE-DOMINANT	DOMINANT
i, i^6, i$^6_4$	iv, iv^6, iv$^6_4$	V, V^6, V$^6_4$
VI, VI^6	VI, VI^6, VI$^6_4$	vii°6
iv$^6_4$	ii°6	iv
	(III, III^6, III$^6_4$)	**i$^6_4$**

TABLE II.7 *The function of inverted triads in the harmonic minor mode*

minor mode, you can count on its being presented in first inversion throughout this material (and for most of the music you are likely to encounter). Determining the inversion of the other triads will continue as before. Listen to and identify the scale degree in the bass. Listen to and identify the chord's quality. Be aware of the triadic possibilities for any given combination of bass note and quality. Use tendency and stability to identify inversion in those few cases where more than one possibility exists.

CLASS DRILLS

According to the preceding limitations, what are the triadic possibilities in the minor mode for each of the following bass-note and chord-quality combinations?

1. $\hat{1}$, M   2. $\hat{2}$, M   3. $\hat{3}$, m   4. $\hat{4}$, °   5. $\hat{5}$, M

6. #$\hat{6}$, °   7. b$\hat{7}$, M   8. $\hat{7}$, °   9. $\hat{2}$, °   10. $\hat{4}$, m

11. $\hat{6}$, M   12. b$\hat{7}$, M   13. $\hat{1}$, m   14. $\hat{3}$, M   15. $\hat{5}$, m

Now you should be ready to test your abilities on triads presented aurally. Remember to think of the following:

1. Scale degree in the bass
2. Chord quality
3. Tendency and stability, where more than one possibility exists

CLASS DRILLS

A. Using Roman and Arabic numerals, identify the function and inversion of each chord that you hear.

A minor

1.   2.   3.   4.   5.   6.   7.   8.

9.   10.   11.   12.   13.   14.   15.

C minor

16.   17.   18.   19.   20.   21.   22.   23.

24.   25.   26.   27.   28.   29.   30.

B. Using Roman and Arabic numerals, identify the function and inversion of each chord that you hear. Each chord will be played in a different key.

1.   2.   3.   4.   5.   6.   7.   8.

9.   10.   11.   12.   13.   14.   15.   16.

HOME EXERCISES

1 Make sure that you know the quality of each triad in the diatonic minor collection in every key, and be certain that you can spell each one quickly and accurately. Watch out for double sharps and for infrequently sharped notes that function as leading tones but that do not appear in the key signatures.

2 Sing and play the triads and their inversions sequentially up the harmonic minor scale,

according to the model:

$$\hat{1}–\hat{3}–\hat{5}, \quad \hat{3}–\hat{5}–\hat{1}, \quad \hat{5}–\hat{1}–\hat{3};$$
$$\hat{2}–\hat{4}–\hat{6}, \quad \hat{4}–\hat{6}–\hat{2}, \quad \hat{6}–\hat{2}–\hat{4}; \text{ etc.}$$

Watch out for the rather awkward transition between the VI and the vii° series. Why is this transition awkward?

Learning to Hear Function

UNIT **36**

Minor-mode Progressions Incorporating Inverted Triads

*A*s before, it seems like a good idea to begin by practicing with three-chord miniprogressions. Try categorizing them by progression type (open, closed, or circular) as you identify bass line, function, and inversion.

CLASS DRILLS

Dictation: Write down the bass line of each three-chord progression that you hear, and provide a complete harmonic analysis (Roman and Arabic numerals) under each bass note.

1.

2.

3.

4.

© 1997 Ardsley House, Publishers, Inc.

5.

6.

7.

8.

9.

10.

11.

12.

13.

14.

15.

16.

17.

18.

19.

20.

21.

22.

23.

24.

25.

26.

27.

28.

Now, try some longer musical sentences. Bass line, chord Quality, Analysis, and Inversion (BQAI) continue to be an effective systematic approach to taking harmonic dictation successfully.

CLASS DRILLS

Dictation: **Write down the bass line of each progression that you hear, and provide a complete harmonic analysis (Roman and Arabic numerals) under each bass note.**

1.

2.

3.

4.

5.

6.

7.

8.

If cadences, motions from tonic, etc. are beginning to sound somewhat formulaic, that's good! Most tonal music follows and/or expands upon these simple formulae. Indeed, the awareness and comprehension of exceptions to the rules require recognition of and adherence to them. After all, you are hearing nothing that you have not heard before; you're simply putting a name to the familiar. Let's continue in the following exercises.

CLASS DRILLS

Dictation: **Write down the bass line of each progression that you hear, and provide a complete harmonic analysis (Roman and Arabic numerals) under each bass note.**

1.

2.

3.

4.

5.

6.

Characteristics of Minor-mode Triads

Note that in the diatonic minor-mode collection of triads we find the only naturally occurring example of two major triads whose roots lie just a half step apart—namely, V and VI. This makes for a unique sound whenever a deceptive cadence is effected in the minor mode and also whenever the VI chord exercises its pre-dominant function and progresses to V. Listen to the progressions that your instructor will now play.

We have observed that the collection of triads in the minor mode possesses a number of peculiar characteristics:

1. Two diminished triads.

2. Two major triads a half step apart.

3. Two consecutive triads whose roots lie an augmented 2nd apart (VI and vii°⁶).

4. Perhaps most surprising of all, despite our being in the minor mode, *minor triads are the least prevalent.*

These distinguishing features contribute to ease of recognition of minor-mode progressions.

Let's again try some longer progressions. The details mentioned before and the recurrence of certain three-chord harmonic modules should sound quite familiar and, hopefully, should be more recognizable by now.

CLASS DRILLS

Dictation: **Write down the bass line of each progression that you hear, and provide a complete harmonic analysis (Roman and Arabic numerals) under each bass note.**

1.

2.

3.

4.

5.

6.

7.

8.

HOME EXERCISES

1 Listen to some music written in the minor mode, particularly pieces from the Classical era. Listen carefully to the bass, and try to identify the harmonic progressions in the music.

2 Following the guidelines for harmonic motion given earlier, construct your own chord progressions in the diatonic minor. Make them at least seven chords long. Perhaps your instructor can use these class-generated progressions as the basis for further harmonic dictation.

Melody

UNIT 37

Soprano and Bass Lines in the Minor Mode

*T*he soprano and bass lines assembled here will challenge and develop many of the skills you have been working on throughout your study of functional hearing. Remember that studying and singing this music is a means to an end, not an end in itself. The goal and intention of this approach is that through attentive work on the pages that follow, you can significantly increase your ability to comprehend the harmonic, melodic, rhythmic, and structural aspects of music before you actually perform it or hear it performed by others. In addition, as you perform, you will begin to hear and listen analytically: you will have a greater understanding of how the voices interact and will be more certain about the harmonies they imply.

To accomplish all of this will take lots of time and energy as well as a commitment to refining your skills to the highest level possible—and that is often difficult in the midst of a hectic semester, filled with lots of work!

CLASS DRILLS

A. *Sight-singing*: Study, analyze, sight-sing, practice, and perform each duet.

B. *Dictation:* **Write down the soprano and bass lines that your instructor presents.**

1.

2.

3.

4.

C. *Error detection*: **Your instructor will play several examples for you. Compare what you hear with what is written on the corresponding staves that follow.**

  i. **Circle any pitch or rhythm which seems to be incorrect.**
  ii. **Correct any pitch or rhythm so that it matches what you hear.**

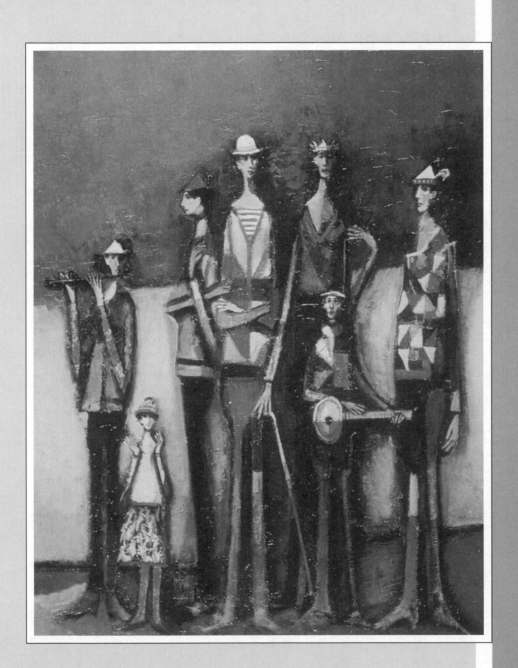

Hearing Quality, Function, and Inversion in Seventh Chords

Learning to Hear Chords

UNIT **38**

Seventh Chords in the Major Mode

Classifying Seventh Chords

Walter Piston often referred to the vii° chord as an "incomplete dominant." Its dominant function is equal to that of the V chord, but it lacks freedom of motion because of the presence of the tritone, which Piston called the most tonal of intervals, and which demands proper resolution of its two strong tendency tones, $\hat{7}$ and $\hat{4}$ ($\hat{7} \to \hat{1}$ and $\hat{4} \to \hat{3}$). The strongest chord results when we *combine* the V and the vii° into one chord, the *dominant seventh chord* (V^7). In the V^7, the strong tendency of the tritone to resolve to the tonic and mediant scale degrees is present, along with the power of the dominant to suggest movement toward a chord with tonic function.

It should come as no surprise that the V^7 is the oldest and most common diatonic **seventh chord**. Most seventh chords first appeared when **passing tones** formed the intervals of major, minor, and diminished 7ths above the roots of diatonic triads (and then resolved downward); but eventually, they came to be accepted as harmonic entities in their own right. Example III.1 reviews the results of placing an additional 3rd on top of each diatonic triad in the major mode.

A **major seventh chord** (M7) is a major triad with a major 7th above the root. The I^7 and IV^7 are, therefore, major seventh chords. A **dominant seventh chord** (V^7) is a major triad with a minor 7th above the root. The V^7 is the *only* diatonic dominant seventh chord within a given key. We use the symbol V^7 to denote a dominant seventh chord, since the only place one encounters this particular configuration of intervals (though not this chord quality) is on $\hat{5}$, whether the mode is major or minor. A **minor seventh chord** (m7) is

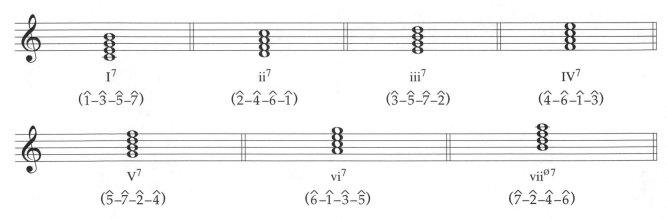

EXAMPLE III.1 *Diatonic seventh chords in C major*

a minor triad with a minor 7th above the root. The ii^7, iii^7, and vi^7 are all minor seventh chords. A half-diminished seventh chord ($^{\o7}$) is a diminished triad with a minor 7th above the root. The only diatonic **half-diminished seventh chord** is the $vii^{\o7}$. A diminished seventh chord ($^{\circ7}$) is a diminished triad with a diminished 7th above the root; but this chord exists diatonically only in the harmonic minor, and will be addressed in Unit 40. Table III.1 summarizes this information about seventh chords.

Identifying Chord Quality

Here are a few hints for identifying the chord quality of the diatonic seventh chords. Major seventh chords contain the major 7th as their most characteristic interval. The inversion of the major 7th is the minor 2nd; it is a distinctive dissonance found only in the major seventh chord. Admittedly, the sense of dissonance is somewhat ameliorated by the simultaneous presence of the major triad. Actually, there is more *color* than dissonance in this sonority. Many a jazz ballad has made good use of this color, with great stability felt on the I^7.

The V^7 is such a strong dominant that it sounds as if it *must* move immediately to the tonic. As mentioned, it is also the most common and, therefore, the most familiar sounding of the seventh chords.

The minor seventh chord has a peculiarly neutral sound. The minor 7th does not sound as strongly dissonant as it does in the dominant seventh chord since the tritone is absent in the minor seventh chord. Like the major seventh chord, its pitch content comprises two perfect 5ths in root position (root ↔ 5th, 3rd ↔ 7th); but it lacks the striking dissonance of the major 7th or minor 2nd. For this reason, the minor seventh chord has a vague major quality about it, especially in first inversion. Indeed, in first inversion it *is* a major triad (3rd–5th–7th), but with an added major 6th above the bass. The minor seventh chord is a "workhorse" in some respects, a utilitarian sonority sometimes incorporated because of the uncertainty of identity that it often creates.

The half-diminished seventh chord, by contrast, is almost exotic in quality. It is still a strong dominant and, like the V^7, contains the characteristic tritone, which demands resolution. The $vii^{\o7}$ possesses a whole-tone quality, perhaps because of the 4th, 6th, and 7th scale degrees and their concomitant intervals. But the half-diminished seventh chord is still not used as commonly as the other seventh chords, and consequently, it sounds somewhat fresh in comparison with them.

Let's now try to identify just the *quality* of each seventh chord, removed from any diatonic context.

CHORD	QUALITY
I^7	M7
ii^7	m7
iii^7	m7
IV^7	M7
V^7	V^7
vi^7	m7
$vii^{\o7}$	$\o7$

TABLE III.1 *Quality of seventh chords in the major mode*

CLASS DRILLS

A.   **Identify the quality of each of the root-position seventh chords that you hear.**

1.	2.	3.	4.	5.	6.
7.	8.	9.	10.	11.	12.

B. **Identify the quality of each of the seventh chords that you hear without regard to its inversion.**

1.   2.   3.   4.   5.   6.

7.   8.   9.   10.   11.   12.

First Inversion of Seventh Chords

As was the case with triads, hearing which scale degree is in the bass aids in the identification of seventh chords since it limits the number of possibilities. For now, we will leave these chords in root position, except for the vii°7, which will be placed in first inversion ($^{ø6}_{5}$). Since putting the 3rd of the chord in the bass will create a 3rd, a 6th, *and* a 5th above the bass, the complete figured bass designation for any first-inversion seventh chord is $^{6}_{5}$, regardless of quality. The usual practice is to abbreviate this figure as $^{6}_{5}$ when indicating any seventh chord in first inversion—hence the symbol vii$^{ø6}_{5}$.

The melodic exercise in Example III.2 will help you to recall the sound of any seventh chord in root position. Sing it, play it, and memorize it. Note that each successive seventh chord requires a change of only one half step in just one chord member.

EXAMPLE III.2   *The "Seventh Chord Anthem"*

CLASS DRILLS

Identify the function of each of the seventh chords that you hear without regard to its inversion.

1.   2.   3.   4.   5.   6.

7.   8.   9.   10.   11.   12.

13.   14.   15.   16.   17.   18.

19.   20.   21.   22.   23.   24.

Other Inversions of Seventh Chords

Now let's consider *all* of the diatonic seventh chords in various inversions. As discussed earlier, placing any seventh chord in first inversion creates a 6th, a 5th, and a 3rd above the bass, and is figured $^{6}_{5}$. Next, placing any seventh chord in second inversion creates a 6th, a *4th*, and a 3rd above the bass (figured $^{4}_{3}$); placing it in third inversion, which is obviously possible only with seventh chords or larger extended tertiary sonorities, creates a 6th, a 4th, and a *2nd* above the bass (figured $\frac{4}{2}$ or, occasionally, just $_2$).

Here is how function is affected by inverting seventh chords, which are ordered from least to most flexible:

1. Third-inversion seventh chords, because of the 7th in the bass, tend to move down by step in the bass, usually to a first-inversion chord whose root lies a perfect 4th above the root of this chord. Thus,

$$V_2^4 - I^6 \qquad I_2^4 - IV^6 \qquad vi_2^4 - ii^6$$

2. First-inversion seventh chords tend to resolve up by step in the bass, usually to a root-position chord whose root also lies a perfect 4th above the root of this chord. Thus,

$$V_5^6 - I \qquad I_5^6 - IV \qquad ii_5^6 - V$$

3. Second-inversion seventh chords display a bit more freedom in their resolution tendencies in that the bass may move up by step, usually to a first-inversion chord whose root lies a perfect 4th above the root of this chord, or down by step, usually to a root-position chord whose root, similarly, lies a perfect 4th above the root of this chord. Thus,

$$V_3^4 - I^6 \qquad V_3^4 - I \qquad ii_3^4 - V \qquad ii_3^4 - V^6$$

4. Root-position seventh chords exhibit the greatest freedom in their motion, although the addition of the 7th often reinforces their tendency to move forward through the circle of fifths. Hence, it is quite common for a root-position seventh chord to progress to another root-position chord, up a 4th or down a 5th, as the following illustrates:

$$V^7 - I \qquad I^7 - IV \qquad iii^7 - vi \qquad vi^7 - ii$$

Proper use of an *inverted* seventh chord dictates that its bass move by step, usually according to the preceding guidelines. However, the *root-position* seventh chords may move by leap or step.

$$vi^7 - V^7 \qquad vi^7 - V^6 \qquad I^7 - V_4^6$$

Arpeggiating seventh chords leads to unique melodic activity, as the inversions will invariably place a step somewhere in the arpeggio. It's not a bad idea to become familiar with the quality of each seventh chord by arpeggiating them in each inversion. Think of them as little melodies, and memorize them for recognition and reproduction.

CLASS DRILLS

Sing the indicated scale degrees up and back down, in succession.

1. M7: $\hat{1}-\hat{3}-\hat{5}-\hat{7}-\hat{5}-\hat{3}-\hat{1}$, $\quad \hat{3}-\hat{5}-\hat{7}-\hat{1}-\hat{7}-\hat{5}-\hat{3}$, $\quad \hat{5}-\hat{7}-\hat{1}-\hat{3}-\hat{1}-\hat{7}-\hat{5}$, $\quad \hat{7}-\hat{1}-\hat{3}-\hat{5}-\hat{3}-\hat{1}-\hat{7}$

2. V7: $\hat{5}-\hat{7}-\hat{2}-\hat{4}-\hat{2}-\hat{7}-\hat{5}$, $\quad \hat{7}-\hat{2}-\hat{4}-\hat{5}-\hat{4}-\hat{2}-\hat{7}$, $\quad \hat{2}-\hat{4}-\hat{5}-\hat{7}-\hat{5}-\hat{4}-\hat{2}$, $\quad \hat{4}-\hat{5}-\hat{7}-\hat{2}-\hat{7}-\hat{5}-\hat{4}$

3. m7: $\hat{2}-\hat{4}-\hat{6}-\hat{1}-\hat{6}-\hat{4}-\hat{2}$, $\quad \hat{4}-\hat{6}-\hat{1}-\hat{2}-\hat{1}-\hat{6}-\hat{4}$, $\quad \hat{6}-\hat{1}-\hat{2}-\hat{4}-\hat{2}-\hat{1}-\hat{6}$, $\quad \hat{1}-\hat{2}-\hat{4}-\hat{6}-\hat{4}-\hat{2}-\hat{1}$

4. $ø_5^6$: $\hat{2}-\hat{4}-\hat{6}-\hat{7}-\hat{6}-\hat{4}-\hat{2}$ (no other inversions as yet)

Using Quality and Inversion to Identify Seventh Chords

Recognizing the function and inversion of a diatonic seventh chord requires identifying the bass (thus limiting the possibilities to four), discerning the quality (further reducing the possibilities), listening to the tendency (especially of the bass), and, primarily as a way of checking your answer, determining the inversion through melodic analog (arpeggiating upward from the bass). Here are two sample procedures:

1. You recognize $\hat{2}$ in the bass. Thus, you realize, the chord could be a ii^7, a vii$^{\varnothing 6}_5$, a V$^4_3$, or a iii$^4_2$. You hear the chord as being somewhat neutral (*not* dominant) in quality, and decide that it's a minor 7th chord. Therefore, it must be a ii^7 or a iii$^4_2$. The bass note sounds dissonant and tends downward; the chord sounds unstable; thus, it is a iii$^4_2$!

2. You recognize $\hat{1}$ in the bass, so the chord could be a I^7, a vi$^6_5$, a IV$^4_3$, or a ii$^4_2$. There is a strong dissonance present, so you determine that the chord is a major 7th; it could be a I^7 or a IV$^4_3$. The chord sounds quite unstable and yet it has no obvious bass tendency; it could move up or down by step. It must be a IV$^4_3$!

CLASS DRILLS

List all the diatonic seventh chords that are consistent with the following observations.

	SCALE DEGREE HEARD IN THE BASS	CHORD QUALITY	BASS TENDENCY	STABILITY
1.	$\hat{2}$	V^7		
2.			Down by step	Unstable
3.	$\hat{3}$			
4.		∅7		
5.		M7	Up by step	Unstable
6.	$\hat{5}$	m7		
7.	$\hat{3}$	M7		
8.		m7	None	Stable
9.	$\hat{6}$	M7		
10.	$\hat{1}$	m7		

Now let's try to identify diatonic seventh chords by function and inversion (Roman and Arabic numerals). Keep all of the foregoing in mind, and don't get discouraged. With just a little practice, you will find these easier to recognize than simple diatonic triads.

CLASS DRILLS

A. Identify the function and inversion of each seventh chord that you hear.

C major

1.	2.	3.	4.	5.	6.	7.

A major

| 8. | 9. | 10. | 11. | 12. | 13. | 14. |

F major

| 15. | 16. | 17. | 18. | 19. | 20. | 21. |

D major

| 22. | 23. | 24. | 25. | 26. | 27. | 28. |

B. Identify the function and inversion of each seventh chord that you hear.

1.	2.	3.	4.	5.	6.	7.
8.	9.	10.	11.	12.	13.	14.
15.	16.	17.	18.	19.	20.	21.
22.	23.	24.	25.	26.	27.	28.

HOME EXERCISES

1 Sing by arpeggiating all diatonic seventh chords in all inversions until you are facile with this on your instrument and at the keyboard, in various keys, without the aid of written music.

2 Practice singing the "Seventh Chord Anthem" (Example III.2, page 178) by transposing it sequentially around the circle of fifths. Again, use your instrument and a keyboard.

Learning to Hear Function

UNIT 39

Major-mode Progressions Incorporating Seventh Chords

*A*dding a 7th to every triad in a diatonic progression yields a stilted and artificial harmonic style. Sevenths are used to emphasize a function (as in V^7), to incorporate an extra note into the harmony (as in I^4_2, a tonic chord with a downward passing tone in the bass, or in the I^7, where the passing tone is above the bass), or to lend extra harmonic color to the tonal palette. For these reasons many seventh chords are used somewhat sparingly, although the dominant seventh chord is easily as prevalent as the V itself. The following progressions illustrate these considerations in that they mix diatonic seventh chords with diatonic triads. The use of these chords and their inversions has a significant impact on our ability to create smooth and effective bass lines, even at the level of three-chord miniprogressions. By way of example, the descending bass line $\hat{1}$–$\hat{7}$–$\hat{6}$, when harmonized only with diatonic triads, has the following possible harmonizations:

$$\text{I–V}^6\text{–vi} \qquad \text{I–iii}^6_4\text{–vi} \qquad \text{vi}^6\text{–iii}^6_4\text{–vi} \qquad \text{vi}^6\text{–V}^6\text{–vi}$$

The use of seventh chords greatly increases the options available to us, even when confining ourselves to the diatonic collection. With the same $\hat{1}$–$\hat{7}$–$\hat{6}$ bass line and allowing the addition of a 7th to only the second chord in each example, we now have the following possibilities:

$$\text{I–I}^4_2\text{–IV}^6 \qquad \text{I–V}^6_5\text{–vi} \qquad \text{I–iii}^4_3\text{–vi} \qquad \text{vi}^6\text{–V}^6_5\text{–vi} \qquad \text{vi}^6\text{–iii}^4_3\text{–vi}$$

Now it is your turn. How many harmonic possibilities can you find for each of these bass-line fragments?

CLASS DRILLS

A. Harmonize each bass line using diatonic seventh chords and triads.

1. $\hat{1}$–$\hat{2}$–$\hat{3}$ **2.** $\hat{4}$–$\hat{5}$–$\hat{1}$ **3.** $\hat{4}$–$\hat{5}$–$\hat{6}$ **4.** $\hat{6}$–$\hat{7}$–$\hat{1}$

B. *Dictation*: Write down the bass line of each three-chord progression that you hear, and provide a complete harmonic analysis under each bass note. (Additional staves are provided at the back of the book.)

1.

2.

3.

4.

5.

6.

7.

8.

9.

10.

11.

12.

13. ⸻

14. ⸻

15. ⸻

16. ⸻

17. ⸻

18. ⸻

19. ⸻

20. ⸻

21. ⸻

22. ⸻

23. ⸻

24. ⸻

As you already know, longer progressions can be thought of as collections of these miniprogressions. One cannot overestimate the importance of the bass line in determining a progression of any length. Using a combination of triads and seventh chords, how might you interpret the bass line in Example III.3?

Here are a few of the more obvious possibilities:

$$\text{I–I}^4_2\text{–IV}^6\text{–V–V}^4_2\text{–I}^6\text{–V}^4_3\text{–I}$$
$$\text{I–iii}^4_3\text{–vi–vi}^4_2\text{–ii}^6\text{–vi}^4_3\text{–vii}^{\varnothing 6}_5\text{–I}$$
$$\text{I–V}^6_5\text{–ii}^4_3\text{–V–V}^4_2\text{–I}^6\text{–vii}^{\varnothing 6}_5\text{–I}$$

How would you be able to discriminate between these three options? In every case, *quality* is the deciding factor. Functionally, they are fairly similar. Where *are* the functional differences? the similarities?

Let's proceed to the identification of longer diatonic progressions that incorporate added 7ths. Remember that *you can always work backward from* **cadences**. And remember to check your work by examining your results to see if they conform to what we know about function and tendency.

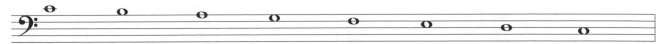

EXAMPLE III.3 *A diatonic bass line*

CLASS DRILLS

Dictation: **Write down the bass line of each progression that you hear, and provide a complete harmonic analysis under each note.**

1.

2.

3.

4.

5.

6.

7.

8.

9.

10.

11.

12.

13.

14.

15.

16.

17.

18.

19.

20.

HOME EXERCISES

1. Write a chord progression consisting of seven to thirteen chords, using diatonic triads and seventh chords. Perhaps your instructor can use it as additional material for dictation; otherwise, try giving the dictation to a classmate.

2. Harmonize the following bass lines, using a combination of diatonic triads and seventh chords:

(a)

(b)

(c)

(d)

Learning to Hear Chords

UNIT
40

*Seventh Chords
in the Minor Mode*

ooking at the diatonic seventh chords in the harmonic minor, we find the following collection:

$$i^7 = m^7 \qquad ii^{\emptyset 7} = {}^{\emptyset 7} \qquad III^7 = M^7 \qquad iv^7 = m^7$$
$$V^7 = V^7 \qquad VI^7 = M^7 \qquad vii^{\circ 7} = {}^{\circ 7}$$

Again, only the dominant-function chords (V^7 and $vii^{\circ 7}$) use the leading tone, $\sharp\hat{7}$; therefore, the seventh chord built upon the tonic is a minor seventh chord ($\hat{1}-\flat\hat{3}-\hat{5}-\flat\hat{7}$). There are two minor seventh chords (i^7 and iv^7), two major seventh chords (III^7 and VI^7) and, as expected, one V^7. Since the triad built upon $\hat{2}$ is diminished, adding $\hat{1}$ to it (as the 7th above the root) creates a ${}^{\emptyset 7}$ chord, namely, $ii^{\emptyset 7}$. And it is in the harmonic form of the minor that we find the only diatonic occurrence of a diminished seventh chord, $vii^{\circ 7}$.

*The Diminished
Seventh Chord*

Since the $vii^{\circ 7}$ is the only new chord quality to consider (the familiar ones just appear at different diatonic locations), let's begin by addressing this sonority. It is a diminished triad with a *diminished* 7th added above the root. This has the rather remarkable effect of making the $vii^{\circ 7}$ a totally symmetrical chord: from root to 3rd is a minor 3rd, from 3rd to 5th is a minor 3rd, and from 5th to 7th is *another* minor 3rd. Moreover, from 7th up to root is an augmented 2nd, the **enharmonic equivalent** of a minor 3rd!

Like all diminished chords, we shall use this one only in the first inversion ($vii^{\circ 6}_5$); but even then a slight problem arises. An astute observer will note that, because of its **symmetry**, one cannot truly *distinguish by ear* the inversion of a diminished seventh chord. It will

© 1997 Ardsley House, Publishers, Inc.

always sound like a stack of minor 3rds, as though it were in root position. Furthermore, any given diminished seventh chord will have three additional **spellings** that yield the same pitches, all of which are enharmonically equivalent. See Example III.4.

Thus, the vii°$^6_5$ is the most common form and most clearly reflects the function of the vii°7 in the harmonic minor mode. Certainly, this spelling does not make it any easier to discern the inversion of the chord. It helps to know that we will always encounter this chord in first inversion, so we can be sure of its identity. If you hear $\hat{2}$ in the bass and a diminished seventh chord, it will be a vii°$^6_5$. For now, if you think you hear any other scale degree in the bass in conjunction with a diminished seventh chord, either you have heard incorrectly or the chord is a vii°7 with a **secondary function** (see Unit 47).

There is one final point to consider. The diminished seventh chord has *two* tritones, so it is the least stable chord that we have yet encountered (or that we are likely to encounter). It is extremely specific in its resolution requirements, more so than even the half-diminished seventh chord. Its sound is probably more familiar than that of other seventh chords, and almost as familiar as the V7. This should help us to distinguish its quality from that of a half-diminished seventh chord.

Identifying seventh chords in the harmonic minor mode follows essentially the same procedure that we developed for the major. Of course, the various chord qualities are associated with different diatonic locations in the minor mode, with the single (though important) exception of the V7.

EXAMPLE III.4 *A diminished seventh chord with its three enharmonically equivalent respellings*

CLASS DRILLS

Considering only the harmonic minor mode, determine all the possible diatonic seventh chords suggested by the data in the chart below.

	SCALE DEGREE HEARD IN THE BASS	CHORD QUALITY	BASS TENDENCY	STABILITY
1.	$\hat{3}$	M7		
2.	$\hat{3}$	m7		
3.	$\hat{5}$	M7	Downward	Unstable
4.		V7	Upward	
5.	$\hat{2}$	°7		
6.	$\hat{4}$		Neutral	Stable
7.	$\flat\hat{7}$		Neutral	Unstable
8.		ø7		
9.	$\hat{1}$	M7		
10.	$\hat{6}$			

Let's try this type of exercise in a harmonic context. Remember the quality of each seventh chord found in the minor, and you should have little or no trouble.

CLASS DRILLS

A. **Identify the function and inversion of each seventh chord that you hear in the context of the minor mode.**

C minor

| 1. | 2. | 3. | 4. | 5. | 6. | 7. |

A minor

| 8. | 9. | 10. | 11. | 12. | 13. | 14. |

F minor

| 15. | 16. | 17. | 18. | 19. | 20. | 21. |

D minor

| 22. | 23. | 24. | 25. | 26. | 27. | 28. |

B. **Identify the function and inversion of each seventh chord that you hear in the context of the minor mode.**

| 1. | 2. | 3. | 4. | 5. | 6. | 7. |

| 8. | 9. | 10. | 11. | 12. | 13. | 14. |

| 15. | 16. | 17. | 18. | 19. | 20. | 21. |

| 22. | 23. | 24. | 25. | 26. | 27. | 28. |

HOME EXERCISES

Through all their inversions and in succession, arpeggiate all the seventh chords found in the harmonic minor mode, as we did in the Class Drills on page 179, where we concentrated on the major mode. Play them on your instrument and at the keyboard, and move sequentially through the circle of fifths. Remember the two forms of $\hat{7}$ as you do this: $\flat\hat{7}$ for III^7 and i^7, and $\sharp\hat{7}$ for V^7 and vii$^{\circ 6}_5$.

Learning to Hear Function

UNIT **41**

Minor-mode Progressions Incorporating Seventh Chords

ecause of the peculiarities of the harmonic minor mode, harmonic motion is a bit more limited and, therefore, can be a bit more predictable. For example, there are only three harmonizations of an open progression that moves downward in the bass from $\hat{1}$ to $\hat{6}$ ($\hat{1}$–♭$\hat{7}$–♭$\hat{6}$):

$$i - III_4^6 - VI \qquad i - III_3^4 - VI \qquad i - i_2^4 - iv^6$$

Since we wish to avoid the augmented second in the bass, we must use ♭$\hat{7}$ to get to ♭$\hat{6}$, and only the III and i^7 chords use the lowered 7th scale degree. There are other restrictions, most notably those caused by the presence of the two diminished chords. And, of course, there is the ever-present tendency of movement toward the relative major, made all the more likely by the strong tendency that $ii^{\varnothing 6}_5$ has toward III.

CLASS DRILLS

Dictation: Write down the bass line of each three-chord miniprogression that you hear, and provide a complete harmonic analysis under each bass note.

1.

2.

3.

4.

5.

6.

7.

8.

9.

10.

11.

12.

13.

14.

15.

16.

At this point, hearing and identifying extended diatonic progressions should be much easier for you because practice, combined with knowledge and expectation, can render seemingly difficult tasks familiar. Test your abilities with the series of extended progressions in the ensuing Class Drills, all of which incorporate diatonic seventh chords from the harmonic minor mode.

CLASS DRILLS

Dictation: Write down the bass line of each progression that you hear, and provide a complete harmonic analysis under each bass note.

1.

2.

3.

4.

5.

6.

7.

8.

9.

10.

11.

12.

HOME EXERCISES

Harmonize the following bass lines, using a combination of diatonic triads and seventh chords from the harmonic minor mode.

1.

2.

3.

4.

5.

6.

UNIT 42

Sequence

A **sequence** in music occurs when recognizable sections of the music are repeated at higher or lower pitch levels. The term "sequence" also refers to the technique of using sequences. To be a true sequence, the melody, rhythm, and harmony must be repeated at the different pitch levels. The purpose or goal of a sequence is to lengthen a phrase, although entire phrases can be sequenced as well. A sequence frequently leads to a cadence. Although it is certainly not restricted to these limitations, repetition of a sequential pattern generally moves by step or around the circle of fifths. It is in sequences whose pattern of repetition follows the circle of fifths that we often find the allowable exception to our steadfast prohibition of diminished triads (vii°) and seventh chords (vii^{ø7}, vii$^{°7}$) in root position. The same, of course, holds true for ii° and ii^{ø7} in the minor mode. See Example III.5.

EXAMPLE III.5 *A piece exhibiting melodic, rhythmic, and harmonic sequence*

© 1997 Ardsley House, Publishers, Inc.

Recognizing Sequence When listening to a piece containing a sequence, there are two critical steps in understanding what we hear. The first is to detect the use of sequence itself; mere repetition of some detail in the music does not necessarily signify a sequence. The second is to determine the *pattern*; that is, what constitutes the sequential unit, how the music is sequenced (up or down by steps, 3rds, 4ths, etc.), and how many repetitions there are. In Example III.5, the sequential unit is two measures in length, the pattern is ascending by step, and there are two repetitions of the sequential unit.

CLASS DRILLS

A. In the following short harmonic progressions determine whether or not harmonic sequence is present.

1. $I–ii–ii^6–V–vi–V^6–I$

2. $I–I^6–IV–IV^6–V–V^6–I$

3. $i–iv–III–VI–iv–V–i$

4. $i–V–VI–III–iv–i–ii^\circ–V^7–i$

5. $I–V_4^6–I^6–ii–vi_4^6–ii^6–IV–I_4^6–IV^6–V–ii_4^6–V^6–I$

6. $i–i^6–ii^{\circ 6}–III–III^6–VI–i_4^6–V^7–i$

7. $I–ii_2^4–V^6–I_2^4–IV^6–vi^7–V–iii_5^6–vi–V^6–I$

8. $i–i_2^4–VI–VI_2^4–iv–iv_2^4–ii^\circ–ii^{\varnothing 4}_2–V^6–V^7–i$

B. Determine the pattern of the sequences contained within the following harmonic progressions.

1. $I–IV–vii^\circ–iii–vi–ii–V–I$

2. $I–I^6–IV–ii–ii^6–V–iii–iii^6–vi–IV–IV^6–V^7–I$

3. $I–V–ii–vi–iii–vii^\circ–IV–V^7–I$

4. $i–V_4^6–i^6–iv–VI–III_4^6–VI^6–ii^\circ–iv–i_4^6–iv^6–V–i$

5. $I–ii^6–iii–IV^6–V–vi^6–vii^\circ–I^6–ii–V^7–I$

6. $i–iv–V–ii^\circ–V–VI–III–VI–V^7–i$

7. $I–I_2^4–IV^6–iii–iii_2^4–vi^6–V–V_2^4–I^6–vii^{\circ 6}_5–I$

8. $i–i^6–iv–V^7–ii^\circ–ii^{\circ 6}–V–VI^7–III–III^6–VI–V^7–i$

HOME EXERCISES

1. Identify sequence in the music you are playing, singing, and listening to. Try to determine the patterns involved.

2. Take the following simple succession of notes and sequence it diatonically (a) by ascending 4ths and (b) by ascending steps until you return to the starting pitch (with allowances for changing octaves when the pattern moves out of your vocal range). You can use this procedure on just about any measure of any etude that you are practicing or playing as a warmup.

Learning to Hear Function

UNIT

43

Sequence in Progressions Incorporating Seventh Chords

N ow that we have had a bit of fun locating sequence and iden-tifying sequential patterns, it is time to apply what we have learned to larger harmonic progressions that may incorpo-rate sequence. (Recognizing sequential patterns can be helpful be-cause once identified, you can allow the pattern to dictate some of the harmonies involved.) A word of caution, however. Don't be fooled by a bass line with a sequential pattern—it may not necessarily be part of an actual sequence. Remember that sequence involves har-mony *and* melody (including bass lines). A sequence cannot go on forever, either; it must break for cadence. Listen carefully for this break. Needless to say, the following progressions for dictation might be using diatonic seventh chords as well.

CLASS DRILLS

A. *Dictation*: **Write down the bass line of each harmonic progression that you hear, and provide a complete harmonic analysis under each bass note.**

1.

2.

3.

4.

© 1997 Ardsley House, Publishers, Inc.

5.

6.

7.

8.

9.

10.

11.

12.

B. *Dictation*: **Write down the longer harmonic progressions that you hear by writing out the bass line and providing a complete harmonic analysis under each bass note.**

1.

2.

3.

4.

5.

6.

HOME EXERCISES

As we have defined it thus far, the minor mode does *not* lend itself particularly well to sequential treatment within the boundaries of diatonicism. Why not?

Melody

UNIT

44

Sequence and Implied Seventh Chords

*T*he following exercises should be approached as in previous units concerned with sight-singing and dictation. In addition, you should be able to identify sequence when it occurs and use this recognition to facilitate your performance and/or dictation; that is, you should hear and sing sequenced material in its entirety rather than concentrate on individual details. The same techniques for identification and recognition of seventh chords apply.

CLASS DRILLS & HOME EXERCISES

A. *Sight-singing*: Study, analyze, sight-sing, practice, and perform the following melodies.

5.

J. S. Bach

6.

B.   *Dictation:* **Write down the melodies that your instructor plays.**

1.

2.

3.

4.

5.

6.

7.

8.

C. *Error detection*: Your instructor will play three examples for you. Compare what you hear with what is written on the corresponding staves that follow.

   i. Circle any pitch or rhythm that seems to be incorrect.

   ii. Correct any pitch or rhythm so that it matches what you hear.

Rhythm

UNIT **45**

Asymmetric Meters

*A*symmetric **meters** are meters whose time signatures have a numerator that is a **prime number** greater than 3. Since time signatures with numerators greater than 13 are rather impractical (to say the least), we will limit ourselves, accordingly, to asymmetric meters such as $\frac{5}{4}$ and $\frac{7}{8}$.

These meters divide so that the given time signature is the "sum" of other time signatures with prime numerators (and common denominators). Thus,

$$\frac{5}{4} = \frac{2}{4} + \frac{3}{4} \quad (\text{or } \frac{3}{4} + \frac{2}{4}) \qquad \frac{7}{8} = \frac{2}{8} + \frac{2}{8} + \frac{3}{8} \quad (\text{or } \frac{2}{8} + \frac{3}{8} + \frac{2}{8} \text{ or } \frac{3}{8} + \frac{2}{8} + \frac{2}{8})$$

Metric stress is placed according to these divisions, which are generally indicated by the composer, by using notated accents, **beamed groupings**, and other means. Succeeding bars of $\frac{5}{4}$ might be indicated as

$$\frac{2}{4} + \frac{3}{4}, \qquad \frac{3}{4} + \frac{2}{4}, \qquad \frac{2}{4} + \frac{2}{4} + \frac{1}{4}$$

and so on. Of course, cross accents can also be written within the context of an asymmetric meter. See Examples III.6 and III.7.

Patterns of Accents

Reading rhythms written in asymmetric meters is a matter of following the metric accents as well as the notated ones. If a regular pattern of accents is established in the music, then it is much easier to read, hear, perform, and conduct the asymmetry of the meter. Those pieces written in asymmetric meters wherein a regular pattern is *not* established can be considered *Augenmusik*, in which the irregular patterns are presented more for a different visual effect

EXAMPLE III.6   *Three divisions of a $\frac{5}{4}$ bar*

EXAMPLE III.7   *Cross accents within $\frac{7}{8}$ meter*

© 1997 Ardsley House, Publishers, Inc.

than for any substantive aural effect. It could easily have been barred into a more standard time signature and **cross-accented**, or written in a more standard time signature with just an occasional interpolation of a different time signature when absolutely necessary (**mixed meter**).

In many instances musicians "ignore" the bar lines anyway, and play the rhythms and associated accents one after the other, perhaps adding an unnotated accent on written **downbeats** of measures. The point is that reading and performing in asymmetric meters *should* be no more difficult than in more standard meters. If a pattern develops, recognize that pattern and keep up with it until it changes or ends. Think of the $\frac{5}{4}$ theme, written by Lalo Schifrin for the '60s television program, "Mission Impossible," shown in Example III.8. Or consider the persistently repeating rhythmic pattern, or **ostinato**, at the opening of "Mars," from Gustav Holst's *The Planets* (Example III.9).

Occasionally, patterns in the more standard time signatures are reaccented into groupings that can suggest an asymmetric meter when repeated frequently. Once heard, who could forget Leonard Bernstein's "America" from *West Side Story* (Example III.10)? The pattern regroups $\frac{6}{8}$ into its $\frac{3}{4}$ derivative (a practice often called **hemiola**) over and over in a rhythmically compelling and dramatically charged fashion. Likewise, Dave Brubeck's "Blue Rondo à la Turk" turns $\frac{9}{8}$ into a $\frac{3}{4} + \frac{3}{8}$ tour de force of bravura asymmetric rhythm and pattern.

With a little practice, the reading of such details will pose no particular problems. The meters themselves are rarely the obstacles; what is found *between* the bar lines can stump us once in a while. Let's begin with a few one-part exercises before we move on to two-part rhythms with asymmetric meters.

EXAMPLE III.8   *The rhythmic pattern found in the theme for "Mission Impossible"*

EXAMPLE III.9   *The opening rhythmic ostinato of "Mars" from* The Planets

EXAMPLE III.10   *The rhythmic ostinato of "America" from* West Side Story

CLASS DRILLS

Perform the following rhythms. Use the syllable *ta*, and make sure that releases are just as accurate as attacks.

© 1997 Ardsley House, Publishers, Inc.

Not so hard and kind of fun? The changing accents keep you on your toes, and the asymmetric patterns are even kind of exciting. So now let's turn to two-part exercises of the same sort. They can be realized by individuals vocalizing one line while clapping or tapping the beginning (or attack) of each note in the other line. They could also be used to practice rhythmic ensemble by realizing them as duets. Finally, they are suitable for use as two-part dictations.

CLASS DRILLS

Perform these two-part studies by yourself, in pairs, or in groups.

9.

10.

HOME EXERCISES

1 Practice your scales by applying a regularly repeating pattern of asymmetric accents (1–2, 1–2, 1–2–3, etc.) to them, and following the pattern without breaking it. This may also alleviate some of the tediousness inherent in scale practice and, as an added bonus, it will actually improve your technique.

2 Search for some music written in asymmetric meters. Does it have a pattern of accents? Practice by reading it, or at least reading its rhythms.

Melody

UNIT 46

Soprano and Bass Lines Incorporating Sequence and Implied Seventh Chords

T hough you may approach the following melodies and dictations as you did in previous units, it is again recommended that you recognize sequences and outlined seventh chords in their entirety, and use this identification to develop a more refined aural comprehension.

CLASS DRILLS

A. *Sight-singing*: Study, analyze, sight-sing, practice, and perform each duet.

3.

G. F. Handel

4.

J. S. Bach

5.

G. F. Handel

B. *Dictation*: **Write down the soprano and bass lines that your instructor plays.**

1.

2.

3.

4.

5.

6.

7.

8.

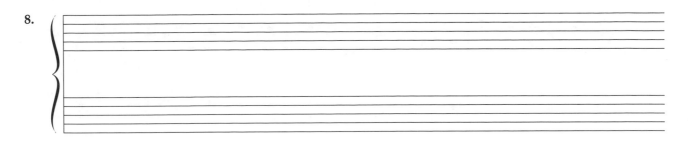

C. *Error detection*: Your instructor will play three examples for you. Compare what you hear with what is written on the corresponding staves that follow.

   i. Circle any pitch or rhythm that seems to be incorrect.

   ii. Correct any pitch or rhythm so that it matches what you hear.

3.

© 1997 Ardsley House, Publishers, Inc.

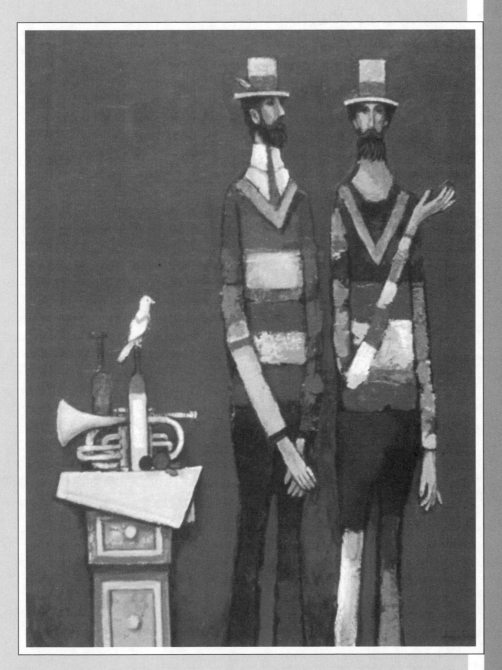

*Hearing
Secondary
Functions
and
Modulations*

Learning to Hear Function

UNIT 47

Secondary Dominants

Secondary dominant is the term used to indicate a chord that is not diatonic but that is nevertheless related to a diatonic chord as its dominant, that is, as its V, V⁷, vii°, viiø⁷, or vii°⁷. For example, in C major, $\hat{2}$ is D. If we temporarily assume that $\hat{2}$ is the tonic, then the tonic triad is a D-minor triad, and its dominant triad would be an A-major triad (A–C♯–E). The A-major triad is not a diatonic chord in C major because the C♯ that constitutes the 3rd of the A-major triad does not exist diatonically in C major. The A-major triad is **borrowed** from the key of the ii chord, D minor, where it exists and functions as V.

All of the chords in the major diatonic collection, except I and vii°, have secondary dominants. The dominant of I is never secondary, and being a diminished triad, vii° cannot function as the tonic chord in any key. Therefore, it obviously cannot have a dominant. Each secondary-dominant chord has at least one nondiatonic note relative to the **home key**, except the V of IV. As we saw earlier, the I chord can have a dominant function with respect to IV because all the scale degrees constituting V in the key of IV ($\hat{5}$, $\hat{7}$, and $\hat{2}$) are common to the key of I ($\hat{1}$, $\hat{3}$, and $\hat{5}$). Example IV.1 looks systematically at the secondary dominant of each diatonic triad in the major mode.

EXAMPLE IV.1 *The secondary V for each appropriate diatonic triad in the major mode*

EXAMPLE IV.2 *The secondary vii° for each appropriate diatonic triad in the major mode*

© 1997 Ardsley House, Publishers, Inc.

Similarly, Example IV.2 examines the secondary vii° of each diatonic triad in the major mode.

Of course, the secondary V⁷ of each diatonic triad is the combination of that triad's secondary V and vii°. The use of these secondary dominants expands the number of pitches available to twelve:

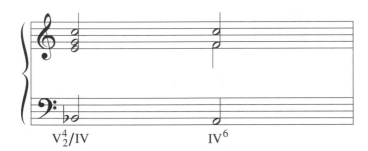

This collection is enharmonically equivalent to the chromatic scale. The appearance of these chromatically altered notes, especially in the bass, greatly aids in the identification of their associated secondary-dominant chords. For example, suppose that you hear a $\sharp\hat{2}$ in the bass. We find this note as the leading tone in the secondary dominants of iii; so the bass will more than likely move upward to $\hat{3}$. If so, then the $\sharp\hat{2}$ is the bass of a V⁶/iii (*not* the bass of a vii°/iii, as we are still limited to *first*-inversion diminished chords). Note that in almost all cases, the altered notes are leading tones. The exceptions are $\sharp\hat{4}$ in V⁶₄/iii and vii°⁶/iii, and $\flat\hat{7}$ in V⁴₂/IV. In the latter case, the $\flat\hat{7}$ is the **upper leading tone**, and should resolve downward to the 3rd of the IV chord, as shown in Example IV.3.

As the 5th of the V/iii and the 3rd of the vii°/iii, $\sharp\hat{4}$ may move upward to root-position iii or downward to first-inversion iii, as in Example IV.4.

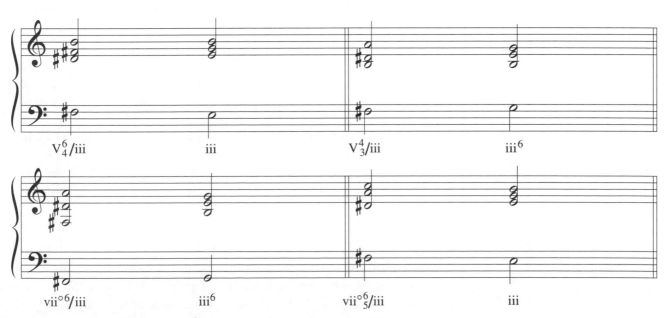

EXAMPLE IV.3   *The 7th of the V⁴₂/IV resolving downward to the 3rd of the IV⁶*

EXAMPLE IV.4   *Resolutions of $\sharp\hat{4}$*

Thus, in the case of $\#\hat{1}$, $\#\hat{2}$, $\#\hat{5}$, or $\flat\hat{7}$ in the bass, you will have a pretty good idea of the associated harmony (V^6/ii or V^6_5/ii, V^6/iii or V^6_5/iii, V^6/vi or V^6_5/vi, and V^4_2/IV, respectively), and in the case of the $\#\hat{4}$ you can determine the harmony from the context. If $\#\hat{4}$ moves up by half step to a root-position major chord, the associated harmony must be the secondary dominant of V in first inversion (V^6/V). If it moves up by step to a first-inversion minor chord or down by step to a root-position minor chord, it must be a V^6_4/iii, a V^4_3/iii, a vii$^{\circ 6}$/ii, or a vii$^{\circ 6}_5$/iii.

What if the chromatically altered note is *not* in the bass? As you can guess by this point, chord quality will most certainly provide a helpful clue. All the secondary dominants are by nature either major, diminished, dominant seventh, half-diminished seventh, or diminished seventh in quality. So if you encounter a chord quality with a bass note not normally (diatonically) associated with it, you may be able to deduce the identity of the harmony. For example, suppose you hear $\hat{7}$ in the bass with a major chord above it. Which secondary harmony is implied? Suppose you hear $\hat{1}$ in the bass, with the sound of a V^7. Again, which secondary harmony is implied? Let's try a game of harmonic sleuth. Given the following data, what diatonic *and* secondary harmonies may be implied?

CLASS DRILLS

Determine the harmonic possibilities suggested by the given collection of data. Secondary dominants should be considered.

	SCALE DEGREE HEARD IN THE BASS	CHORD QUALITY	BASS TENDENCY	STABILITY
1.	$\hat{3}$	M		
2.	$\#\hat{1}$			
3.	$\#\hat{4}$	$\circ$		
4.	$\hat{6}$	M		
5.	$\flat\hat{7}$		Downward	Unstable
6.	$\hat{2}$	M		
7.	$\#\hat{4}$	M	Upward	
8.	$\hat{7}$	M		
9.	$\hat{2}$	V^7	Downward	Unstable
10.	$\hat{5}$	V^7	Downward	Unstable
11.	$\#\hat{5}$			
12.	$\hat{7}$	$\circ$	Upward/ downward	Unstable
13.	$\hat{1}$		Downward	Unstable
14.	$\hat{3}$	V^7	Upward	
15.	$\#\hat{2}$		Upward	

As another preliminary exercise, listen to secondary dominants and, in your mind's ear, hear the triad to which they resolve. Then identify that diatonic triad. At first, concentrate only on root-position secondary V and V^7 chords.

CLASS DRILLS

Hearing only its secondary dominant, identify the diatonic chord of resolution.

C major

1.   2.   3.   4.   5.

D major

6.   7.   8.   9.   10.

F major

11.   12.   13.   14.   15.

G major

16.   17.   18.   19.   20.

Now let's try the same thing using secondary dominants and dominant seventh chords in various inversions. Remember, the goal of these exercises is to identify the *diatonic* triad of which these harmonies are secondary dominants.

CLASS DRILLS

Hearing only its secondary dominant, identify the diatonic chord of resolution.

A major

1.   2.   3.   4.   5.

E major

6.   7.   8.   9.   10.

E♭ major

11.   12.   13.   14.   15.

F major

16.   17.   18.   19.   20.

The next step is to identify the inversion of the secondary dominant. The process is the same as that for any diatonic dominant or dominant seventh chord: listen for its tendency and resolution. In the next Exercise Set, we'll also include diminished chords in first inversion. If you hear a diminished chord, determine whether a 7th (and which type of 7th) has been added, and with which diatonic triad it is associated as a vii^{o6}, vii$^{\varnothing 6}_{5}$, or vii$^{o6}_{5}$.

CLASS DRILLS

Identify the secondary dominant that you hear by identifying its inversion and its resolution (V^6_5/___ or vii°/___).

B♭ major

1.	2.	3.	4.	5.

C major

6.	7.	8.	9.	10.

E♭ major

11.	12.	13.	14.	15.

F major

16.	17.	18.	19.	20.

D major

21.	22.	23.	24.	25.

E major

26.	27.	28.	29.	30.

G major

31.	32.	33.	34.	35.

A major

36.	37.	38.	39.	40.

As a reminder, if the chromatically altered notes $\sharp\hat{1}$, $\sharp\hat{2}$, or $\sharp\hat{5}$ appear in the bass, then the secondary dominant must be V^6/ii or V^6_5/ii, V^6/iii or V^6_5/iii, or finally V^6/vi or V^6_5/vi, respectively. If $\flat\hat{7}$ is in the bass, the secondary dominant must be V^4_2/IV. A $\sharp\hat{4}$ in the bass could imply a V^6/V or V^6_5/V, or it could also imply a V^6_4/iii, V^4_3/iii, vii°^{6}/iii, or vii°$^6_5$/iii. The resolution will tell you definitively which of these two categories of secondary dominants you are hearing. Otherwise, chord quality is your chief means of discernment.

In the ensuing exercises, you will hear the chord of resolution following its secondary dominant. The resulting two-note bass line should make the identification of the secondary dominant easier.

CLASS DRILLS

Identify the secondary dominant that you hear, its inversion, and the diatonic triad of resolution with this inversion.

C major

1.	2.	3.	4.

5.	6.	7.	8.

D major

9.	10.	11.	12.
13.	14.	15.	16.

F major

17.	18.	19.	20.
21.	22.	23.	24.

G major

25.	26.	27.	28.
29.	30.	31.	32.

E major

33.	34.	35.	36.
37.	38.	39.	40.

HOME EXERCISES

1 Be able to arpeggiate the root-position V^7 of any scale degree (except $\hat{7}$) in the major mode. First, sing the major scale, then choose any note from it. Starting a perfect 4th below this note, arpeggiate a V^7 chord upward and downward, and end by moving back (resolving) to the original scale degree that you chose. Do this on $\hat{1}$ through $\hat{6}$, successively. Practice this exercise on your instrument and also at the keyboard, in all major keys.

2 Repeat Exercise 1 using secondary diminished seventh chords. Remember that major triads will follow secondary half-diminished seventh chords, whereas minor triads will follow secondary diminished seventh chords.

Learning to Hear Function

UNIT 48

Progressions Incorporating Secondary Dominants

Major Mode Harmonic progressions that utilize secondary dominants can often prove easier to identify because the chromatic notes and the changes in chord quality that they effect are quite striking and stand out to those listening. By comparison, progressions that are restricted to exclusively diatonic contexts offer fewer listening clues and often create an amorphous, **pandiatonic** impression on the listener, an impression created when even all the dissonances come from the same scale and when the individual characters of each scale degree seem to be equalized. This is what contemporary American composer Ross Lee Finney often calls "**white-note music**." In such a context it's simply harder to hear the harmonic details. The use of secondary dominants helps to alleviate this problem and provides more aural cues. We'll start with a few miniprogressions, most of which are either open or closed, owing to the extremely strong *pre-dominant* function of all secondary dominants.

CLASS DRILLS

Dictation: Write down the bass line of each three-chord progression that you hear, and provide a complete harmonic analysis under each bass note. (Additional staves are provided at the back of the book.)

1.

2.

3.

4.

5.

6.

7.

8.

9.

10.

11.

12.

13.

14.

15.

16.

© 1997 Ardsley House, Publishers, Inc.

17.

18.

19.

20.

21.

22.

23.

24.

25.

26.

27.

28.

29.

30.

31.

32.

33.

34.

35.

36.

Listen to what happens when we incorporate secondary dominants into larger progressions. Remember that since secondary dominants have such a strong pre-dominant function, they will either move to another pre-dominant (as in V^7/ii–ii, vii^{o6}_{5}/iii–iii, or V^4_2/vi–vi^6) or they will move directly to a dominant (as in V^7/V–V or $vii^{ø6}_{5}/V$–I^6_4). Don't forget to listen for altered scale degrees in the bass and for changes in diatonic chord qualities.

CLASS DRILLS

Dictation: **Write down the bass line of each progression that you hear, and provide a complete harmonic analysis under each bass note.**

1.

2.

3.

4.

5.

6.

7.

8.

Minor Mode   Now let's consider these sounds and concepts in the minor mode. The principles remain the same; only the diatonic locations of specific chord qualities are different. In the minor mode we find secondary dominants available at the following diatonic locations:

$$V^7 \text{ and } vii^{\o 7} \text{ of III} \qquad V^7 \text{ and } vii^{\o 7} \text{ of iv}$$
$$V^7 \text{ and } vii^{\o 7} \text{ of V} \qquad V^7 \text{ and } vii^{\o 7} \text{ of VI}$$

Of course, the ii° and vii° chords, being diminished, do not allow for the possibility of a secondary dominant. Let's begin by identifying three-chord progressions in the minor mode.

CLASS DRILLS

Dictation: **Write down the bass line of each three-chord progression that you hear, and provide a complete harmonic analysis under each bass note.**

1.

2.

3.

4.

5.

6.

7.

8.

9.

10.

11.

12.

13.

14.

15.

16.

17.

18.

19.

20.

21.

22.

23.

24.

25.

26.

27.

28.

29.

30.

In the minor mode, longer progressions employ secondary dominants in much the same manner as those in the major. Remember the tendency to move toward the relative major, made all the more efficacious through the availability of secondary dominants on III and VI.

CLASS DRILLS

Dictation: **Write down the bass line of each progression that you hear, and provide a complete harmonic analysis under each bass note.**

1.

2.

3.

4.

5.

6. _____

7. _____

8. _____

9. _____

10. _____

11. _____

12. _____

HOME EXERCISES

1. Harmonize the following bass lines, using a combination of diatonic triads, diatonic seventh chords, and secondary dominants:

(a)

(b)

(c)

(d)

2. Write your own chord progressions of seven to thirteen chords each, using secondary dominants, one in the major mode and the other in the minor. Perhaps your instructor will use these progressions as additional material for dictation; otherwise, try giving these dictations to a classmate.

Learning to Hear Function

UNIT 49

Secondary Pre-dominants

Secondary pre-dominants, like secondary dominants, are borrowed from keys other than the tonic. Secondary pre-dominants function with respect to diatonic chords in any given key as either their supertonic, mediant, subdominant, or sub-mediant.

For example, in C major (our home key), $\hat{4}$ is F. If we temporarily assume that $\hat{4}$ is the tonic, then the tonic key and tonic triad are F major. There are four triads that have a pre-dominant function in F major. They are G minor (ii), A minor (iii), B♭ major (IV), and D minor (vi). Of these four triads with pre-dominant function in F major, two triads (G minor, ii/IV; B♭ major, IV/IV) are not diatonic in our home key of C major and two (A minor, iii/IV; D minor, vi/IV) are.

In listening to identify secondary pre-dominants in the context of the home key, those secondary pre-dominants that happen to be diatonic in the home key are unlikely to be heard as secondary pre-dominants, even when they are used in association with their corresponding secondary dominants. On the other hand, those secondary pre-dominants that are *not* diatonic in the home key stand out because they incorporate pitches not found in the home key and consequently are more easily heard. Therefore, we shall not attempt to classify as secondary pre-dominants those chords common to both the secondary and home keys except when we are listening to music that modulates (Units 55–57) or when these chords are functioning as part of secondary **deceptive motion**.

With C major as the example of the home key, all of the possible secondary pre-dominants (supertonic, mediant, subdominant, or submediant) in a major key are listed in Table IV.1. Those secondary pre-dominants that are *not* diatonic in the home key are printed in boldface.

Goal Harmonies

The identification and awareness of secondary pre-dominants will help us to develop a perception of large-scale harmonic movement toward specific harmonic goals. In any given progression, identification of the **goal harmony**—the diatonic triad toward which a secondary dominant and secondary pre-dominant move—will be our biggest clue to the identity of any secondary pre-dominant in question. Work backward from the goal harmony and then, using the note in the bass and the quality of the chord, deduce its identity as follows:

Step 1. $x - y - \text{ii}$

Step 2. $x - y/\text{ii} - \text{ii}$

	$\hat{1}$	$\hat{2}$	$\hat{3}$	$\hat{4}$	$\hat{5}$	$\hat{6}$	$\hat{7}$
Home-key triad	I*	ii	iii	IV	V	vi	vii°†
Secondary tonic (key)		D minor	E minor	F major	G major	A minor	
Secondary supertonic		**ii°/ii** **e°**	**ii°/iii** **f♯°**	**ii/IV** **g**	ii/V a	ii/vi b°	
Secondary mediant		III/ii F	III/iii G	iii/IV a	**iii/V** **b**	III/vi C	
Secondary subdominant		**iv/ii** **g**	iv/iii a	**IV/IV** **B♭**	IV/V C	iv/vi d	
Secondary submediant		**VI/ii** **B♭**	VI/iii C	vi/IV d	vi/V e	VI/vi F	

*The pre-dominants of the tonic key are never considered secondary.

†A diminished triad can never assume a tonic function; so it cannot have a dominant or pre-dominant.

TABLE IV.1 *Secondary pre-dominants of triads in the C-major scale. Those secondary pre-dominants that are* not *diatonic are printed in boldface.*

Step 3. $x - V^7/ii - ii$

Step 4. ♭7 in bass, major chord $- V^7/ii - ii$

Step 5. $VI/ii - V^7/ii - ii$

The use of a secondary pre-dominant prior to its secondary dominant almost always sounds as if a **modulation** has taken place. More commonly (that is, where modulation has *not* occurred), the secondary vi or VI chord might *follow* the secondary dominant, creating a secondary deceptive motion. At first, this use of the secondary vi or VI can be tricky to identify, and it requires recognition of the *sound* of a deceptive motion. That sound, that is, the sound of a V, V^7, vii°, vii°⁷, or vii°⁷ moving to vi or VI (depending on the mode), should be very familiar to you by now and should not pose a problem. Let's practice with a series of three-chord progressions.

CLASS DRILLS

A. *Dictation*: Write down the bass line of each three-chord progression that you hear, and identify the secondary pre-dominant, the secondary dominant, the goal diatonic triad, and their inversions. All of the progressions relate to the home key of C major and should be expressed accordingly.

1.

2.

3.

4.

5. _____

6. _____

7. _____

8. _____

9. _____

10. _____

B. *Dictation*: Write down the bass line of each three-chord progression that you hear, and identify the diatonic triad, the secondary dominant, the secondary pre-dominant, and their inversions. All of these secondary deceptive motions relate to the home key of D major and should be expressed accordingly.

1. _____

2. _____

3. _____

4. _____

5. _____

6. _____

7. _____

8. _____

9. _____

10. _____

Minor Mode   In the minor mode, secondary pre-dominants are associated with III, iv, V, and VI. With A minor as the home key, all the possible secondary pre-dominants are listed in Table IV.2. Those secondary pre-dominants that are *not* diatonic in the home key are printed in boldface.

Identification of these secondary pre-dominants should follow the same procedure for identifying such chords in the major mode. It just requires a little practice.

	$\hat{1}$	$\hat{2}$	$\hat{3}$	$\hat{4}$	$\hat{5}$	$\hat{6}$	$\hat{7}$
Home-key triad	i*	ii°†	III	iv	V	VI	vii°†
Secondary tonic (key)			C major	D minor	E major	F major	
Secondary supertonic			ii/III d	ii°/iv e°	**ii/V** **f♯**	**ii/VI** **g**	
Secondary mediant			**iii/III** **e**	III/iv F	**iii/V** **g♯**	iii/VI a	
Secondary subdominant			IV/III F	iv/iv g	**IV/V** **A**	**IV/VI** **B♭**	
Secondary submediant			vi/III a	**VI/iv** **B♭**	**vi/V** **c♯**	vi/VI d	

*The pre-dominants of the tonic key are never considered secondary.

†A diminished triad can never assume a tonic function; so it cannot have a dominant or pre-dominant.

TABLE **IV.2** · *Secondary pre-dominants of triads in the A-minor scale. Those secondary pre-dominants that are* not *diatonic are printed in boldface.*

CLASS DRILLS

A. *Dictation*: Write down the bass line of each three-chord progression that you hear, and identify the secondary dominant, the secondary pre-dominant, the diatonic triad, and their inversions. All of the progressions relate to the home key of A minor and should be expressed accordingly.

1.

2.

3.

4.

5.

6.

7.

8.

9.

10.

B. *Dictation*: Write down the bass line of each three-chord progression that you hear, and identify the diatonic triad, the secondary dominant, the secondary pre-dominant, and their inversions. All of the secondary deceptive motions relate to the home key of C minor and should be expressed accordingly.

1.

2.

3.

4.

5.

6.

7.

8.

9.

10.

HOME EXERCISES

1 Determine the identity of the following secondary pre-dominants in each of the specified home keys. Be sure that you can spell each secondary pre-dominant accurately.

(a) ii°/ii in A major

(b) III/iii in B major

(c) IV/IV in G major

(d) vi/V in F major

(e) ii°/vi in D major

(f) vi/VI in A minor

(g) IV/V in C minor

(h) III/iv in F♯ minor

(i) iii/III in D minor

2 Practice naming and spelling secondary pre-dominants to all appropriate scale degrees in any key and mode. Facility in this skill will aid you in thinking quickly and easily in two keys simultaneously, an invaluable skill for what is to come.

Learning to Hear Function

Progressions Incorporating Secondary Pre-dominants

*T*he purpose and effect of using both secondary pre-domi-nants and secondary dominants are to emphasize the diatonic chord that is their goal. Often, the term used to describe this effect is **prolongation**, which should not be confused with the lengthening of time or the augmentation of rhythm, al-though those are certainly other means of obtaining this effect. Consider the following progression:

$$I - I_2^4 - VI/ii - V^7/ii - ii - V_5^6/V - V^7 - I$$

In this example, the I is extended through the use of the passing I_2^4, and the V is emphasized through the use of the V_5^6/V. The ii is even further prolonged by the use of its pre-dominant, VI, and its domi-nant seventh, V^7, so much so that the movement to ii sounds like an arrival on the tonic. It is *not* a modulation, however, because other conditions pertaining to cadence and duration would have to be met in order to say that a modulation has truly been effected. In the fol-lowing progressions listen for this phenomenon, this prolonged and heightened sense of arrival, as an indication of the use of secondary pre-dominants. Also, listen for the appearance of secondary decep-tive motion.

CLASS DRILLS

A. *Dictation*: **Write down the bass line of each progression that you hear, and provide a complete harmonic analysis under each bass note.**

1.

2.

3.

4.

5.

6.

7.

8.

B. *Dictation*: **Write down the bass line of each progression that you hear, and provide a complete harmonic analysis under each bass note.**

1.

2.

3.

4.

5.

6.

7.

HOME EXERCISES

Supply a complete harmonic analysis for each of the following progressions. Remember that when it comes to secondary pre-dominants, there may well be more than one correct analysis. Accidentals apply only to the notes they immediately precede.

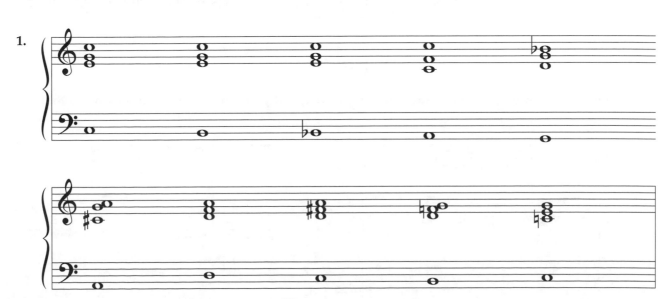

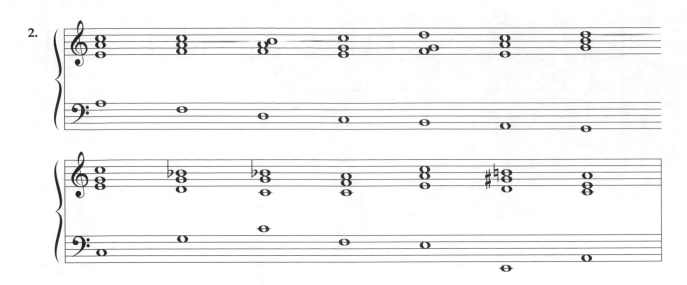

Melody

UNIT 51

Implied Secondary Functions

● ●

*I*n preparation for sight-singing, scan these melodies and look for accidentals that imply secondary functions. Identify those functions as a part of your normal preparatory activity for sight-singing. When writing down music from dictation, be aware of the function of any altered notes you may hear, and use that awareness to help keep you on track—that is, to help prevent you from getting off by a step and involuntarily transposing portions of your dictation.

CLASS DRILLS

A. *Sight-singing*: **Sight-sing, study, analyze, practice, and perform each of the following melodies.**

German folk song

© 1997 Ardsley House, Publishers, Inc.

C. G. Neefe

C. M. v. Weber

G. Paisiello

F. Silcher

German folk song

C. M. v. Weber

W. A. Mozart

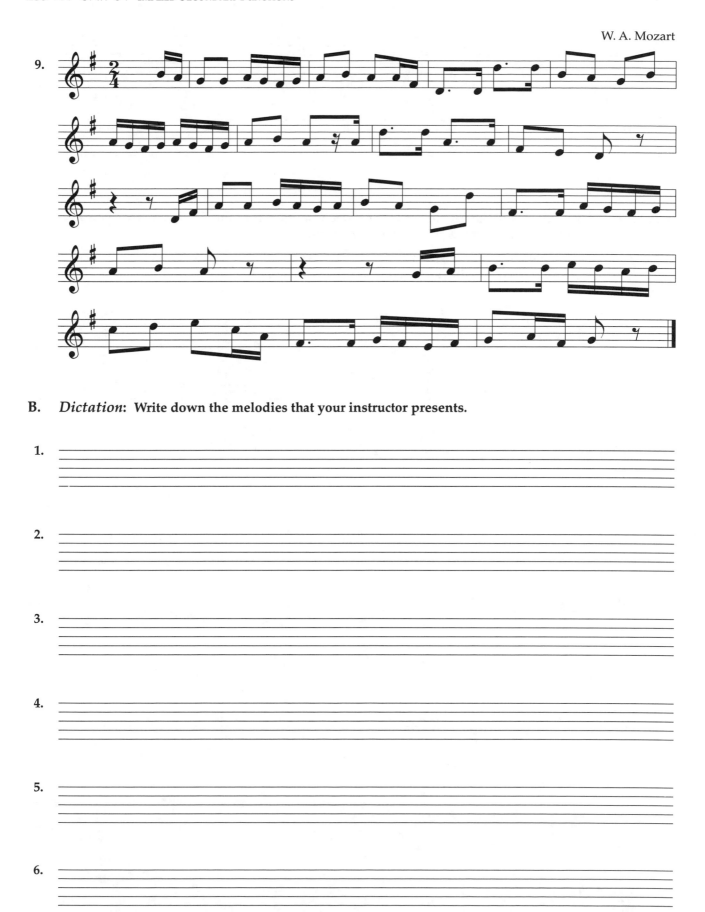

B. *Dictation:* **Write down the melodies that your instructor presents.**

1.

2.

3.

4.

5.

6.

7.

8.

C. *Error detection*: Your instructor will play three examples for you. Compare what you hear with what is written on the corresponding staves that follow.

    i. Circle any pitch or rhythm that seems to be incorrect.

    ii. Correct any pitch or rhythm so that it matches what you hear.

1.

2.

3.

Transposition

UNIT 52

Clefs and Transposing Instruments

*T*ransposition is the process of playing or notating music at a pitch other than that written in the score. Transposition and the use of multiple clefs are two of the more useful skills a musician must acquire. Actually, they involve reading and notation skills more than listening skills. Those of you with "perfect pitch" have been practicing transposition to a certain extent already; in fact, you've been asked to take many of your dictations in C major or A minor, even though the actual key in which your instructor played them was different. Some of you play transposing instruments (whether you are aurally aware of this or not), and some of you play instruments that require you to play in clefs other than the treble (G) clef or the bass (F) clef. Players of bassoons, cellos, violas, trombones, and other instruments are required to play in as many as four different clefs. But did you know that many of the transposing instruments are actually playing in nonstandard clefs?

Consider common E♭ transposing instruments, such as the E♭ and alto clarinets and the alto and baritone saxophones. The *written* note C on these instruments corresponds to the *sounding* note E♭ (the **concert pitch**). Music for these instruments is written in the treble clef, despite the various **ranges** involved. If you substitute a bass clef for the treble clef and leave all else alone, the written C will look like an E. In other words, players of E♭ instruments are reading octave transpositions of the bass clef, with appropriate alterations to the key signatures. If you can read the bass clef (and of course you do), then you can easily transpose and read parts written for E♭ instruments. Simply substitute the bass clef for the treble, locate the correct octave for the particular instrument whose part you are reading, and change the key signature to that of the key (in the same mode) located a minor 3rd higher than the key used in the original treble-clef version. Table IV.3 lists some E♭ transpositions. For other transpositions (see Tables IV.4 and IV.5 on page 242) alterations of the key signatures will *also* be according to the interval of transposition in question.

Another common instrumental transposition is B♭. Standard B♭ instruments include B♭ trumpets and B♭ clarinets as well as soprano and tenor saxophones. This transposition corresponds to the **tenor clef**, which is one of the **C-clefs**, so-called because they locate middle C on the staff. The tenor clef locates middle C as the second line from the top of the staff. A note on this line corresponds to the concert

WRITTEN	SOUNDING
Treble clef, key of C major	Bass clef, key of E♭ major
Treble clef, key of D major	Bass clef, key of F major
Treble clef, key of F minor	Bass clef, key of A♭ minor
Treble clef, key of A minor	Bass clef, key of C minor

TABLE IV.3 *E♭ transpositions*

WRITTEN	SOUNDING
Treble clef, key of C major	Tenor clef, key of B♭ major
Treble clef, key of D major	Tenor clef, key of C major
Treble clef, key of F minor	Tenor clef, key of E♭ minor
Treble clef, key of A minor	Tenor clef, key of G minor

TABLE IV.4 B♭ *transpositions*

pitch heard when a B♭ instrument plays D in the treble clef. Familiarity with this clef enables you to transpose B♭ treble-clef parts just as the bass clef allows you to transpose parts for E♭ instruments. Table IV.4 lists some B♭ transpositions.

The **alto clef** is the most familiar of the C-clefs. It locates middle C on the middle line of the staff. Violists and trombonists read the alto clef regularly. One could reinterpret the alto clef as a treble clef with all notes appearing a step lower on the staff (and sounding an octave lower) or as a bass clef with all notes appearing one step higher on the staff (and sounding an octave higher). Reading the alto clef is not a difficult endeavor, but, like anything else, it requires a bit of practice to achieve fluency. You will have that opportunity soon.

Still another common transposition involves the F instruments, such as English horns and French horns. The corresponding C-clef is the **mezzo-soprano clef**, which locates middle C on the second line from the bottom of the staff. Reading horn parts is then a matter of applying the mezzo-soprano clef to notes written in the treble clef and adjusting the key signature. (Neither the English horn nor the French horn requires an adjustment of the octave.) Table IV.5 lists some F transpositions.

Two other relatively common transpositions occur in orchestral music. Clarinets in A are frequently called for in works with sharp key signatures. Why do you think this is so? Clarinets in A are also used in situations in which a composer might wish to take advantage of their slightly extended lower register. The clarinet in A sounds the A above middle C when it plays the C written an octave higher. Therefore, all of the notes written for the A clarinet sound exactly a minor 3rd lower when played. With this in mind, answer the following questions.

WRITTEN	SOUNDING
Treble clef, key of C minor	Mezzo-soprano clef, key of F minor
Treble clef, key of D major	Mezzo-soprano clef, key of G major
Treble clef, key of F minor	Mezzo-soprano clef, key of B♭ minor
Treble clef, key of A major	Mezzo-soprano clef, key of D major

TABLE IV.5 F *transpositions*

CLASS DRILLS

A. When the clarinet in A has music written in each of the following keys, what are the concert (sounding, nontransposed) keys?

1. C minor   **2.** D major   **3.** F major   **4.** A minor   **5.** B major   **6.** E♭ major

B. When orchestral music is written in each of the following keys, which key signature must be provided for the clarinet in A?

1. F major   **2.** C♯ minor   **3.** B major   **4.** G major   **5.** E minor   **6.** D major

The other transposing instrument to which we are alluding is the alto flute, which is pitched in G. Its written C sounds the G that is a perfect 4th lower. Now answer the following questions.

CLASS DRILLS

A. When the alto flute has music written in each of the following keys, what are the corresponding concert keys?

1. B♭ major   **2.** C minor   **3.** E♭ major   **4.** G minor   **5.** A major   **6.** D♭ major

B. When orchestral music is written in each of the following keys, which key signature must be provided for the alto flute?

1. G major   **2.** E♭ major   **3.** C♯ minor   **4.** A major   **5.** F♯ minor   **6.** E major

Transposing without Clefs

If you successfully completed this last series of exercises, congratulations! You have taken the first and most crucial step toward transposing. The manner in which we determine the answer to the previous questions can be expressed algebraically by the following equation:

$$\frac{C}{\text{Key of transposing instrument}} = \frac{\text{Transposed key}}{\text{Concert key}}$$

For a natural horn in D, the equation becomes:

$$\frac{C}{D} = \frac{F}{x}$$

Solving for x, the result is obviously G (since C is to D as F is to G). This formula yields every transposed note as well as the corresponding key signature for any transposition you need to make.

To transpose with facility you need to be able to think in two keys at once. This is not as hard as it may sound; professional musicians do it all the time. It merely requires the ability to recognize $\hat{5}$, for example, in one key and produce $\hat{5}$ in another (and remain consistent). Clefs can facilitate this process, as can solfège, or any other method that you may internalize. Practice, as was said, is the most important thing. As a matter of course, horn players and trumpeters must transpose in a variety of keys, frequently on a moment's notice.

HOME EXERCISES

1. Transpose the following melody into each of the indicated keys, using the treble clef.

(a) B♭ major

(b) E♭ major

(c) F major

(d) A major

(e) G major

2. Rewrite the following melody in each of the indicated clefs and octaves.

(a) Alto clef, down an octave

(b) Tenor clef, down an octave

© 1997 Ardsley House, Publishers, Inc.

(c) Mezzo-soprano clef, at pitch

3. Transpose the following harmonic progression into each of the indicated keys.

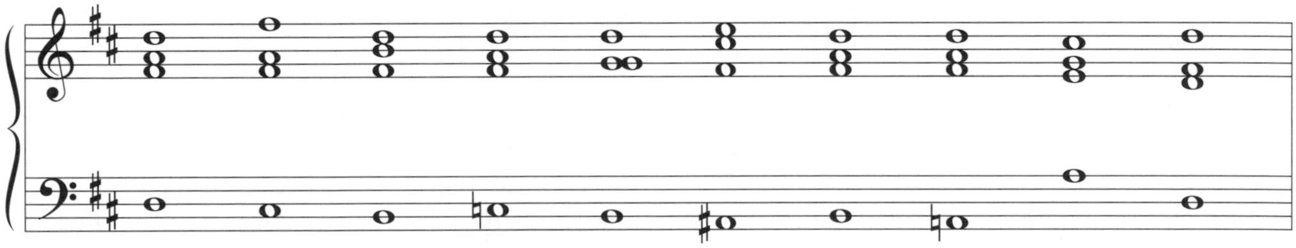

(a) E major

(b) A♭ major

(c) B major

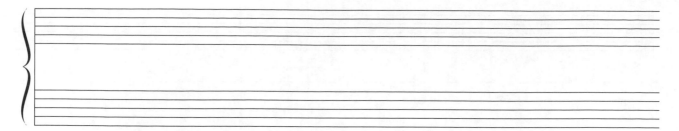

(d) F major

4. If we wish to hear the D above middle C, how would it have to be written for each of the following instruments?

   (a) Viola   **(b)** B♭ trumpet   **(c)** Alto saxophone   **(d)** Alto flute

   (e) B♭ bass clarinet   **(f)** English horn   **(g)** Clarinet in A

5. Transposition is the ideal skill to practice away from the classroom or the aural-skills lab. There are many ways to practice on your own. You might read music on your instrument for an instrument whose music is written in a different clef, transposing octaves as necessary and convenient. Read your regular warmups and etudes transposed to various levels. Work upward or downward chromatically, or proceed around the circle of fifths. If you are a singer, perform these exercises at the keyboard, too.

6. Mentally apply any clef you wish to practice (other than the treble or bass clef) to the beginning of one of the staves (a)–(j), which follow, and read aloud the letter names of the notes, according to the clef you have chosen. Keep a steady tempo throughout the line and do not stop for any reason. In each line, once you have achieved complete accuracy at a relatively slow tempo, gradually increase your tempo with each successive attempt. After you have mastered each line with a specific clef, repeat this process for the same line, using a different clef. Only after you have practiced with several different clefs on the same staff should you proceed to the next line.

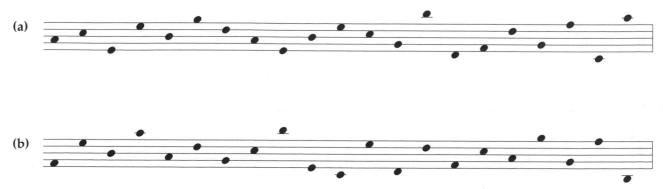

© 1997 Ardsley House, Publishers, Inc.

Transposition

UNIT 53

Transposing at Sight

Remember that middle C, no matter where it may be located on the staff by a particular clef, always falls on a *line*.[1] This observation alone is a big clue in interpreting any clef that may be presented to you. Where is middle C located on the staves in Example IV.5?

Reading these clefs is akin to locating middle C and then relating the lines of the staff to those of a more familiar clef. Some of the lines may be thought of as extending **ledger lines** across the width of the staff; conversely, you may add imaginary staff lines above or below the new staff to help orient yourself. All the clefs, except those that involve octave transpositions, are segments of the eleven-line **great staff**, as shown in Example IV.6. Let's try reading some melodies placed in clefs other than the treble (G) clef or the bass (F) clef.

EXAMPLE IV.5 *Locating middle C*

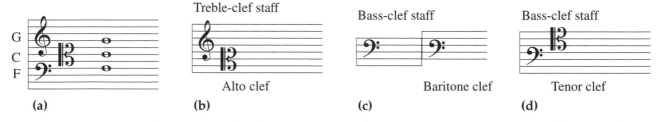

Treble-clef staff

(a) (b) (c) (d)

Alto clef Baritone clef Tenor clef

Bass-clef staff Bass-clef staff

EXAMPLE IV.6 **(a)** *The eleven-line great staff with G, C, and F clefs* **(b)** *The alto clef on the treble-clef staff extended*
(c) *The baritone clef on the bass-clef staff extended* **(d)** *The tenor clef on the bass-clef staff extended*

1. There is a practice in some English choral music to notate the tenor part using a C-clef that locates middle C in the second *space* from the top, so that notes are read *exactly* like standard **ottava** treble-clef parts, which are written an octave above the pitches actually sung. Obviously, this is an unusual exception to the line rule. There is also a rarely encountered type of **baritone clef** that uses a C-clef and locates middle C on the top line.

CLASS DRILLS

A. Sing each of the following melodies at sight. Vocalize the correct pitches using the letter name of each note. Omit the words "sharp," "flat," or "natural," except in the case of a nondiatonic note.

C. de Morales

10.

H. Purcell

11.

G. F. Handel

12.

C. Saint-Saëns

13.

W. A. Mozart

14.

R. Schumann

15.

G. P. da Palestrina

16.

F. Schubert

17.

W. A. Mozart

18.

G. P. da Palestrina

19.

B. Locate concert-pitch middle C for each of the following transposing instruments. (Recall that transposing is similar to reading a clef.)

1. E♭ clarinet _____
2. B♭ trumpet _____
3. G alto flute _____
4. F horn _____
5. B♭ tenor saxophone _____
6. A clarinet _____
7. B♭ bass clarinet _____
8. E horn _____
9. D trumpet _____
10. E♭ baritone saxophone _____
11. D♭ piccolo _____
12. A♭ horn _____
13. B trumpet _____
14. E♭ alto clarinet _____

As you can see, in transposition it is important to be aware of the specific octave in which an instrumental part is intended to sound because not all instruments of the same transposition locate *concert* middle C in the same octave. This is illustrated in Example IV.7.

And not all transposing instruments place middle C on a *line*, as shown in Example IV.8.

It is important that you be aware of the *actual* octave of the part you are examining, even though you may sight-sing the following exercises in an octave of convenience. Practicing these exercises according to the directions given in the Home Exercises on page 259 will be particularly beneficial.

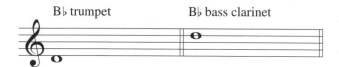

EXAMPLE IV.7 *Concert middle C as written for two different B♭ instruments*

EXAMPLE IV.8 *Concert middle C as written for two different transposing instruments*

CLASS DRILLS

Sing each of the following melodies at sight, transposing as indicated. Choose an octave of convenience and vocalize on the letter names only, minus any associated sharps, flats, or naturals. Be aware of the actual octave of the part you are singing, even if you are singing in an octave other than the part written.

D♭ piccolo

3.

A♭ trumpet

4.

D trumpet

5.

Horn in E

6.

HOME EXERCISES

1 Read the exercises in this unit on your instrument, switching octaves as is necessary. Practice both clef and transposition studies. As a corollary to this, you should take any of the melodic exercises from this book and read them up a whole step, down a whole step, up a minor 3rd, down a minor 3rd, up a perfect 4th, and down a perfect 4th. If you are a singer, try reading them similarly, but vocalizing the pitches, using the transposed note names.

2 To become truly adept, you should transpose the exercises in this unit at the keyboard and in the correct octave. Keyboard proficiency is *not* a prerequisite for this activity; in fact, they are all single-part studies. Greater proficiency and musicality will result regardless of your major instrument.

Rhythm

UNIT 54

More about Composite Rhythm

$\mathcal{T}$he performance and dictation of two-part rhythms present some interesting challenges. First, coordination of two hands, voice and hands, hands and feet, or all of the above may be necessary. Percussionists and keyboard players take such coordination for granted, but for many singers and instrumentalists it offers a formidable obstacle. Second, dictation of simultaneous rhythms requires the listener to perceive the "composite rhythm." We hear this way subconsciously, so we merely need to be *consciously* aware of what we are hearing and then write it down. Even though we have worked with these concepts earlier, we can refine our techniques further.

Performance

Let's address practice first. To practice the performance of two-part rhythms, it is best to vocalize one of the parts; the syllable *ta* is an old fallback. This allows us to concentrate not only on the attack, but also on the sustain and release of a note. The other part must be tapped (which we recommend) or clapped, unless, of course, you are capable of singing more than one independent line.

Next, we consider coordinating the two parts. Performance of two parts simultaneously is aided by an awareness of the linear and vertical arrangement of most printed music. In the linear dimension, the spacing of the notes reflects the relative real-time distance between notes when performed. In the vertical dimension, the alignment of multiple parts performed simultaneously usually indicates precisely when notes are to sound together and when they are to sound by themselves. Thus, as you consider Example IV.9, quickly assimilate both the linear and vertical relationships among the notes of the two parts. In Example IV.10(b), the composite rhythm, the result of superimposing one part on the other, is shown.

In other words, there are times when you vocalize, times when you tap, and times when you do both. All this is done, of course, relative to the prevailing beat (which can be supplied unobtrusively

© 1997 Ardsley House, Publishers, Inc.

EXAMPLE IV.9   *Two simultaneous rhythms*

EXAMPLE IV.10 **(a)** *The two rhythms of Example IV.9 occupying the same line* **(b)** *The composite rhythm of Example IV.9*

by the foot). Performing two-part rhythms is easy to describe, but doing it is another matter altogether. It takes practice, and that is certainly one of the objectives of this unit.

CLASS DRILLS

Perform each of the following two-part rhythms by singing one part on any pitch using the syllable *ta* and tapping or clapping the other part.

Once you are able to tackle the preceding exercises with some surety and success, you should be ready to go on to slightly more challenging pieces. You may try vocalizing the top part and tapping the bottom part in one measure, and then reverse the procedure on each successive measure to enhance your facility. Be aware of the composite rhythm, and allow the vertical alignment and the linear spacing to guide your performance of the two parts. Never, under any circumstances, lose track of the beat or tempo. If you stumble on a particular rhythm, *keep going* (as you have been told throughout this book). Finish the reading, go back and work on trouble spots, and then try again until you have mastered the exercise. Use slower tempi throughout the following exercises until all the rhythmic details are secure.

CLASS DRILLS

Perform each of the following two-part rhythms by singing one part on any pitch using the syllable *ta* and tapping or clapping the other part.

Dictation As you know by now, taking dictation can be considered the obverse of the performance process. It reinforces your performance capability and trains your ears to listen analytically. It is necessary for these reasons. With regard to two-part rhythmic dictation, you have two options. The obvious one is to focus on each line separately while trying to ignore the other line so that you won't be distracted by it. It must be admitted that this approach is the recourse of many, if not most, students. Though it seems to make sense, ask yourself, "Is this how we *listen* to music?" Of course not! Imagine concentrating intensely on the bassoon line in Beethoven's Symphony no. 6 and trying not to be distracted by the violins!

The second option, the preferable approach, is to write down the music as we hear it: the resultant of all of the aural information presented to us sequentially in time. It is the composite rhythm that compels us, even though we might wish to concentrate on a particularly attractive component now and then.

An illustration of what might be played for you by your instructor is given in Example IV.11, and the corresponding composite rhythm, with the beams and flags merged into one part, is given in Example IV.12. So let's begin by listening carefully to the resultant of both parts, and practice writing down *only* the composite rhythm.

EXAMPLE IV.11 *The rhythmic duet played*

EXAMPLE IV.12 *The composite rhythm heard*

CLASS DRILLS

Dictation: Listen to the two-part rhythms that your instructor presents, and write down the composite rhythm of each piece.

1.

2.

3.

4.

5.

6.

7.

8.

9.

Now let's proceed to write down two-part rhythmic pieces in their entirety. It will help to write down the composite rhythm (Examples IV.11 and IV.12) first, and then to notate those elements that sound only in the top part, only in the bottom part, or in both parts, as demonstrated in Example IV.13. Finally, as shown in Example IV.14, separate the notes into two parts, and then make sure that you represent the durations and releases of each component part accurately.

EXAMPLE IV.13 *The composite rhythm analyzed*

EXAMPLE IV.14 *The rhythmic duet written*

CLASS DRILLS

Dictation: **Listen to the two-part rhythms that your instructor presents, and write down each part.**

1.

2.

3.

4.

5.

6.

7.

8.

9.

10.

11.

12.

HOME EXERCISES

Try performing the two-part dictations that you have completed in this unit. As well as tapping and clapping, try playing them with two hands on two well-spaced notes on a keyboard.

Fundamentals

UNIT 55

Modulation

• •

Modulation vs. Tonicization

Modulation is the process whereby a key is replaced by firmly establishing a new tonic. The process of modulation can be brief or extended, simple or complex, but all modulations (as opposed to temporary **tonicizations**) are distinguished by three factors:

1. Time spent in the new key

2. Cadence on the new tonic (confirming the new key)

3. The use of a secondary pre-dominant (often a **pivot chord** that is diatonic in the **home key** as well) and a *secondary dominant* to initiate movement to the new tonic

The last factor is seldom important in certain types of **chromatic**, "**common-tone**," **enharmonic**, or **abrupt modulations**.

At this time, we will examine modulations that occur between **closely related keys**, that is, keys whose signatures differ from the home key by at most one accidental or whose tonic chords are diatonic to the home key. If C major is taken as the home key, such closely related keys could be:

◆ F major (IV in C major, 1-flat difference)

◆ G major (V in C major, 1-sharp difference)

◆ A minor (vi in C major, **relative minor**)

If A minor is taken as the home key, closely related keys could be:

◆ D minor (iv in A minor, 1-flat difference)

◆ E major (V in A minor, 3-sharp difference)

◆ C major (III in A minor, relative major)

◆ E minor (not diatonic to A minor, but related through the circle of fifths, 1-sharp difference)

Common-Chord Modulation

The type of modulation described here is a **common-chord modulation**, that is, one using a pivot chord that is diatonic in both the home key and the new key. As stated before, the pivot chord is often a pre-dominant in the new key. When this pivot chord is first heard, it is often impossible to anticipate either that modulation is about to occur or that this chord is diatonic in both keys. The aural equivalent of hindsight is necessary to identify the pivot chord correctly in these cases. Look at and listen to Example IV.15.

When we first hear the ii chord, we have no expectations other than those normally created by its pre-dominant function. Even after the ensuing move to vi via its secondary dominant, we don't know whether this is just a temporary tonicization of vi, as we've heard in previous units, or a modulation. Only after spending some musical time in the key of vi and hearing a circular progression in vi, do we realize that a brief modulation has occurred. Then we can analyze what we heard, as shown in Example IV.16.

Modulation is another means of *prolonging* a chord or function. In the preceding progression, vi was prolonged by modulating to A minor and by the amount of musical time spent in this key. This concept leads to more complicated and interesting structural results, as we will see later. Meanwhile, in the following exercises, try to listen for the answers to the following questions:

1. Did a modulation actually occur? (Why or why not?)

2. If so, to which closely related key did the progression modulate?

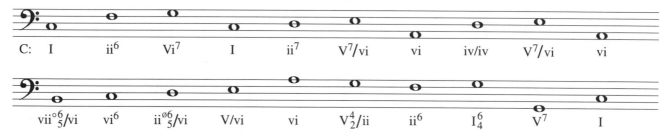

EXAMPLE IV.15 *A harmonic progression with an analysis that does not reflect modulation*

C major: $\text{I} - \text{ii}^6 - \text{V}^7 - \text{I} - \text{ii}^7 - \text{V}^7/\text{vi} - \text{vi} \ldots$ $\qquad$ $\text{vii}^{\varnothing 6}_5 - \text{V}/\text{vi} - \text{vi} - \text{V}^4_2/\text{ii} - \text{ii}^6 - \text{I}^6_4 - \text{V}^7 - \text{I}$

A minor: $\qquad\qquad\quad$ $\text{iv}^7 - \text{V}^7 \quad - \text{i} \ - \ \text{vii}^{\circ 6}_5 - \text{i}^6 \ - \text{ii}^{\varnothing 6}_5 - \text{V} \ - \ \text{i} \ldots$

EXAMPLE IV.16 *An analysis of Example IV.15 reflecting common-chord modulation*

CLASS DRILLS

Determine whether or not a modulation occurs in each of the following harmonic progressions. Justify your answer. If a modulation occurs, identify the key to which the progression moves. Also, perform an analysis showing the modulation (and return, if any).

1. $\text{I} - \text{V}^4_3 - \text{I}^6 - \text{ii}^6 - \text{V}^6_5/\text{V} - \text{V} - \text{vi} - \text{V}^6_5 - \text{I}$

2. $\text{I} - \text{I}^4_2 - \text{vi} - \text{V}^7/\text{V} - \text{V} - \text{V}^4_2 - \text{I}^6 - \text{vii}^{\circ 6}_5 - \text{I}$

3. $I - ii_2^4 - V_5^6 - I - ii^6/IV - V^7/IV - IV - V_3^4/IV - IV^6 - IV/IV - V^7/IV - IV - V_5^6/V - I_4^6 - V^7 - I$

4. $i - ii^{o6} - V^7 - i - V_5^6/III - III - VI - V^7/III - i - ii^6/III - V^7/III - III - VI - i_4^6 - V^7 - i$

5. $i - i_4^6 - iv - iv^6 - i_4^6 - V_5^6/VI - VI - V^7 - V_2^4 - i^6 - iv - i$

6. $i - V_2^4/iv - iv^6 - i_4^6 - V_5^6/V - V - vii^{o6}_5/V - V^6 - IV/V - V^7/V - V - V_2^4 - i^6 - vii^{o6}_5 - i$

7. $I - IV - V^7 - I - ii^{o6}/vi - V^7/vi - vi - iv/vi - V^7/vi - V_2^4/vi - vi^6 - V_5^6 - I - IV_4^6 - I$

8. $i - V_3^4 - i^6 - V_5^6/iv - iv - i_4^6 - iv^6 - i_4^6 - V^7 - i$

As you have probably noticed, time plays an important role in modulation; the modulatory examples given in the preceding Class Drills contain more harmonies and thus occupy more musical time than is required for the nonmodulatory examples. This observation is almost by way of an apology for the exercises that will follow in subsequent units. If we are to establish the home key *and* establish the new key (and possibly return to the home key), then longer harmonic progressions are a necessity. So be it; but before we go on to identify such longer modulatory progressions, let's practice the basics some more.

CLASS DRILLS

Provide a complete harmonic analysis of the following progressions. Make sure to indicate modulatory passages clearly. Accidentals apply only to the notes they immediately precede.

1.

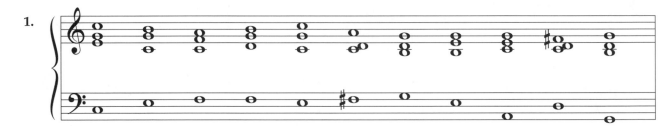

2.

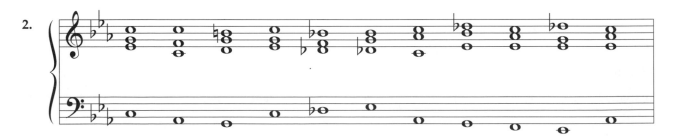

3.

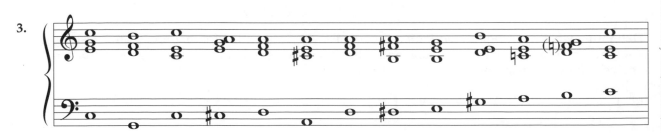

8.

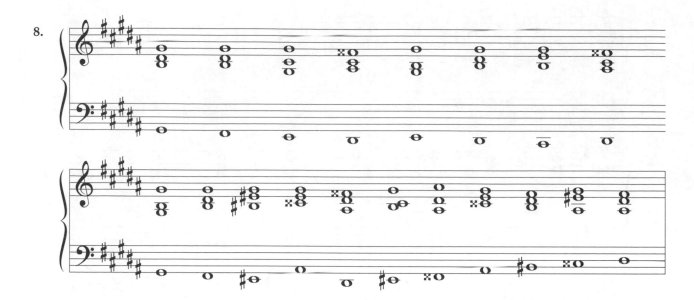

HOME EXERCISES

Write two harmonic progressions of eleven to seventeen chords each, as indicated.

(a) In the major mode, modulating to IV.　　　　**(b)** In the minor mode, modulating to III.

Learning to Hear Function

UNIT 56

Progressions That Modulate

ow let's attempt to identify, by ear, all the harmonic elements in progressions incorporating modulation. In each exercise of the following Class Drills, the process of modulation is initiated, but not completed. The progression arrives at a new key; however, a clear and complete modulation is not heard because the new tonic is not confirmed by a strong cadence in the new key. Listen for the final chord in each case; each final chord is diatonic and represents a modulatory goal closely related to the home key. Identifying the final chord should make it easy for you to work backward from the end and thus identify the harmonies that move there. Concentrate on the bass line at first, as well as the harmonic logic implied therein.

© 1997 Ardsley House, Publishers, Inc.

CLASS DRILLS

Dictation: **Write down the bass line and supply a complete harmonic analysis of each open modulatory progression that you hear. Be sure to label the possible pivot chords, if any, in both keys.**

1.

2.

3.

4.

5.

6.

7.

8.

9.

10.

11.

12.

13.

14.

15.

16.

In the next series of exercises we begin with shorter progressions (Exercises 1–11 are about as short as they can be and still modulate); then we move toward longer ones. On first listening, try to identify only where the modulation occurs and the key to which the progression modulates. Then notate the bass line and add the details of your analysis. Check this analysis carefully to make sure that it follows harmonic logic.

CLASS DRILLS

Dictation: **Write down the bass line and supply a complete harmonic analysis of each modulatory progression that you hear. Make sure that the modulatory sections are correctly notated and that pivot chords (if any) are identified in both keys.**

1.

2.

3.

4.

5.

6.

7.

8.

9.

10.

11.

12.

13.

14.

15.

16.

HOME EXERCISES

Most tonal pieces of any length use modulation to enhance harmonic interest and to prolong structural harmonies. As you listen to music in other classes, in your ensembles, on your stereo system, and at concerts, try to locate the modulatory sections of the music and to identify the functional name of the tonic of these sections, relative to the home key. This will have the added effect of converting you into a more **active** (as opposed to a passive) listener.

Melody

UNIT 57

Melodies and Duets That Modulate

*A*s you perform these exercises, try not only to recognize, but also to *feel*, each new tonal center when a modulation occurs, and be aware of the feeling of impending return to the original tonic. In the case of dictations, first recognize the new tonal centers and then try to determine the modulatory procedures; that is, determine which altered notes were involved and how they were used. Be aware that several examples appear to modulate but actually do not. It is essential to develop your ability to differentiate between music that modulates and music that does not.

CLASS DRILLS

A. *Sight-singing*: Study, analyze, sight-sing, practice, and perform the following melodies and duets.

J. S. Bach

"O Gott, du frommer Gott"

Neu ordentlich Gesangbuch, 1646

H. Carey

C. H. H. Parry

4.

"Den des Vaters Sinn geboren"

Hundert Arien, 1694

5.

J. Clarke

6.

J. S. Bach

7.

J. S. Bach

8.

J. S. Bach

W. A. Mozart

F. Schubert

11.

B. *Dictation*: **Write down the melodies and duets your instructor presents.**

1.

2.

3.

4.

5.

6.

7.

8.

AREA

UNITS 58–64

*Hearing
and
Performing
in
Multiple
Parts*

Dictation

UNIT 58

Guidelines for Four-Part Dictation

Soprano and Bass Lines

Successfully completing four-part dictation requires combining all of the skills you have developed so far: melodic dictation, bass lines and harmonic dictation, rhythmic dictation (to a limited extent), and part writing. A "bottom up" approach is recommended, since we've spent so much time working on harmonic dictation. At first, let's limit ourselves to just soprano and bass lines, the outer voices, using only triads in a simple diatonic context. Write down the bass voice first, then the soprano. It is astonishing how much information can be inferred from just these two voices: A 5th outlines a triad in root position; a 4th indicates a triad in second inversion. A 3rd limits our options to a triad in root position or in first inversion; a 6th suggests a triad in first or second inversion. Of course, an octave allows three triadic possibilities.

Consider the bass and soprano of the harmonic progression in Example V.1. We surmise that the first and last dyads represent I chords because we can be fairly certain that this is a circular progression in C major. The perfect 5th of the second simultaneity must be IV. The major 3rd of the third simultaneity could be V or iii⁶. Since iii is less likely than V to follow IV, let's assume that the third harmony is a V chord. The minor 3rd that follows could be a vi or a IV⁶, and since it follows a V (or even the unlikely iii⁶), it is probably the vi, as we generally follow dominant-function chords with tonic-function chords. However, it must be mentioned that style and practice often take precedence over the "rules": For a bass line such as this, whose movement can be described as $\hat{5}-\hat{6}-\hat{7}-\hat{1}$, the 6th scale degree is often harmonized as IV⁶, despite its pre-dominant function. The next minor 3rd must be V⁶ because the other option, vii°, is improbable, given our avoidance of diminished chords in any but first inversion. This leads to the hypothetical analysis presented in Example V.2.

EXAMPLE V.1 *The bass and soprano of a harmonic progression*

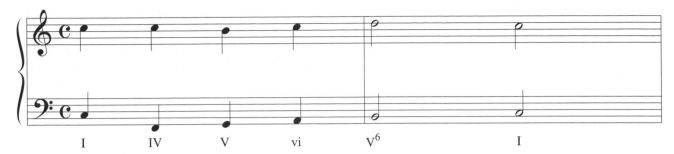

EXAMPLE V.2 *A hypothetical analysis*

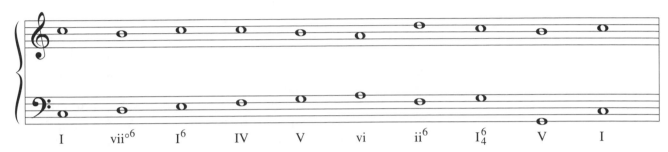

EXAMPLE V.3 *A dictation model*

Voice Leading

When one knows the outer voices (soprano and bass), there is usually very little doubt as to what the implied harmonic progression is; thus, the notes that will be found in the inner voices (alto and tenor) are suggested by the soprano and the bass. In these cases, you can then apply what you know of proper **voice-leading** (part-writing) rules and project what the possibilities for the inner voices will be. Then you can follow these parts aurally and make changes where your projections diverge from what you hear. Consider the dictation model in Example V.3.

Your instructor will furnish you with the starting pitches for all four voices. Assuming that your instructor gives the voicing in Example V.4, we begin to extrapolate the inner voices from the information we've already acquired.

The second chord is vii°⁶, so we know that an F is found in an inner voice and that the D must be doubled. The E in the alto probably moves to the D because the G in the tenor most likely moves to F. (Why?) If we assume that this is so, the I⁶ chord requires a G, and the standard doubling would be of the C. In the second chord the D that we have placed in the alto likely goes to C because the F in the tenor returns to G. (After all, its resolution, E, was taken by the bass.) Next, the IV chord requires an A and an F, doubling the root. Since the G is back in the tenor and will move smoothly to A, it is possible that the C now in the alto will skip to the F.

At this point, remember that the motion between root-position triads whose roots are a step apart (IV–V–vi) can sometimes be problematic. The V chord requires a D and the possible doubling of the G. This might be handled by returning the tenor to a unison on the G with the bass, while allowing the alto to skip back down to D. In

Soprano
Alto

Tenor
Bass

EXAMPLE V.4 *Starting pitches for the dictation model*

the next harmonic motion the vi chord needs an E and a C to be complete. The tenor should not cross the bass (and thus *become* the bass); we expect that it will skip up to C, permitting the alto to complete the triad with an E. However, this creates **parallel fifths** between the alto and the bass, and your instructor (not to mention the authors of this book) wouldn't do that to you! Secure in the conviction that a parallel 5th will *not* occur, we must reevaluate our hypothetical voicing of the fifth and sixth chords.

The 3rd determines the quality of the triad in most cases, and it (along with the root) is absolutely necessary to define the triad. Therefore, let's put the C in the alto of the vi chord, and rather than have the tenor leap up by a 6th to the E (and cross the alto), double the bass with a unison A. However, another problem results: **parallel unisons** between the tenor and the bass! Doubling the third (C) in the alto (commonly done with minor chords, particularly in a deceptive motion) is perhaps a better idea since this would create no flagrant violations of the rules of **counterpoint**.

Let's continue: the ii^6 requires an A and preferably a doubling of the D in the soprano. Doubling that D in the alto and putting the A in the tenor seems to be the path of least resistance. And that would allow the alto to move to E on the I_4^6 and the tenor to double the bass of that $_4^6$ chord (at the unison again). For the penultimate chord, the tenor can maintain the common-tone G as the bass changes octaves, and the alto can complete the triad with a move to D. Resolving the V chord is easy. The tenor again maintains the common tone to provide the 5th, G, and the alto can return to E to provide the 3rd. Example V.5 shows what we've extrapolated.

We can more easily follow and check an extrapolated inner part on subsequent hearings than when we follow it without any written reference. Suppose that we follow the tenor part and find that the performance diverged from our extrapolated part at the ii^6 chord, so that the actual tenor is as shown in Example V.6. How would this affect the alto?

A quick reevaluation and adjustment of the alto might yield the re-creation illustrated in Example V.7. This looks okay in context—at

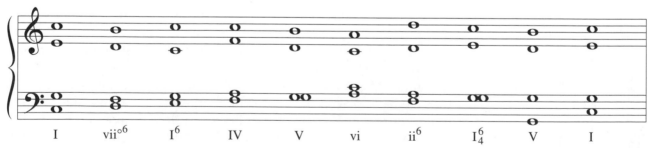

| I | vii°⁶ | I⁶ | IV | V | vi | ii⁶ | I₄⁶ | V | I |

EXAMPLE V.5 *Initial hypothesis for the dictation model*

EXAMPLE V.6 *The actual tenor of the dictation model*

least there are no obvious breaches of the rules. So now we follow the alto aurally to check it. Sure enough, as we listen, we find that the alto, as performed, diverged from our hypothetical line on the sixth chord (vi); it moved to the A above, rather than to the C below. See Example V.8.

The purpose of this rather lengthy illustration is to demonstrate that the inner parts are easier to hear and to notate if we have some idea of where they should (or might) go. This process takes far longer to read about than actually to do. Obviously, some skill and facility at part writing will help; so keep up with your theory studies!

In the following Class Drills, Exercise Set A will help you to gain confidence in evaluating harmonic options quickly. Then Exercise Set B will help you practice extrapolating possible inner parts.

EXAMPLE V.7 *Adjustment of the alto for the dictation model*

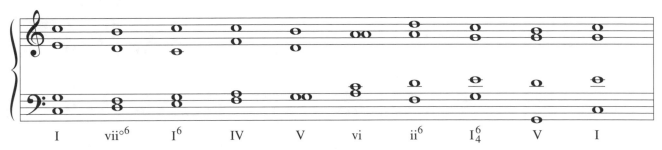

EXAMPLE V.8 *The dictation model realized*

CLASS DRILLS

A. In each exercise, determine the possible harmonic progressions suggested by the soprano and bass lines, using only diatonic triads. Exercises 1–3 are in C major; Exercises 4–6 are in A minor.

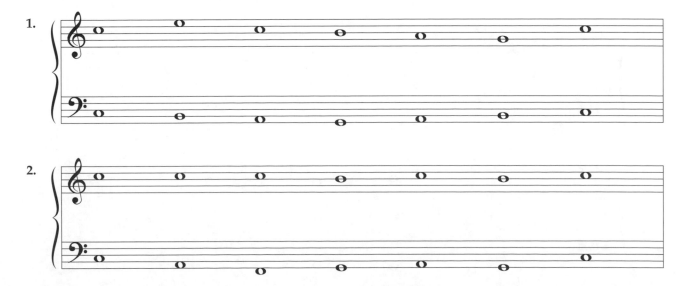

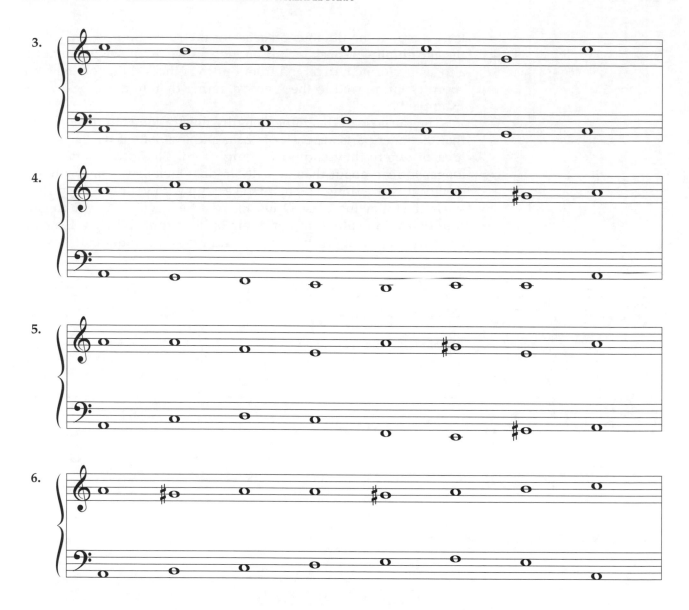

B. In each exercise, determine a possible harmonic progression suggested by the soprano and bass lines, using only diatonic triads. Then supply inner parts that are consistent with your hypothetical progression. Exercises 1–3 are in D major; Exercises 4–6 are in C minor.

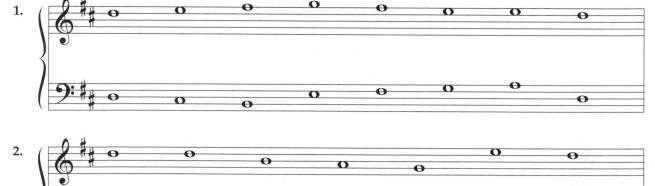

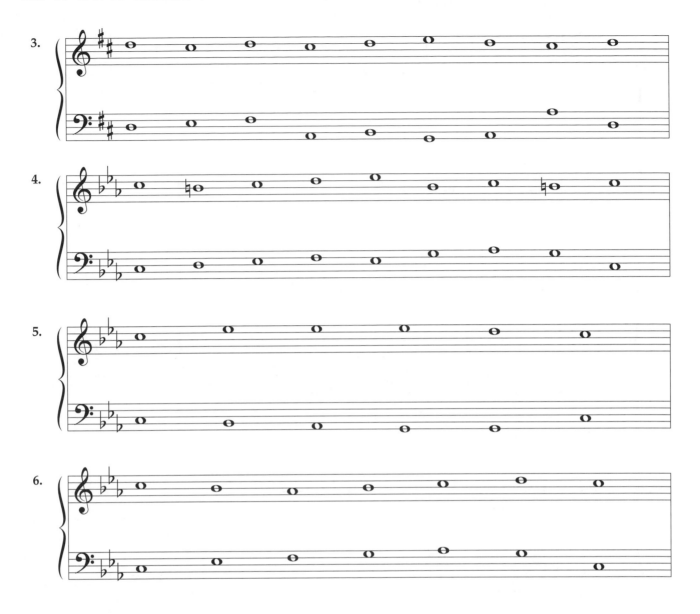

HOME EXERCISES

These exercises may seem a bit like theory homework; however, you can never get enough practice of these time-honored skills. Realize each of the following progressions in four parts (**SATB**).

1. $I - vii^{\circ 6} - I^6 - ii^6 - V - vi - I_4^6 - V - I$

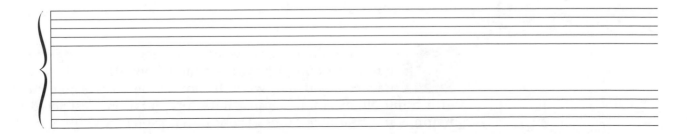

2. $\text{i} - \text{III}_4^6 - \text{VI} - \text{i}_4^6 - \text{iv} - \text{V} - \text{i}$

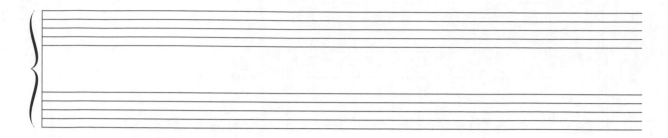

3. $\text{I} - \text{vi} - \text{ii}^6 - \text{vi}_4^6 - \text{ii} - \text{V}^6 - \text{I}$

4. $\text{i} - \text{V}_4^6 - \text{i}^6 - \text{iv} - \text{V} - \text{i} - \text{iv}_4^6 - \text{i}$

Dictation

UNIT

59

Four-Part Homophony

N ow that we have established a method for writing down four-part **homophony**, it's time to put the method into practice. As usual, we will move progressively, starting with **homophonic** (note against note) presentations restricted to diatonic and triadic textures. These initial exercises will be small chorale excerpts of three to five chords each. Since rhythm is not an issue here, you may as well take all the parts down as consecutive whole notes, for ease of reading as well as notation. Spread your writing out and make sure the parts line up vertically. Such simple issues as spacing and alignment can often affect your work.

CLASS DRILLS

Dictation: **Write down the four parts that you hear, and provide a complete harmonic analysis for each excerpt. Your instructor will give you the key and also the starting pitches for all four parts. (Additional staves are provided at the back of the book.)**

1.

2.

3.

4.

5.

6.

7.

8.

It is but a small step to write down longer pieces. Apply the methods from the preceding unit, listen carefully, and be sure to check your results for errors in voice leading and in harmonic analysis.

CLASS DRILLS

Dictation: Write down the four parts that you hear, and provide a complete harmonic analysis for each exercise. Your instructor will furnish you with the key and also the starting pitches for all four parts.

1.

2.

3.

4.

5.

6.

Incorporating Diatonic Seventh Chords

Our part writing quickly becomes cramped because of the limitations imposed by triadic restrictions. Let's consider the possibilities afforded by the use of diatonic seventh chords. There are a few new implications therein. For example, a 5th between the soprano and bass doesn't necessarily outline a root-position chord; it can also outline a seventh chord in first inversion with the 7th of the chord above the bass. A 4th can imply a second-inversion chord, but it can also suggest a third-inversion chord with the 3rd above the bass. On the other hand, the interval of a 2nd or 7th *does* define the chord. If the interval is a 7th, it is in root position with the 7th in the higher voice; if the interval is a 2nd (or 9th, which is, of course, a compound 2nd), then it is in third inversion with the root in the upper voice. Since the 7th is rarely, if ever, doubled, then an octave between the bass and soprano still limits our options to three chords, whether or not a diatonic 7th is present.

CLASS DRILLS

A. What are the possible diatonic harmonies for each of the following soprano and bass combinations? Include all the diatonic seventh-chord options.

C major

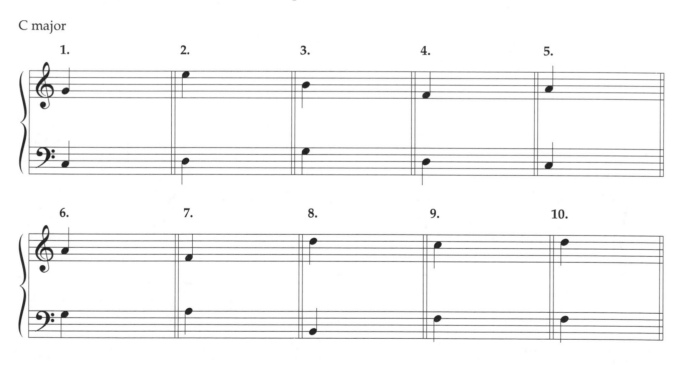

C minor

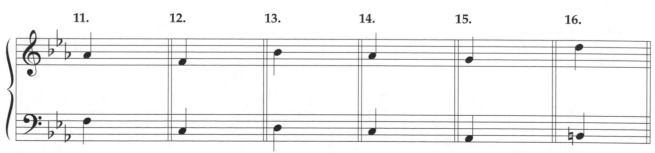

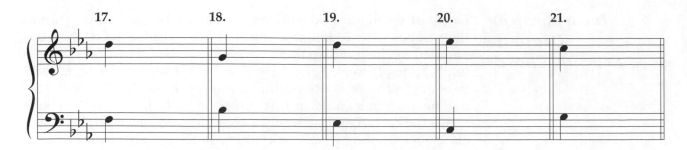

B. *Dictation*: Write down the four parts that you hear, and provide a complete harmonic analysis for each exercise. Your instructor will give you the key and also the starting pitches for all four parts. Remember the tendencies of the 7ths and 3rds of chords as you try the next series of brief excerpts.

1.

2.

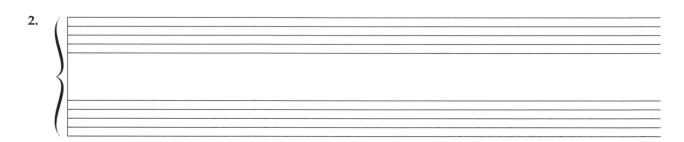

3.

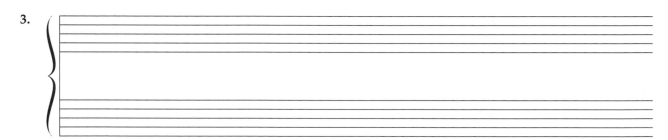

4.

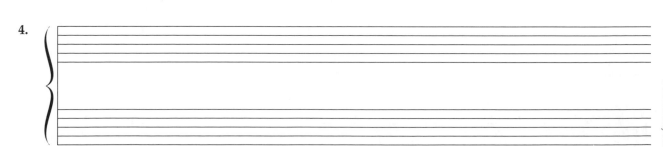

5.

C. *Dictation*: **Write down the four parts that you hear, and provide a complete harmonic analysis for each exercise. Your instructor will give you the key and also the starting pitches for all four parts.**

1.

2.

3.

4.

5.

HOME EXERCISES

Realize the following progression in homophonic four-part counterpoint.

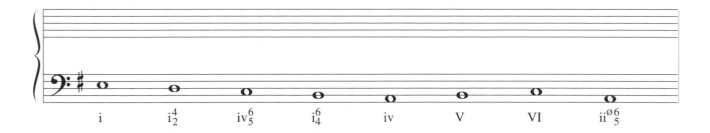

i   i$_2^4$ iv$_5^6$ i$_4^6$ iv   V   VI   ii$^{ø6}_5$

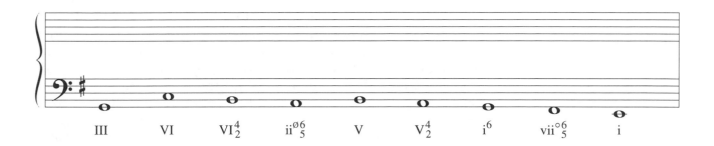

III   VI   VI$_2^4$ ii$^{ø6}_5$ V   V$_2^4$ i^6 vii$^{o6}_5$ i

Dictation

UNIT 60

Adding Nonchord Tones to Four-Part Homophony

Nonchord Tones
Now that we've had some practice at four-part dictation, we can introduce **nonchord tones** into the texture. Nonchord tones add linear interest and smoother voice leading; they also add decoration to harmonic events—and thus prolongation. They can be classified into two broad divisions: chromatic and diatonic. Within these divisions are various types of nonchord tones. We will concern ourselves with *diatonic* nonchord tones for the moment.

An **auxiliary tone** (**neighbor note**) moves by step (up or down) from a chord member and returns to it, thus decorating, drawing attention to, heightening the importance of, and *prolonging* the chord tone and the prevailing harmony. A **passing tone** moves by step (up or down) from a chord member and continues by step in the same direction to another chord member, always filling in the interval of a 3rd. Passing tones may be accented (on the beat) or unaccented (between beats). An **appoggiatura** is a nonchord tone that is approached by leap from a chord member and is then left by step (usually in the direction opposite that of the leap) to a chord tone. An **escape tone** (*échappée*) is just the opposite; it is a nonchord tone, usually falling on a weak beat, that is approached by step from a chord member and then left by leap (usually a 3rd) to a chord tone. Both appoggiaturas and escape tones may be accented or unaccented; however, the appoggiatura is usually accented, whereas the escape tone is usually not. One type of nonchord tone that *requires* metric accent is a **suspension.** With this device, a chord tone is held through a change of harmony, where it becomes a nonharmonic dissonance, suspended over the bass of the new harmony. It then resolves down by step, in the same voice, to a chord tone. While it is a chord tone (relative to the first harmony), the note is called a **preparation**; when it becomes dissonant relative to the new harmony, the resulting nonchord tone is called a **suspension**; finally, the note to which it resolves is called a **resolution**. A suspension that resolves up is often referred to as a **retardation.** The opposite of a suspension is an **anticipation**, in which a chord tone moves (usually by step) to a nonchord tone that is sustained into the next harmonic change, wherein it becomes a chord member. This device is often used to ornament cadences, and suspensions are often used to emphasize and highlight cadences. These various nonchord tones are illustrated in Example V.9.

The use of nonchord tones can often make an inner voice more independent, and thus easier to distinguish. These tones also rely on

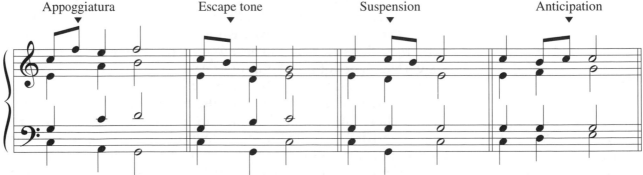

EXAMPLE V.9 *Types of nonchord tones*

specific aspects of rhythm (long vs. short note values) or at least meter (stressed vs. unstressed beats). Let's listen to and identify the various types of nonchord tones in small four-part excerpts.

CLASS DRILLS

Dictation: **Write down each four-part excerpt that you hear, and provide a complete harmonic analysis. Circle any nonchord tone and label its type. Sing these chorales in class after they have been successfully notated.**

1.

2.

3.

4.

5.

6.

7.

8.

Suspensions   Special attention should be given to the use of suspensions since they often play an important role at cadences and at other structural points. Suspensions are labeled according to the intervals formed above the bass. The most common suspensions are the 4–3, the 7–6, the 2–3 (a bass suspension), and the 9–8 (often found in combination with the 4–3 or 7–6). These suspensions are illustrated in Example V.10. Now and again, they are used in combination with a **change of bass**, as illustrated in Example V.11. In these cases, the analytic label for the suspensions remains as if the bass had not moved. We should, perhaps, spend a little time and practice listening to and identifying the various types of suspensions in four-part contexts.

© 1997 Ardsley House, Publishers, Inc.

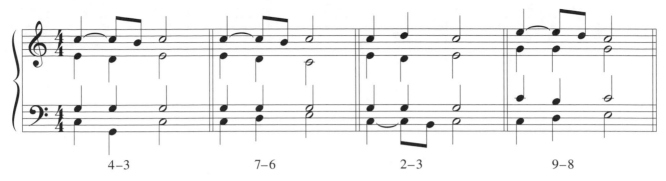

4–3   7–6   2–3   9–8

EXAMPLE V.10   *Types of suspensions*

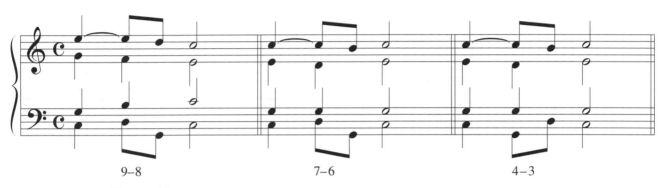

9–8   7–6   4–3

EXAMPLE V.11   *Change of bass*

CLASS DRILLS

Dictation: Write down each four-part excerpt that you hear, and provide a complete harmonic analysis. Circle each suspension and label its type. Sing these chorales after you have successfully completed them.

1.

2.

3.

4.

Now let's practice with longer four-part textures that incorporate diatonic nonchord tones. You may find these easier than the four-part dictations of the previous units because the nonchord tones often "catch your ear" and highlight inner parts that otherwise blend in with the overall harmonic texture. In addition, the four-part dictation techniques you have already acquired and developed should stand you in good stead.

CLASS DRILLS

Dictation: Write down each four-part excerpt that you hear, and provide a complete harmonic analysis. Circle any nonchord tone and label its type. Sing these chorales in class after they have been completed successfully.

1.

2.

3.

4.

HOME EXERCISES

Using the following four-part homophonic progression, add nonchord tones to create smoother lines and to ornament the texture tastefully. Be sure to include at least one suspension.

Melody

UNIT 61

Compositions for Ensembles

Before you sing the following ensemble pieces, make sure that you locate and identify all dissonances as a part of your normal preparation. It is suggested that you pay particular attention, both in performance and in dictation, to how suspensions are used. You should be able to sing all parts with ease, not just those that are written for your voice or instrument. Listen closely to understand how the part you are singing contributes to the harmony at any given moment. Identify any note you are singing as the root, third, fifth, or seventh, or as a nonchord tone.

© 1997 Ardsley House, Publishers, Inc.

CLASS DRILLS

A. *Sight-singing*: With your classmates, study, analyze, sight-sing, practice, and perform each of the following three-, four-, and five-part compositions.

"Ach Gott, erhor' mein Seufzen!"

Praxis pietatis, 1662, harm.
J. S. Bach

"Come, Ye Sons of Art"

H. Purcell

voi - ces___ and___ in - stru - ments play, to
voi - ces___ and in - stru - ments___ play, to
voi - ces and in - stru - ments play, to

ce - le - brate, to ce - le - brate this tri - um - phant day.
ce - le - brate, to ce - le - brate this tri - um - phant day.
ce - le - brate, to ce - le - brate this tri - um - phant day.

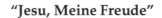

"Jesu, Meine Freude"

J. Crüger, harm.
J. S. Bach

3.

Soprano

Alto

Tenor

Bass

"Jesu, Meine Freude"

J. Crüger, harm.
J. S. Bach

4.

"Jesu, Meine Freude"

J. S. Bach

"Ach Gott, wie manches Herzeleid"

J. Clauder, harm.
J. S. Bach

6.

"Lift Thine Eyes"

F. Mendelssohn

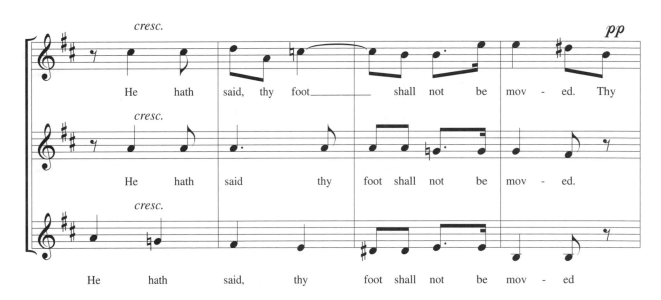

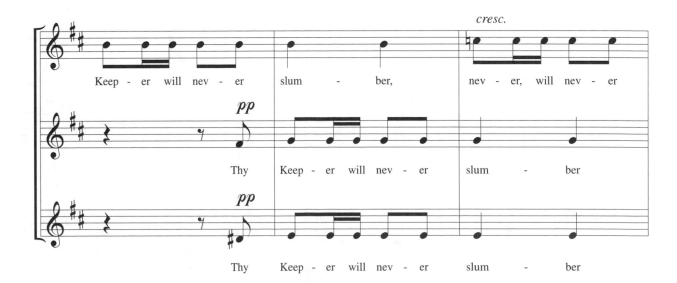

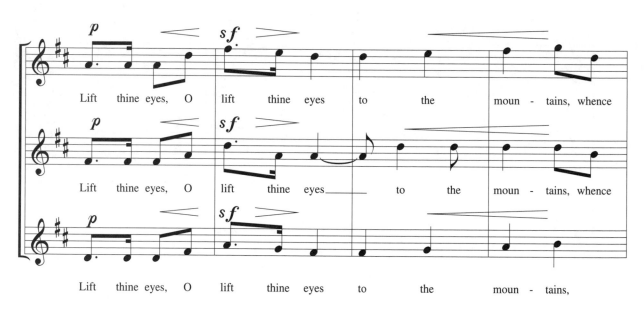

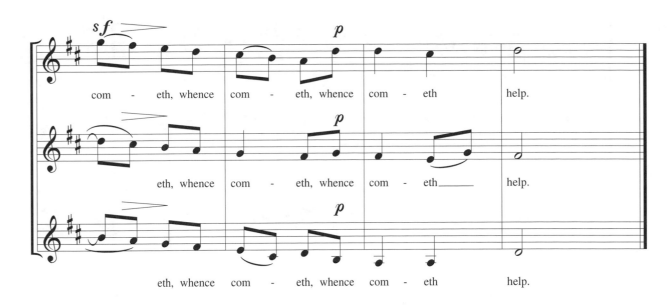

"Jesu, Meine Freude"

J. S. Bach

B. *Dictation*: Write down each four-part composition that you hear, and provide a complete harmonic analysis under the staff. Circle and label nonchord tones, if any.

1.

2.

3.

4.

5.

6.

7.

© 1997 Ardsley House, Publishers, Inc.

8.

Fundamentals

UNIT

62

Canon and Imitation

Analyzing Canons

The word *canon* means rule or principle. When **canon** is used to name or describe imitative music, we mean that there is a rule governing the composition and performance of this type of music. The rule always refers to conditions regarding musical time and intervallic distance. *Time* in this context refers to the number of beats and/or measures after which the first voice (the ***dux***, or *leader*) is joined in imitation by a subsequent voice (the ***comes***, or *follower*) or voices. *Distance* here refers to the interval, relative to the leader's starting pitch, at which the follower or followers imitate. The canon (or rule) for the **perpetual canon** "Row, Row, Row Your Boat" is generally expressed as being *at the two measures and the unison*; that is, the **imitation** by the second voice commences after two measures and at the interval of an octave/unison.

Have you ever noticed how "Row, Row, Row Your Boat" just peters out for an "ending"? In order to avoid writing such perpetual canons, composers must cease using imitation at some point in the music. What follows the cessation of imitation is called **free counterpoint**, and leads inevitably to cadence. When analyzing an imitative work, we look for this **break for cadence**; when listening to imitative music, we should be aware of the break, just as we should be aware of the canon (rule) itself. Some canonic pieces are difficult to identify aurally as canons; they may use less obvious imitative procedures such as **inversion** (imitating by mirroring the intervals of the *dux*), **retrograde** (imitating through reversing the order of the pitches and rhythms of the *dux*), or **retrograde inversion** (often called *cancrizans*, or **crab canon**), a retrograde of the inversion. Of these three contrapuntal procedures, inversion is the easiest to detect because it at least preserves the rhythm of the *dux* in the imitation. In addition, there are two basic *rhythmic* permutations that are occasionally used: **augmentation** (the note values of the *dux* are proportionally longer in the *comes*) and **diminution** (the note values of the *dux* are proportionally shorter in the *comes*). All five of these devices can be used in various combinations. In general, the greater the time interval between the *dux* and the *comes*, the harder it is to detect imitative procedure. And the more of these five standard contrapuntal permutations that are used, the more difficult it is to detect imitation.

Writing Canons   The best way to understand canonic writing is to attempt its practice. First, determine your canon, that is, your intervals of time and distance. Then write the parts of your canon concurrently. For example, a canon at the measure and at the 5th above might begin as in Example V.12.

After the first measure of the *dux* is written, we must stop immediately and write the corresponding notes into the *comes* in the next bar. Now we are able to write the second measure of the *dux*, reconciling it with the extant notes in the *comes*. Once this is done, we put these new notes into the *comes*, a 5th higher, as in Example V.13.

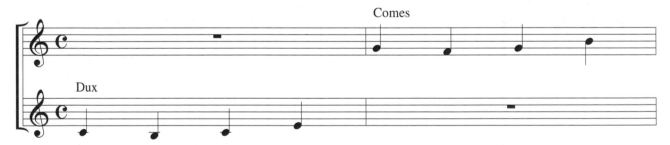

EXAMPLE V.12   *The first step in writing a canon at the measure and at the fifth above*

EXAMPLE V.13   *The second step in writing a canon at the measure and at the fifth above*

This process is repeated until the decision is made to break for cadence. Nonimitative free counterpoint is written until cadence is achieved. See Example V.14, in which the double bars in the middle show the break in the imitation.

EXAMPLE V.14 *The final step in writing a canon at the measure and at the fifth above using free counterpoint to complete it*

CLASS DRILLS

A. Write a canon for alto and tenor voices in F major and $\frac{4}{4}$ time at the measure and a half and at the 4th below. The canon should be approximately twelve bars in duration. Perform it in class and evaluate it.

B. **Answer the following questions.**

1. If you were to go about writing a canon in retrograde inversion, how should you proceed?

2. What will eventually happen in a canon with the *comes* written in diminution?

3. What will eventually happen in a canon with the *comes* written in augmentation?

4. If you were to write a canon at the unison and disallow any **voice crossing**, what would be the result?

C. **Each of the following melodies will allow for canonic performance with proper dissonance treatment. Try to find the canon for each one. There may be more than one successful canon per melody. Perform them according to the canon(s) that you determine and evaluate the results.**

Imitative counterpoint as a driving force in music enjoyed its heyday in the **Renaissance** and Baroque eras. Nevertheless, we are all accustomed to the sounds created by this contrapuntal procedure, regardless of the style or era of music with which we are most familiar. Let's listen now to some short canons in order to identify the time and distance rules in operation (or anything else we might detect aurally).

CLASS DRILLS

Listen to each short canon, and determine the time and distance governing the imitation—the canon. Then write down these canons, and perform them in class.

1.

imitation at the _____ and at the _____

2.

imitation at the _____ and at the _____

3.

imitation at the _____ and at the _____

4.

imitation at the _____ and at the _____

HOME EXERCISES

Listen for instances of imitation in the music around you, and try to identify the governing principles. Composers of every style and genre of music for at least five hundred years, including composers of the present day, have used imitation frequently as a structural and expressive device. To name only a very few examples of canonic procedure from a cross section of music history, see J. S. Bach's "Canonic Variations on *Von Himmel Hoch*," BWV 769; Johannes Brahms's Sonata for Violin and Piano, Op. 100, first movement; Marcel Dupré's "Variations on a Noël," Op. 21; Igor Stravinsky's "A Prayer" from *A Sermon, a Narrative and a Prayer*, and Leonard Bernstein's Overture to *Candide*.

Melody

UNIT 63

Canon and Imitative Counterpoint

*B*efore attempting to perform the following exercises, it will certainly help to take the time to recognize and analyze the canonical procedures involved. But in dictation, an aural analysis of the canon will prove to be the most important step in its successful realization. As always, you should be able to sing each part of the various exercises. Listen analytically for the harmonic implications of the combined parts, and determine when your part is the most crucial one in defining the harmony.

CLASS DRILLS

A. *Sight-singing*: With your classmates, study, analyze, sight-sing, practice, and perform each of the following canons.

F. J. Haydn

© 1997 Ardsley House, Publishers, Inc.

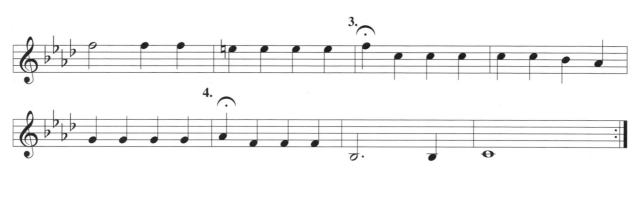

F. J. Haydn

F. J. Haydn

H. L. Hassler

5.

H. L. Hassler

H. L. Hassler

B. *Dictation*: **Write down the canons presented by your instructor.**

1.

2.

3.

4.

5.

6.

7.

8.

Rhythm

UNIT
64

Canon and Hocket

Canon and other forms of imitative counterpoint will now be considered from a purely rhythmic standpoint. **Hocket** is a rhythmic contrapuntal device that we have already been using, but not in a strict sense and without a definition of the term. Medieval theorists defined hocket as a contrapuntal device wherein one voice sings while another voice is silent. The name is derived from the Latin *hoquetus*, meaning hiccup. In its simplest form one voice alternates single notes and rests, while a second voice fills in the rests of the first voice, and vice versa. See Example V.15.

It must be mentioned that the device was a favorite of composers who wrote **catches**, innocent-looking **rounds** intended for glee clubs, designed so that, when sung, the hocket technique reorders the lyrics in such a manner that bawdy references are made. Needless to say, such is not *our* intent. Hocket is an interesting rhythmic device in its own right, and is one way of propelling a composite rhythm. In Part A of the following Class Drills, a few hocket canons are presented for performance and sight-reading practice. In Part B, for the purpose of dictation, simpler versions of these rhythms are given. These dictations are in strict canon, so diagnosing the canonic procedure will prove of inestimable value. Part C presents additional rhythmic catches for analysis and practice. Part D presents further melodic catches.

© 1997 Ardsley House, Publishers, Inc.

EXAMPLE V.15   *A simple hocket*

CLASS DRILLS

A. Read the following rhythmic duets at sight by dividing into groups or pairs, or by individually singing one line on the syllable *ta* while tapping the *ictus* of the other. Try to discover the operating principle behind each canon.

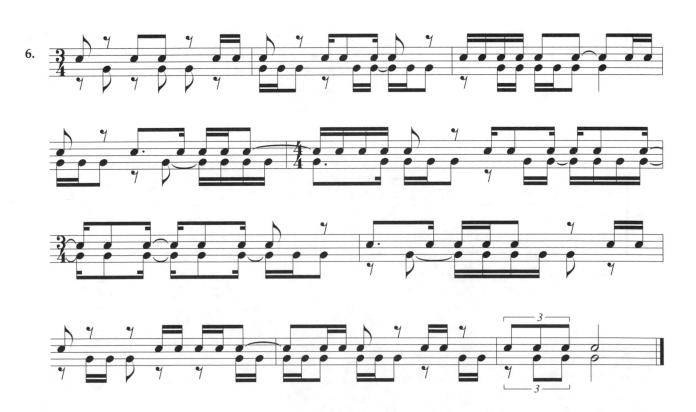

7.

8.

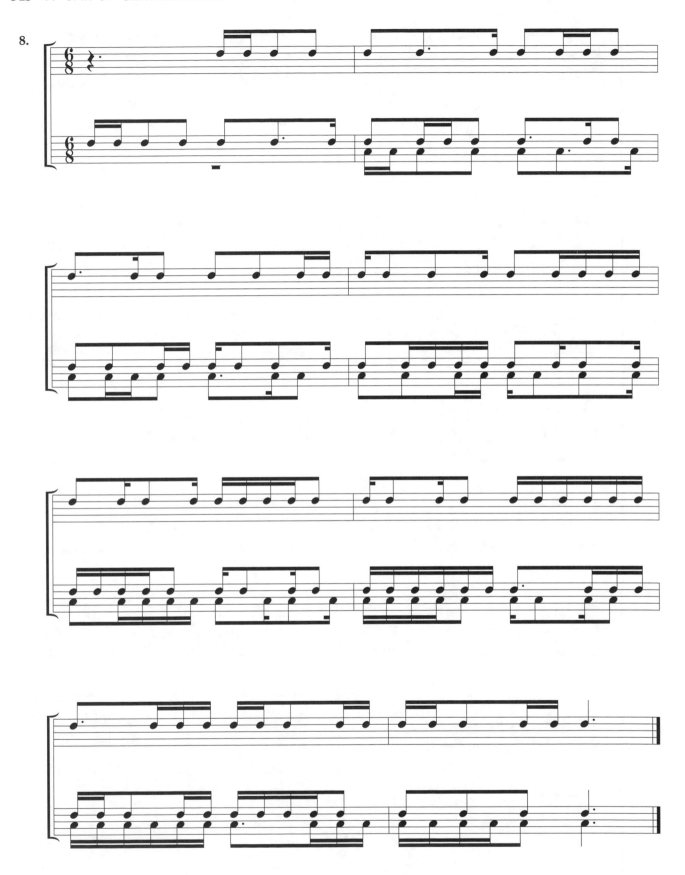

9.

© 1997 Ardsley House, Publishers, Inc.

B. *Dictation*: **Write down each two-part rhythm that you hear.**

1.

2.

3.

4.

5.

6.

C.   *Sight-singing*: With your classmates, study, analyze, sight-sing, practice, and perform each of the
following rhythmic catches.

D. *Sight-singing*: **With your classmates, study, analyze, sight-sing, practice, and perform each of the following catches.**

H. Purcell

1.

Come, come, let us drink, let us drink,

let us drink, let us drink: 'Tis in vain_____ to

think Like_____ fools_____ on grief or

sad - ness; Let our mo - ney fly,_____

_____ And our sor - rows dye:_____ All

world - ly care is mad - ness But

wine, wine, wine, wine,

wine_____ and good cheer Will, in spite of our

fear, In - spire_____ our heart with

J. Blow

2.

I   know   bro - ther   tar.   I

know,   bro - ther   tar,   those   French   durst   not   stand   us,   Nor   the

das - tard - ly   Ir - ish   once___   ven - ture   to   land   us;   If   we

bang   not___   such   scoun - drels   may   a   storm___

___   rise___   and   strand   us.

But   the   bo - son's   shrill   whi - stle   cries

all,   all,   all,   all   hands___   a   loft,   boys,   And   a

boat   full___   of   punch   is   a   rich   mor - ning's   draught,   boys;

Now tope we cat har - pin, now tope we cat

har - pin, and then fore ans aft, boys. Bro - ther

Bluff, Bro - ther Bluff, 'tis a gal - lon, 'tis a

gal - lon that now, now, now, now is a - sink - ing, To our

land - men who ne - ver yet___ knew what was shrink - ing, We'll

co - ver our des - cent with huz - zas, huz - zas, and

down_____ drink - ing.

H. Purcell

3.

1.

Now, now we are met and hu - mours a -

gree,   Call,   call   for   wine,   and

lose   no   time,   but let's   mer - ry   be.   Fill,

fill   it   a - bout,   to   me   let   it

come,   Fill   the   glass   to   the   top: I'll

drink   ev - 'ry drop su - per - na_____ cu - lum.   A

health   to   the   King,   round,   round   let   it

pass,   Fill   it   up,   and   then   drink   it

off   like   men,   ne - ver   balk   your   glass.

HOME EXERCISES

Solve the following canon so that maximum hocket is effected. Perform it by singing one part on the syllable *ta* while clapping the other part. (There may be more than one solution.)

Fundamentals

UNIT 65

Chromaticism

Decorative Chromaticism

Chromaticism is a term that embraces a wide variety of practices. It generally means the opposite of diatonicism, referring to the use of nondiatonic pitches within the context of tonality. When we worked with secondary functions, we were already working with chromaticism. In the case of secondary functions, the chromatic notes affected the harmonic resources available. But chromatic notes do not necessarily have to be harmonic in either nature or implication.

Chromatic pitches might be used in a purely decorative manner, for instance. Chromatic auxiliaries might be used in place of the diatonic neighbor notes examined earlier, as in Examples VI.1 and VI. 2. They may be used as passing tones as well. See Examples VI.3 and VI.4. Chromatic appoggiaturas and escape tones may also be used, as in Examples VI.5 and VI.6.

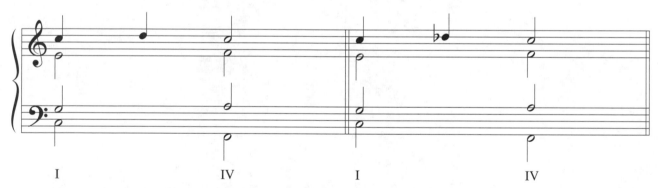

EXAMPLE VI.1 *A diatonic neighbor note replaced by a chromatic auxiliary in the soprano*

EXAMPLE VI.2 *A diatonic neighbor note replaced by a chromatic auxiliary in the tenor*

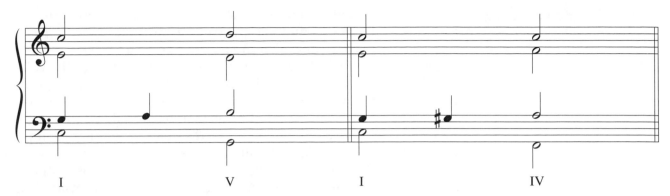

EXAMPLE VI.3   *A diatonic passing tone followed by a chromatic passing tone in the tenor*

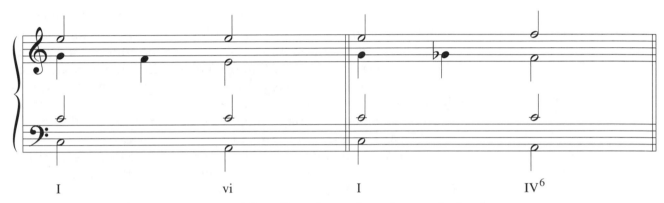

EXAMPLE VI.4   *A diatonic passing tone followed by a chromatic passing tone in the alto*

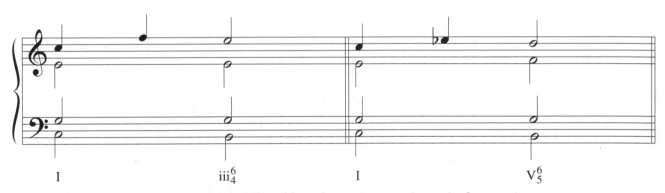

EXAMPLE VI.5   *A diatonic appoggiatura followed by a chromatic appoggiatura in the soprano*

EXAMPLE VI.6   *A diatonic escape tone replaced by a chromatic escape tone in the tenor*

Modal Borrowing

Like any ornament, a chromatic nonchord tone tends to emphasize the note it decorates and the prevailing harmony of which the decorated pitch is a part. Chromatic ornaments add extra color to otherwise diatonic textures and may improve or even alter the voice leading. Another means of adding chromatic color is through the use of **modal borrowing**. This practice presupposes that all of the notes and chords of the **parallel minor** can be available in the major mode (and vice versa, to a more limited extent). A familiar example of this is the so-called **Picardy third**, wherein the final tonic chord in a minor-mode piece is altered to become major. When this happens, $\hat{3}$ is "borrowed" temporarily from the parallel major. Consider the following progression:

$$\text{I} - \text{vii}^{\circ 6}_{5} - \text{I}^6 - \text{ii}^6_5 - \text{V}^7 - \text{vi} - \text{iv} - \text{V}^7 - \text{I}$$

The $\text{vii}^{\circ 6}_{5}$ and the iv chords use $\flat\hat{6}$, borrowed from the parallel minor. Both $\text{vii}^{\circ 6}_{5}$ and iv are examples of chords commonly borrowed from the harmonic form of the parallel minor. The various chords of the parallel minor that can be used in a major-mode piece together with the numerous possible secondary dominants and predominants put at our disposal a formidable arsenal of harmonic resources. Compare the major-mode chords with their parallel-minor counterparts, as shown in Table VI.1.

Table VI.1 illustrates that $\hat{3}$ and $\hat{6}$ are the scale degrees most frequently altered through modal borrowing, with the addition of $\flat\hat{7}$ for III and i^7 chords. In each case except the V, V^7, and vii° chords, the quality changes from the major-mode chord to its minor-mode alter ego. However, the *function* of those chords borrowed from the parallel mode remains the same. Let's hear what happens when we replace diatonic harmonies with chords from the parallel mode.

$$\text{I} - \text{V}^4_2/\text{IV} - \mathbf{IV^6} - \text{V} - \text{V}^4_2 - \text{I}^6 - \mathbf{ii^6_5} - \text{V}^7 - \mathbf{vi} - \text{I}^6_4 - \text{V}^7 - \text{I}$$

$$\text{I} - \text{V}^4_2/\text{IV} - \mathbf{iv^6} - \text{V} - \text{V}^4_2 - \text{I}^6 - \mathbf{ii^{\varnothing 6}_5} - \text{V}^7 - \mathbf{\flat VI} - \text{I}^6_4 - \text{V}^7 - \text{I}$$

$$\text{i} - \text{V}^6_5/\text{III} - \text{III} - \mathbf{ii^{\varnothing 6}_5} - \text{V}^7 - \mathbf{VI} - \text{V}^7 - \text{i} - \text{VI} - \text{i}^6_4 - \text{V}^7 - \text{i}$$

$$\text{i} - \text{V}^6_5/\text{III} - \text{III} - \mathbf{ii^6_5} - \text{V}^7 - \mathbf{\sharp vi} - \text{V}^6_5 - \text{i} - \text{VI} - \text{i}^6_4 - \text{V}^7 - \mathbf{I}$$

C Major			C Minor		
$\hat{1}$	$\text{I}^{(7)}$	$\text{C} - \text{E} - \text{G} (-\text{B})$	$\text{C} - \text{E}\flat - \text{G} (-\mathbf{B\flat})$	$\text{i}^{(7)}$	$\hat{1}$
$\hat{2}$	$\text{ii}^{(7)}$	$\text{D} - \text{F} - \text{A} (-\text{C})$	$\text{D} - \text{F} - \mathbf{A\flat} (-\text{C})$	$\text{ii}^{\circ(\varnothing 7)}$	$\hat{2}$
$\hat{3}$	$\text{iii}^{(7)}$	$\text{E} - \text{G} - \text{B} (-\text{D})$	$\mathbf{E\flat} - \text{G} - \mathbf{B\flat} (-\text{D})$	$\text{III}^{(7)}$	$\hat{3}$
$\hat{4}$	$\text{IV}^{(7)}$	$\text{F} - \text{A} - \text{C} (-\text{E})$	$\text{F} - \mathbf{A\flat} - \text{C} (-\mathbf{E\flat})$	$\text{iv}^{(7)}$	$\hat{4}$
$\hat{5}$	$\text{V}^{(7)}$	$\text{G} - \text{B} - \text{D} (-\text{F})$	$\text{G} - \text{B} - \text{D} (-\text{F})$	$\text{V}^{(7)}$	$\hat{5}$
$\hat{6}$	$\text{vi}^{(7)}$	$\text{A} - \text{C} - \text{E} (-\text{G})$	$\mathbf{A\flat} - \text{C} - \mathbf{E\flat} (-\text{G})$	$\text{VI}^{(7)}$	$\hat{6}$
$\hat{7}$	$\text{vii}^{\circ(\varnothing 7)}$	$\text{B} - \text{D} - \text{F} (-\text{A})$	$\text{B} - \text{D} - \text{F} (-\mathbf{A\flat})$	$\text{vii}^{\circ(7)}$	$\hat{7}$

TABLE VI.1 *A comparison of the triads (and seventh chords) built on each scale degree of the C-major and C-minor scales. Nondiatonic notes are shown in boldface.*

Note that, as with secondary chords, the function of most modally borrowed chords is that of a pre-dominant; the exceptions are the seventh chord built on $\hat{7}$ and the (borrowed) tonic chord. Do you begin to sense a pattern here? Don't you find it interesting that the majority of the new harmonies becoming available are used to expand (prolong) the pre-dominant function? Indeed, one of the effects of the development of chromatic music is that the musical space between tonic and dominant, never too distant in, say, Scarlatti's time, became longer and

Tonic	Pre-dominant	Dominant
I, I^7, i, i^7	ii, ii^7, ii°, ii^{Ø7}	V, V^7
vi, vi^7, **VI**, **VI**^{7}	IV, IV^7, iv, iv^7	vii°, vii^{Ø7}, vii^{o7}
IV$^6_4$, iv$^6_4$	vi, vi^7, **VI**, **VI**^{7}	IV, iv
	(iii, iii^7, **III**, **III**^{7})	
	V^7**/ii**, **vii**^{o7}**/ii**	
	V^7**/IV**, **vii**^{Ø7}**/IV**	
	V^7**/vi**, **vii**^{o7}**/vi**	
	(**V**^{7}**/iii**, **vii**^{o7}**/iii**)	
	ii°/ii, **iv/ii**, **VI/ii**	
	ii/IV, **IV/IV**	
	(**ii°/iii**)	

TABLE VI.2 *Another update of the list of functions*

longer as the harmonic language increased in sophistication and complexity toward the end of the nineteenth century, so much so that the relationship between tonic and dominant gradually became lost in much music of the twentieth century. Be that as it may, let's revisit our function chart and bring it up to date in Table VI.2.

The list is by no means exhaustive, but it has grown rapidly. We will add to this chart one more time. It may surprise you to learn that there are other harmonic functions beyond the three given in Table VI.2. However, for the time being we'll limit our analyses to these three.

HOME EXERCISES

1. Realize the following progression in four parts, and then add chromatic and diatonic nonchord tones. Be sure to include at least one suspension. When you are finished, sing the results in class.

$$i - vii^{o6} - i^6 - V^6_5/iv - iv - V^6_5/V - V - V^4_2 - i^6 - V^4_3 - i$$

2. In the following progression substitute some chords borrowed from the parallel minor and realize the new version in four parts. Perform the results at the keyboard and judge the effect. Perform the results in ensemble with your classmates.

$$I - V^6_5 - I - I^4_2 - V^4_2/IV - IV^6 - V^4_2/ii - ii^6_5 - I^6_4 - V^7 - I - IV^6_4 - I$$

Learning to Hear Function

UNIT

66

Progressions
Incorporating Chromaticism

ow the fun can really begin! Progressions that incorporate modal borrowings *and* secondary functions are certainly much less predictable than those restricted to the diatonic. They might take an unexpected turn at any moment: they might modulate or imply a modulation that doesn't actually occur. The only thing you can count on is that these harmonies will still follow the precepts already established; eventually you will hear a final cadence. It is no wonder that many a modern theorist has nicknamed the use of these types of progressions "slippery chromaticism."

However, you *do* have the knowledge and skills available to tame all but the fiercest of progressions. And, luckily, these additional chords are so striking as to make them all the more easily identifiable. Just to make sure, let's begin with some small harmonic excerpts involving modal borrowings.

CLASS DRILLS

Dictation: Write down the bass line of each progression that you hear, and provide a complete harmonic analysis under each bass note. (Additional staves are provided at the back of the book.)

1.

2.

3.

4.

5.

6.

7.

8.

9.

10.

11.

12.

13.

14.

15.

16.

17.

18.

19.

20.

21.

22.

23.

24.

The next series of exercises consists of longer progressions for dictation. Write down the bass lines, listening carefully for modal borrowings, secondary dominants and pre-dominants, diatonic seventh chords, and modulation. If modulation occurs, indicate it properly.

CLASS DRILLS

Dictation: Write down the bass line of each progression that you hear, and provide a complete harmonic analysis under each bass note.

1.

2.

3.

4.

5.

6.

7.

8.

9.

10.

11.

12.

We should also practice writing all four parts. Looking at the soprano, realizing the functional implications of the bass, and fulfilling the voice-leading requirements of any tendency tones and chromatic notes should aid you in accomplishing this task. In the following Class Drills, Exercises 5–8 contain nonchord tones (diatonic as well as chromatic).

CLASS DRILLS

Dictation: Write down all four parts of each piece that you hear, and provide a complete harmonic analysis under the bass.

1.

2.

3.

4.

5.

© 1997 Ardsley House, Publishers, Inc.

6.

7.

8.

Locate some of the chorales harmonized by J. S. Bach (the Riemenschneider collection is excellent for this purpose) and play them at the keyboard, or sing them with three or more friends.

Melody

UNIT
67

Incorporating Chromaticism

*I*n tonal music, accidentals other than those found in the key signature fall into one of three categories: chromatics with secondary function, decorative chromatics, or chromatics borrowed from the parallel mode. The first and last categories primarily encompass chord tones, whereas the second is usually concerned with nonchord tones. The context can ordinarily be relied upon to clarify the usage; that is, metric accent, the surrounding notes, and harmonic rhythm all play a part in helping you to determine whether a particular chromatic note is secondary in function, decorative, or borrowed. Being able to recognize and categorize the nature of a chromatic note quickly helps in hearing and singing it, since its function relates to the musical context in which it is found. In Example VI.7 circle all the chromatics. Then provide a Roman numeral analysis of the harmony. Categorize all the accidentals, and label the type of any nonchord tones. The Class Drills that follow this example contain all three types of chromatics.

Symphony No. 5

P. I. Tchaikovsky

EXAMPLE VI.7 *An excerpt for analysis*

CLASS DRILLS

A. *Sight-singing—secondary functions*: Study, analyze, and sight-sing the following melodies using a system of diatonic identification of your choice or one specified by your instructor. The chromatics all result from the implications of secondary functions.

J. Brahms

1.

German folk song

2.

J. Lyra

3.

F. Schubert

4.

L. v. Beethoven

5.

L. v. Beethoven

6.

B. *Sight-singing—modal borrowings:* Study, analyze, and sight-sing each of the following melodies, as in Part A. The chromatics all result from the use of modal borrowings.

F. Schubert

1.

F. Schubert

P. I. Tchaikovsky

F. Schubert

C. *Sight-singing—decorative chromatics*: Study, analyze, and sight-sing each of the following melodies, as in Part A. The chromatics are all decorative in nature.

F. Chopin

D. *Sight-singing—combinations of chromatics*: Study, analyze, and sight-sing each of the following melodies, as in Part A. The chromatics result from a combination of the three previous types.

C. Schumann

3.

F. Schubert

4.

5.

F. Schubert

6.

Fundamentals

UNIT 68

Altered Chords

Altered Dominants

There are a number of new chromatic harmonies that must be introduced at this time. They are often called **altered chords**, as they do not exist diatonically in *any* key and thus require chromatic alterations of diatonic pitches to realize them. The first altered chords to be examined are categorized as **altered dominants**. In this category, for purposes of color or voice leading (or both), a V or V^7 chord is subjected to chromatic alteration, the 5th of the chord being raised or lowered by a half step (V^{+5}, V^{7}_{+5}). These altered dominants are presented in Example VI.8.

The V^{7}_{+5}, with a raised 5th, contains an augmented triad built upon $\hat{5}$. This raised 5th, leading to $\hat{3}$, imbues the dominant chord with another tendency tone. This chord is also frequently used without

EXAMPLE VI.8 *Altered dominants*

the added 7th (V^+). In Example VI.9(a), the V^+ resolves to I; in Example VI.9(b) the V^7_{+5} resolves to vi. Note that these chords are rarely, if ever, encountered in the minor. (Why?)

Please note that hereafter in the text altered dominants with a raised 5th are shown with only a plus sign (V^+), since the plus sign without a numeral following it always refers to the 5th.

The V^7_{-5} uses its lowered 5th as an upper tendency tone to $\hat{1}$. Unlike the V^+, it is quite common in the minor mode. Note that the interval between the 3rd and the 5th of this chord is a diminished 3rd, and its inversion is an augmented 6th. For this reason it is sometimes confused by students with another category of altered chords. (See *Augmented Sixth Chords* on page 375.) However, the difference is that the V^7_{-5} is built on $\hat{5}$, and the interval of the diminished 3rd/augmented 6th resolves to an octave/unison on $\hat{1}$. See Example VI.10.

Neapolitan Sixths

Another interesting category of altered chords is the so-called **Neapolitan sixth** chord ($\flat II^6$). It is a major triad built on $\flat\hat{2}$ and almost always occurs in first inversion (hence the second part of its name). The 3rd of this chord, since it is diatonic, is always doubled, and since $\hat{4}$ is the 3rd of the triad, it is usually associated with cadential movements to I^6_4 or V^7, in which the bass moves up by step. The root ($\flat\hat{2}$) moves to $\hat{1}$ and the 5th ($\flat\hat{6}$) moves to $\hat{5}$. One must be careful to avoid parallel fifths when applying a Neapolitan 6th; the root therefore appears most often above the 5th. Note that a Neapolitan 6th requires two alterations in the major mode, but only one in the minor mode (where it is much more common). Example VI.11 illustrates a few typical cadences involving the Neapolitan 6th chord.

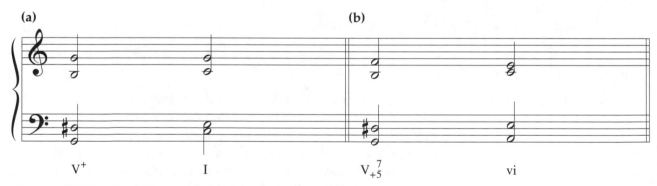

(a)   (b)

V^+ I V^7_{+5} vi

EXAMPLE VI.9 *Resolutions of altered dominants*

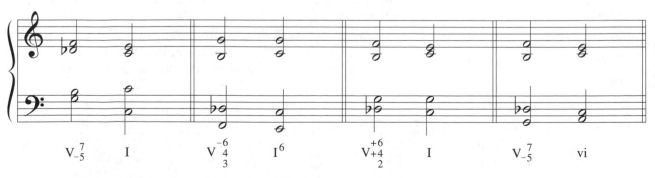

V^7_{-5} I $V^{-6}_{\ \ 4}_{\ \ 3}$ I^6 $V^{+6}_{+4}_{\ \ 2}$ I V^7_{-5} vi

EXAMPLE VI.10 *Resolving inversions of altered dominants*

© 1997 Ardsley House, Publishers, Inc.

Notice the leap of a diminished 3rd (an enharmonic whole step) between D♭ and B in Example VI.11(c). This is a fairly common means of avoiding even more egregious voice-leading problems inherent in the use of the ♭II⁶ chord.

Augmented Sixth Chords

The last category of altered chords to be considered is the group of four known collectively as **augmented sixth** chords because all the chords in this group incorporate this characteristic interval. To understand their construction, it will be easier to begin in the minor mode, where they require the least alteration. Let's start with the simplest one, the **Italian sixth** chord (iv⁺⁶). If you begin with a iv chord in first inversion and then raise the root, the interval of an augmented 6th is created between the 3rd of the chord in the bass (♭6̂) and the raised root above. The iv⁺⁶ is a *strong* pre-dominant (as are the other augmented chords), and it requires that the bass and the raised root above resolve to 5̂. (Find the exception to this in Example VI.12.) The 5th of the chord, 1̂, is always doubled. The *sound* of the Italian 6th chord is that of a (enharmonic) V⁷ chord built on ♭6̂, with the 5th missing. Example VI.12 illustrates how the iv⁺⁶ is customarily used. Listen to how the chord sounds in these contexts.

The next augmented 6th chord, the **German sixth** chord, provides the enharmonic 5th that is "missing" from the Italian 6th chord. It also begins as a iv chord in first inversion, but with an added 7th. Again, we raise the root to create an augmented 6th. All else is the same, except for the added 7th. The German 6th (iv⁺⁶₅) generally resolves the 7th by maintaining it as the 3rd of the next harmony, typically a i⁶₄ in the minor key, or by moving by half step down to 2̂.

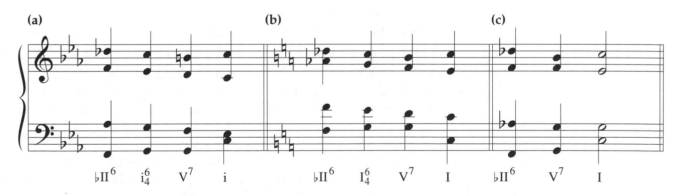

EXAMPLE VI.11 *Cadences involving the Neapolitan sixth*

EXAMPLE VI.12 *Resolutions of the Italian sixth*

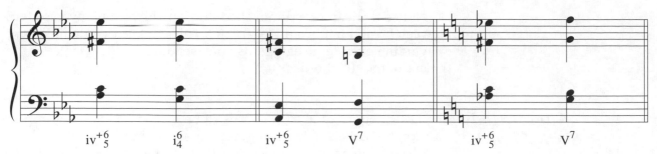

EXAMPLE VI.13   *Resolutions of the German sixth*

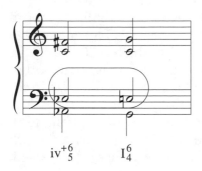

iv⁺⁶₅   I⁶₄

EXAMPLE VI.14   *The cross-relation resulting from the resolution of a German sixth to a I⁶₄ in the major mode*

This last movement almost always creates problems because it is hard to avoid parallel fifths with the bass. For that reason, either the iv$^{+6}_5$ goes to the tonic in second inversion, or on occasion the 7th moves up by step to the 7th of a V^7 chord. See Example VI.13.

The German 6th chord rarely goes to I$^6_4$ in the major mode because of the **cross-relation** between the 7th of the iv$^{+6}_5$ and the 3rd of the I$^6_4$ that would result. See Example VI.14.

Note again that the iv$^{+6}_5$ chord is enharmonically equivalent to a V^7 built on a ♭$\hat6$ (the V^7 of the Neapolitan!) and has the *sound* characteristic of a V^7. It is in its resolution that we are able to hear its identity as an augmented 6th chord.

It seems that there has always been a rivalry between the Germans and the French, so it is only fitting that the French should have their own augmented 6th chord; it is built on $\hat2$. Begin with a ii^{ø7} chord in *second* inversion, and raise the 3rd. Surprise! We end up with ♭$\hat6$ in the bass and ♯$\hat4$ above, just as in the other two augmented 6th chords. The **French sixth** chord $\left(\text{ii}^{+6}_{\ 4\ 3}\right)$ also contains $\hat1$, as did the others. For all intents and purposes, these three augmented 6th chords have virtually the same construction. The ii$^{+6}_{\ 4\ 3}$ does contain the added twist, however, of having $\hat2$, its root, a tritone above the bass. This gives the chord a vaguely "whole-tone" sound (perhaps reminiscent of French **Impressionism**) because there is a major 2nd between the 7th and the root, and the enharmonic equivalent of a major 2nd (the inversion of the augmented 6th) between the raised 3rd and the 5th. The French 6th chord resolves smoothly to the second-inversion tonic chord, the V, or the V^7. See Examples VI.15 and VI.16.

The last of the augmented 6th chords is somewhat unusual. It is the same as the ii$^{+6}_{\ 4\ 3}$ except that it has a raised *root* as well. This creates a rather odd interval above the bass—a doubly augmented 4th.

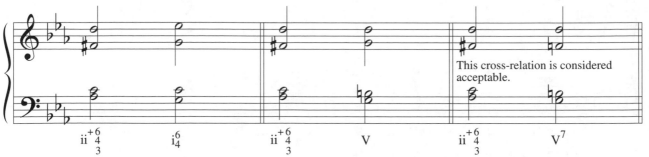

This cross-relation is considered acceptable.

ii⁺⁶₄₃   i⁶₄   ii⁺⁶₄₃   V   ii⁺⁶₄₃   V⁷

EXAMPLE VI.15   *Resolutions of the French sixth in the minor mode*

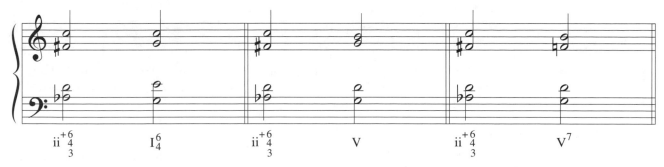

EXAMPLE VI.16 *Resolutions of the French sixth in the major mode*

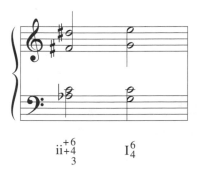

EXAMPLE VI.17 *Resolution of the doubly augmented fourth chord*

And that is the name often given to this chord, the **doubly augmented fourth** chord $\left(\mathrm{ii}^{+6}_{+4\ 3}\right)$. By raising the root, we have created the enharmonic equivalent of the German 6th (iv^{+6}_{5}), which is itself the enharmonic equivalent of a $\mathrm{V}^{7}/\flat\mathrm{II}$. Needless to say, the ear cannot discriminate between differences in spelling alone. But fear not! Remember the problem encountered previously with resolving the German 6th to I^{6}_{4} in the major mode? The doubly augmented 4th chord is designed to overcome that dilemma. No longer need we fear the dreaded cross-relation, as we observe in Example VI.17.

Voila! It sounds the same, yet it is easier to perform (we can *see* the leading-tone effect); moreover, it solves certain problems of voice leading. So, how then can we tell if we're hearing a iv^{+6}_{5} or a $\mathrm{ii}^{+6}_{+4\ 3}$? If the chord in question moves to a major I^{6}_{4}, simply *assume* it is a $\mathrm{ii}^{+6}_{+4\ 3}$. Otherwise, it is much more likely to be spelled as a German 6th chord.

Function of Altered Chords

Let's add these altered chords to our function list (Table VI.3), and see how it has grown.

The Neapolitan 6th and each of the augmented 6th chords are extremely strong pre-dominants; as such, they are usually reserved for articulating cadences at important structural points. This is especially true of the augmented 6ths; they will *make* what follows them sound significant. Listen for these chords, then, in cadential progressions. As style, taste, and voice leading permit, they are generally used judiciously, as are all good seasonings.

Tonic	Pre-dominant	Dominant
I, I^7, i, i^7	ii, ii^7, ii$^\circ$, ii$^{\varnothing 7}$	V, V^7
vi, vi^7, VI, VI^7	IV, IV^7, iv, iv^7	vii$^\circ$, vii$^{\varnothing 7}$, vii$^{\circ 7}$
IV$^6_4$, iv$^6_4$	vi, vi^7, VI, VI^7	IV, iv
	(iii, iii^7, III, III^7)	**V$^+$, V$^7_+$**
	V^7/ii, vii$^{\circ 7}$/ii	**V$^{-7}_5$**
	V^7/IV, vii$^{\circ 7}$/IV	
	V^7/vi, vii$^{\circ 7}$/vi	
	(V^7/iii, vii$^{\circ 7}$/iii)	
	ii$^\circ$/ii, iv/ii, VI/ii	
	ii/IV, IV/IV	
	(ii$^\circ$/iii)	
	$\flat$II^6	
	iv^{+6}, iv$^{+6}_5$	
	ii$^{+6}_{4\ 3}$, ii$^{+6}_{+4\ 3}$	

TABLE VI.3 *The list of functions updated to include altered chords*

HOME EXERCISES

1. The Neapolitan 6th and the augmented 6th chords are often used for modulation to remote keys or even for *enharmonic modulation*. How could they be used for these purposes? Draw up a list of where these chords could take you, relative to the home key.

2. Spell the following chords.

   (a) German 6th in E minor

   (b) $ii^{+6}_{4\ 3}$ in D major

   (c) Italian 6th in B major

   (d) $ii^{+6}_{4\ 3}$ in C minor

   (e) Neapolitan 6th in A major

   (f) iv^{+6} in A major

   (g) French 6th in F minor

   (h) $\flat II^6$ in B♭ major

   (i) iv^{+6}_5 in D minor

   (j) Doubly augmented 4th in E major

Learning to Hear Function

UNIT 69

Progressions Incorporating Altered Chords

*B*ecause altered chords, especially augmented 6ths, have strong cadential implications and because of the striking nature of their sound, they are best used sparingly and to good effect. Again, because of the almost exotic character of their sound, particularly in primarily diatonic contexts, they stand out and provide harmonic "road signs" to any progression in which they are involved. Therefore, altered chords are relatively easy to locate and identify. Indeed, in progressions of any length, it is best to locate the more obvious chords first and then to fill in the details on subsequent hearings.

Suppose that after the first presentation, all you are able to identify with certainty are the following harmonies:

$$i - \underline{\quad} - \underline{\quad} - iv^{+6}_5 - \underline{\quad} - V - i$$

What might you surmise happened in the blank spaces? We *know* that the iv^{+6}_5 chord is a strong pre-dominant and that the next bass note *must* be $\hat{5}$. Since the V chord doesn't occur until one harmonic change later, we can reason that the iv^{+6}_5 is probably followed by a i^6_4 in this case. It might appear at first that the two blanks preceding the German 6th chord could be just about anything; but on the next presentation perhaps you pick up this additional information:

$$i - V^6_5/III - \underline{\quad} - iv^{+6}_5 - i^6_4 - V - i$$

You can surely fill in the remaining blank without another hearing and be almost guaranteed of success if you answer III. If, upon

© 1997 Ardsley House, Publishers, Inc.

subsequent listening, it proves *not* to be III, but rather some minor triad, what might it be? Let's try this method with other progressions incorporating altered chords. We will begin with short excerpts, as has been our custom.

CLASS DRILLS

A. *Dictation*: **In each progression that you hear, identify the function and inversion of each chord.**

1.

2.

3.

4.

5.

6.

7.

8.

9.

10.

B. *Dictation*: **Write down the bass line of each progression that you hear, and provide a complete harmonic analysis under each bass note.**

1.

2.

3.

4.

5.

6.

7.

8.

9.

10.

11.

12.

13.

14.

15.

16.

17.

18.

19.

20.

21.

22.

23.

24.

25.

26.

27.

28.

29.

30.

31.

32.

33.

34.

© 1997 Ardsley House, Publishers, Inc.

HOME EXERCISES

Be much more aware of the music around you. Listen for such things as the use of altered chords and of other unusual harmonies, and take personal satisfaction in your identification of them.

Melody

Implying Altered Chords

*A*ltered harmonies contain many tendency tones, so an acute awareness of these tendency tones and the harmonies that they imply in the following melodies are necessary. Remember that the proper analysis of these altered harmonies may require a consideration of several consecutive measures. As in previous units of this sort, prepare for performance through an analysis of the function of all accidentals. When listening to dictation material, take the time to hear and recognize the use of all implied chromatic harmonies, particularly the ones recently discussed.

CLASS DRILLS

A. *Sight-singing*: Study, analyze, sight-sing, practice, and perform each of the following melodies.

J. S. Bach

A. Braun

B. *Dictation*: Write down the melodies that your instructor presents.

1.

2.

3.

4.

5.

6.

7.

8.

Rhythm

© 1997 Ardsley House, Publishers, Inc.

UNIT **71**

Two against Three

Combining Duplets with Triplets

We have discussed the notion of composite rhythm and have applied the concept to two-part rhythmic dictations. But there is another, even more valuable, use—to aid in the performance of **cross-rhythms**.

What is the composite rhythm that results from playing an eighth-note duplet against an eighth-note triplet? To find out, we apply some elementary arithmetic: we look for the **least common multiple** of 2 and 3. It is, of course, 6. So if we look at the sixteenth-note sextuplet in Example VI.18, we find that, sure enough, it will divide evenly by both 2 and 3.

EXAMPLE VI.18 *Duple and triple divisions of a sixteenth-note sextuplet*

EXAMPLE VI.19 *Generating the composite rhythm of 2 vs. 3 eighth notes*

EXAMPLE VI.20 *Two eighth notes vs. an eighth-note triplet*

Example VI.19 shows us the resultant composite rhythm of 2 vs. 3 because the second eighth note of the duplet falls on the fourth sixteenth of the sextuplet, and the second and third eighth notes of the triplet fall on 3 and 5, respectively. The accents in Example VI.19 illustrate this, and help to generate the composite rhythm shown.

To perform two eighths vs. an eighth-note triplet, then, simply perform the composite rhythm allocated between the two parts, as shown in Example VI.20. Try this method on a few other combinations of 2 vs. 3. A quarter-note triplet against two quarter notes yields the situation in Example VI.21.

This is also how we can perform a half-note triplet accurately. Mentally divide the measure into quarter-note triplets, and play on the first, third, and fifth of a pair of them, as in Example VI.22.

Other Combinations

Other combinations beyond 2 against 3 are admittedly more complex, though the method remains the same. How would we perform quarter-note triplets vs. four eighth notes? The least common multiple of 3 and 4 is 12, so we look at a pair of sixteenth-note sextuplets.

EXAMPLE VI.21 *Generating the composite rhythm of a quarter-note triplet vs. two quarter notes*

EXAMPLE VI.22 *Performing a half-note triplet*

The quarter-note triplet falls on 1, 5, and 9, while the eighth notes fall on 1, 4, 7, and 10, as shown in Example VI.23; the composite rhythm is revealed in Example VI.24.

Now try performing some of these combinations. It may seem like patting your head and rubbing your stomach at the same time. This kind of coordination is similar: it requires practice.

EXAMPLE VI.23   *Generating the composite rhythm of a quarter-note triplet against four eighth notes*

EXAMPLE VI.24   *Composite rhythm of four eighth notes against a quarter-note triplet*

CLASS DRILLS

Perform the following two-part rhythms by tapping the upper part with your right hand and the lower one with your left hand.

© 1997 Ardsley House, Publishers, Inc.

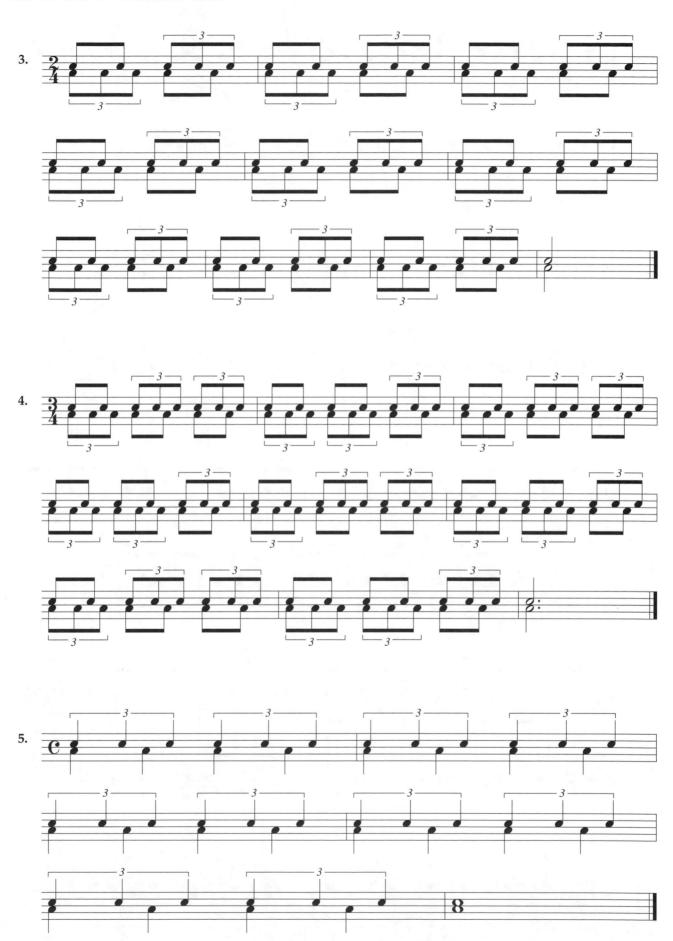

15.

Unless you are a percussionist, you may have found these exercises taxing. Fortunately, most music does not make these demands continuously. We are most likely to encounter such cross-rhythms as more or less isolated instances within a larger context. Nevertheless, we should be flexible enough as musicians to deal with these exigencies when they occur. Pianists who play the works of Brahms and Chopin, to name but two composers, must master these skills. The least-common-multiple approach is also necessary to negotiate most metric modulations. In Renaissance music it is often necessary to move from passages written in $\frac{4}{2}$ (or the Renaissance equivalent) to $\frac{3}{1}$; the proportions are usually 3:1 or 3:2. If the former, then the whole note of the triple meter is three times faster than that of the duple meter; in the latter proportion, the dotted whole of the triple meter is equal to the whole note of the duple meter, a Renaissance metric modulation known as *sesquialtera*.

CLASS DRILLS

Perform at sight each of the following rhythms by yourself, in pairs, or in groups. In each exercise the division of the beat remains constant. *Example:* $\frac{2}{4}$ ♪ = $\frac{3}{8}$ ♪

1.

Finally, here are similar rhythms for dictation. Metric modulation and mixed meter have been excluded because they are open to metric interpretation (in Example VI.25, rhythm (a) could be easily heard as rhythm (b)). Otherwise, heads up! And listen for those cross-rhythms.

EXAMPLE VI.25 *Rhythm (a) can easily be heard as rhythm (b)*

CLASS DRILLS

Dictation: **Write down the one- and two-part rhythms that you hear.**

1.

2.

3.

4.

5.

6.

7.

8.

9.

HOME EXERCISES

Find some music that incorporates mixed meters, and *read* the rhythms; it doesn't matter whether or not this music is intended for your instrument. The music of Stravinsky will prove a fruitful source. Also find some music that uses metric modulation and try performing the rhythms and the tempo changes. Such music may be more difficult to locate, but works by Elliott Carter, Henry Cowell, and Charles Ives contain these devices. Tomás Luís de Victoria and Giovanni Pierluigi da Palestrina, among other Renaissance master composers, can provide you with examples of *sesquialtera*.

Melody

UNIT 72

Ensembles Incorporating Chromaticism

*T*wo-part pieces written in a tonal/chromatic idiom should present no new obstacles when performed. They should contain the same challenges as the single-part melodies encountered in previous units, except that the individual parts themselves may be a bit *less* chromatic, since the two parts "share" in the duty of implying harmony. As dictations, these duets present more opportunities to check your work because you are able to review how the two parts relate to each other and to look for any obvious errors in harmony or counterpoint. Be sure to check your spelling of chromatic notes. Leading tones, especially, need to be notated correctly; proper notation of altered notes will show that you understand their linear and harmonic function. If you fully understand the reasons why Example VI.26 is *correctly* spelled, whereas Example VI.27 is *not*, then you are ready to begin.

EXAMPLE VI.26   *Correct spelling*

EXAMPLE VI.27   *Incorrect spelling*

CLASS DRILLS

A. *Sight-singing*: Sing each of the following ensemble pieces at sight, using the system of diatonic identification that you choose or that is suggested by your instructor. Sing each of them as a duet or in ensemble.

Trio Sonata, BWV 528

J. S. Bach

3.

4.

L. v. Beethoven

5.

"Ave Maria"

G. Verdi

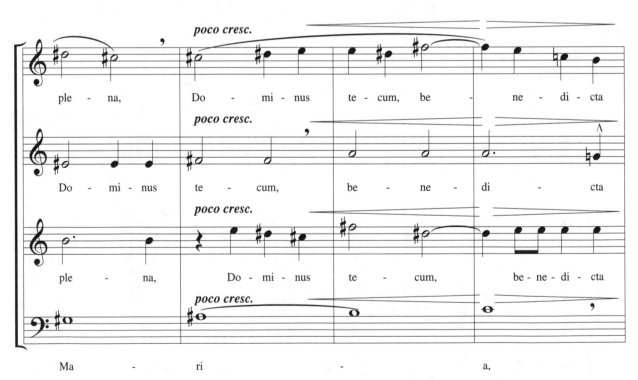

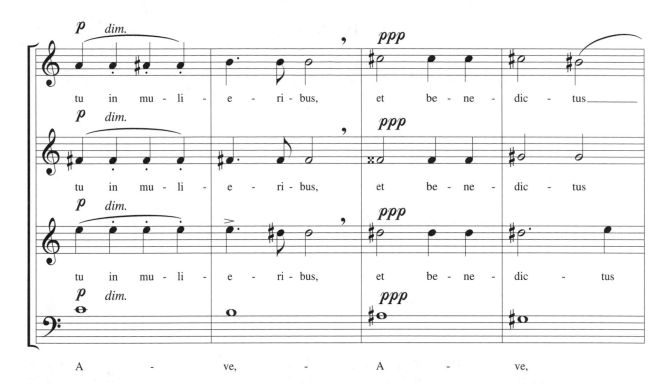

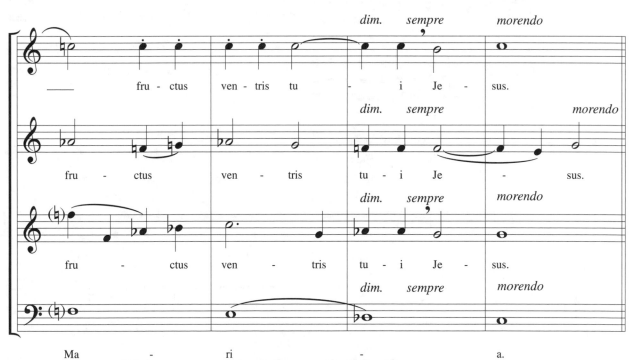

Hail Mary, full of grace,
the Lord is with thee,
blessed art thou among women,
and blessed is the fruit of thy womb, Jesus.

"Der Tanz," D. 826

F. Schubert

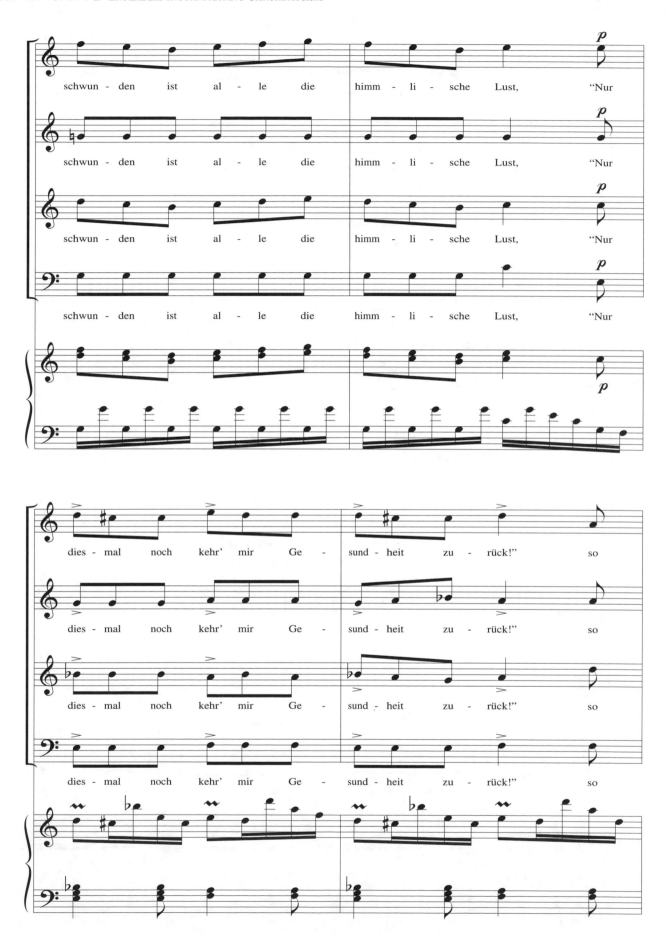

fle - het___ vom___ Him - mel der hof - fen - de Blick!

fle - het vom Him - mel der hof - fen - de Blick!

fle - het vom Him - mel der hof - fen - de Blick!

fle - het___ vom___ Him - mel der hof - fen - de Blick!

Youth are always talking and dreaming a lot
About dancing, carousing, and feasting.
Suddenly they reach their delusive destination,
And that's when you'll hear their sighs and sorrows.

Soon their throats are aching;
soon there'll be pains in their chests,
that is when all heavenly joy has vanished.
"Only once, please, let health return to me!"
This yearning call from heaven sounds!

"Agnus Dei" from *Paukenmesse*

F. J. Haydn

O Lamb of God, who takest away the sins of the world,
have mercy upon us.

"Lacrymosa" from *Requiem*, K. 626

W. A. Mozart

. . . when the world ascends from the ashes, sinful and
ready for judgment.

"Im Herbst"

J. Brahms

Autumn is earnest,
and when leaves are falling,
the heart, as well, begins to sadden.
The countryside is quiet,
as the songbirds silently leave for the south,
as to their graves.

Octet, D. 803

F. Schubert

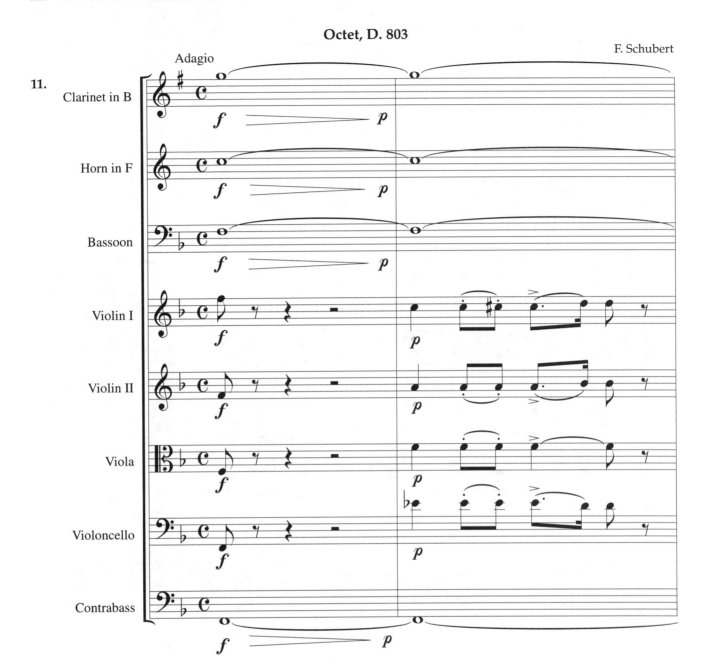

String Quartet, K. 465

W. A. Mozart

12.

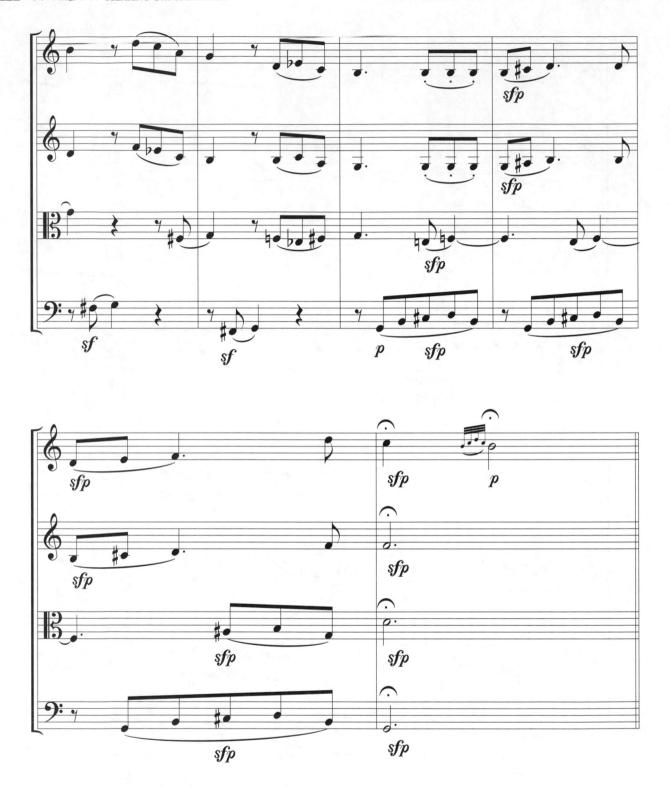

String Quartet, K. 428

Andante con moto

W. A. Mozart

13.

"Ach Gott, vom Himmel sieh' darein"

Erfurter Enchiridion, 1524, harm J. S. Bach

14.

"An Mignon," D. 161

F. Schubert

auf, im - mer mor - gens wie - der

auf.

High above the valleys and the rivers
the sun's carriage appears.
Oh, while moving from east to west
it stirs your sorrows as well as mine,
deep in the hearts, each morning, again and again.

Minuet, K. 355

W. A. Mozart

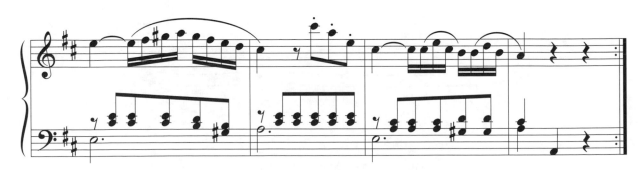

"Es ist genug"

J. R. Ahle, harm. J. S. Bach

B.   *Dictation:* **On two staff lines write down each two-part piece that you hear.**

1.

2.

3.

4.

5.

6.

7.

8.

HOME EXERCISES

1 Harmonize the melodies in Unit 70 on pages 383–385 by supplying a complete harmonic analysis under each system. Make sure that each of your analyses provides a consistent and logical harmonic rhythm and an aurally pleasing result.

2 Where possible, provide a complete harmonic analysis for each of the ensembles pieces in this unit.

Hearing
in
Nonfunctional
Contexts

Fundamentals

UNIT **73**

*Modes
and Nontonal Scales*

T he materials presented in this area are, for the most part, outside the realm of functional harmony and will therefore be presented in only the most elementary fashion. The subject is fascinating and musically attractive; thus, this area could be used as a springboard for further studies in twentieth-century music and in the music of other cultures.

*Ecclesiastical
Modes*

Reference has been made throughout this book to the major and minor modes. These scales and their interval arrangements are actually relatively new devices in Western music. For centuries before their development, music was conceived and written according to the eight **ecclesiastical modes**. These are all analogous to the modern major mode, with the two half steps appearing between different scale degrees. Later, theorists also spoke of three **theoretical modes**: the **Ionian** (much like our major scale), the **Aeolian** (much like our natural minor scale), and the **Locrian** (which would sound much like playing from a given B to the B an octave higher in the key of C major).

Mode I of the eight ecclesiastical modes is also called the **Dorian** mode. It places the half steps between $\hat{2}$ and $\hat{3}$ and between $\hat{6}$ and $\hat{7}$. It can be heard by playing from a given D to the D an octave higher in C major; when C is used as the tonic, this mode appears as in Example VII.1.

Mode III is also called the **Phrygian** mode. It places the half steps between $\hat{1}$ and $\hat{2}$ and between $\hat{5}$ and $\hat{6}$. It can be heard by playing from a given E to the E an octave higher in C major; when C is used as the tonic, this mode appears as in Example VII.2.

EXAMPLE VII.1   *The Dorian mode, beginning on C*

EXAMPLE VII.2   *The Phrygian mode, beginning on C*

© 1997 Ardsley House, Publishers, Inc.

Mode V is also called the **Lydian** mode. It places the half steps between $\hat{4}$ and $\hat{5}$ and between $\hat{7}$ and $\hat{1}$. It can be heard by playing from a given F to the F an octave higher in C major; when C is used as the tonic, this mode appears as in Example VII.3.

Mode VII is also called the **Mixolydian** mode. It places the half steps between $\hat{3}$ and $\hat{4}$ and between $\hat{6}$ and $\hat{7}$. It can be heard by playing from a given G to the G an octave higher in C major; when C is used as the tonic, this mode appears as in Example VII.4.

Modes II, IV, VI, and VIII are so-called **plagal forms** of modes I, III, V, and VII, respectively, and cannot be distinguished orally from the authentic forms. However, they specify or suggest differences in melodic range, and they served as a theoretical basis for composition prior to the tonal era. All of these church modes (as they're also known) are named after ancient Greek communities. Plato mentions them in his *Republic*, but he is referring to the Greek system of *rhythmic* modes, and not the scales just described.

The Pentatonic Scale

Some scale systems eschew the half step altogether. The most widely used mode without half steps is the **pentatonic scale**, which provides the basis for much Asian music. The pentatonic scale exists in two forms, both of which have a number of properties in common, the most obvious characteristic being that they contain only five notes. Theoretically, both forms can be derived by choosing the proper starting note and arranging the five scale degrees successively so that a perfect 5th separates contiguous members. Try it! Furthermore, both forms are structured like the black keys within an octave on the piano: the group of two notes is separated by a minor 3rd from the group of three notes. The two-note group spans a major 2nd. In the three-note group, a major 2nd is spanned from the lowest to the middle note and also from the middle to the highest note. With C used as the "tonic," the two forms of the pentatonic scale are shown in Example VII.5.

EXAMPLE VII.3 *The Lydian mode, beginning on C*

EXAMPLE VII.4 *The Mixolydian mode, beginning on C*

EXAMPLE VII.5 *The two forms of the pentatonic scale, beginning on C*

The Whole-Tone Scale

Another common scale that lacks the half step is the **whole-tone scale**. It is one of a larger group of scales sometimes called **artificial scales** because, when they are examined from any modal or diatonic perspective, they contain altered notes. The whole-tone scale is a six-note scale that consists of nothing but whole steps in succession; when C is used as the "tonic," the whole-tone scale appears as in Example VII.6.

The lack of any half step, along with the perfect (though enharmonic) symmetry of the whole-tone scale, makes this scale difficult to describe tonally. That is, it is difficult to locate a tonic pitch, as there is nothing to differentiate one pitch from another intervallically, and there is no perfect 5th between any of the pitches to yield a tonal authentic cadence.

The Octatonic Scale

Finally, the **octatonic scale** is a perfectly symmetric eight-note scale consisting of alternating whole steps and half steps. Therefore, it is also classified as an artificial scale. It may take one of two forms, depending upon the initial interval (whole or half step). When C is used as the "tonic," the two forms appear as in Example VII.7 (both forms admit a number of enharmonic respellings).

Because of the presence of half steps, one can easily establish a sense of apparent tonic with this scale, and thus it has proved a favorite device of many twentieth-century composers.

Summary

Each of these modes and nontonal scales, like the major and minor scales of the tonal system, has its own distinct sound and character. Lack of familiarity with them gives them their "exotic" flavor, and this fact has been exploited in many nineteenth- and twentieth-century **tone poems**. We should remember, however, that they do not sound exotic in every culture, nor did they sound exotic in every age.

EXAMPLE VII.6 *The whole-tone scale, beginning on C*

EXAMPLE VII.7 *The two forms of the octatonic scale, beginning on C*

CLASS DRILLS

A. Sing and identify each of the following scales and modes.

B. Identify each of the scales that you hear.

1.   2.   3.   4.

5.   6.   7.   8.

9.   10.   11.

HOME EXERCISES

1 Starting on D, write each of the seven scales and modes presented in this unit on the staves provided.

2 **Gregorian chant** has suddenly become popular again. Listen to any of the many fine recordings available, and try to discern the mode of each chant. This is not at all an easy task, as many pieces use a mixture of ecclesiastical and theoretical modes (an early form of modulation). Nonetheless, it is a worthwhile experience.

3 Try playing and singing any of the seven modes and scales of this unit, beginning on any freely chosen pitch. Remember the construction of the chosen mode or scale, and proceed slowly. Familiarity will naturally enhance your capability.

Melody

UNIT
74

*Modes
and Nontonal Scales*

F or both sight-reading and dictation purposes, here are a number of melodies that use the modes and nontonal scales introduced in the preceding unit. It would help if, before singing one of these exercises, you were to determine the mode or scale of the piece. Before you sight-sing the exercise, locate the half steps (if any) and sing the mode or scale first, starting on its "tonic" note.

CLASS DRILLS

A. *Sight-singing*: Sing the following melodies at sight on a neutral syllable, unless directed otherwise by your instructor.

B. Bartók

1.

C. Lampoc

Perotin

G. P. da Palestrina

6.

B. *Dictation*: Write down the melodies that your instructor presents. Listen carefully and, on the first hearing of each, try to identify the mode or scale from which it is derived.

1.

2.

3.

4.

5.

6.

7.

HOME EXERCISES

1. Starting on any pitch you choose, sing or play all seven of the modes or scales with which we have been working in these units.

2. Make up your own artificial scale of six to nine notes. Compose a short melody using your scale, and bring it to class for sight-singing purposes.

Melodic Constructs

UNIT **75**

Pitch-Class Sets

*T*here are many other ways of organizing musical materials besides scales and modes. Other cultures offer a bewildering array of methods and concepts, and composers of the twentieth century have built upon these methods and have created some new ones. Set theory, borrowed from mathematics, has yielded new means of organization and new analytical techniques for tonal music as well. It is not our intention to discuss all of these here; however, it would be interesting and productive to examine the compositional technique that utilizes groups of *pitch classes*. (Any notes with the same letter name, regardless of the octave in which they sound, belong to the same **pitch class**.)

A **pitch-class set** is a collection of from two to twelve pitch classes that is applied **constructivistically** in a composition to yield results other than those obtained through "normal" tonal channels. The results themselves may be tonal (and often are), depending upon the nature of the sets themselves and the manner in which they are used. For our purposes, pitch-class sets also represent another way for our mind's ear to recognize the organization of pitch material. Once we can apprehend and recognize them, then perhaps we will develop a greater appreciation for music written according to these and similar systems. (In music, familiarity does *not* breed contempt; indeed, generally, the opposite is true.)

Pitch-class sets, as we will use them, range in size from two-note (dyad) to six-note (**hexachord**) collections. For example, Bartók's *Mikrokosmos*, vol. I, no. 36, uses tetrachord groupings, and Schoenberg's *Piano Piece*, op. 11, no. 1, provides an example of an early nontonal use of **trichord** procedures. And again, for our purposes, they represent a good source of "musical calisthenics" for our ears and minds.

Herewith, then, are a number of such aural exercises based on pitch-class sets. They are grouped progressively, from dyads to hexachords.

CLASS DRILLS

A. Analyze each line for its specific pitch and interval content. Brackets identify the pitch-class set used. Sing each succession of pitches at sight, using whichever system of vocalization is most comfortable for you or is suggested by your instructor.

2-Note Sets (Dyads)

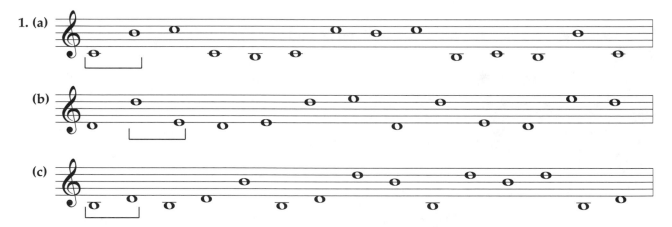

3-Note Sets (Trichords)

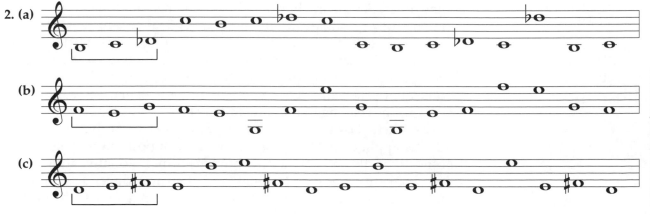

© 1997 Ardsley House, Publishers, Inc.

4-Note Sets (Tetrachords)

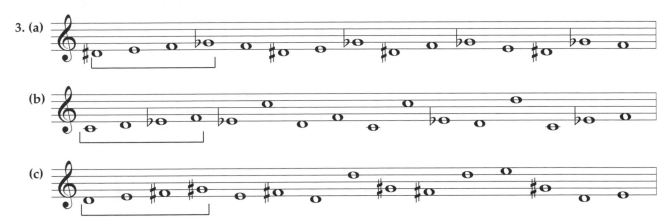

5-Note Sets (Pentachords)

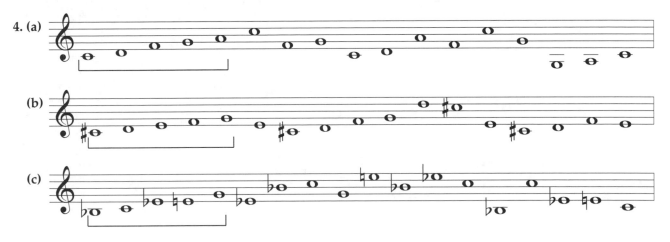

6-Note Sets (Hexachords)

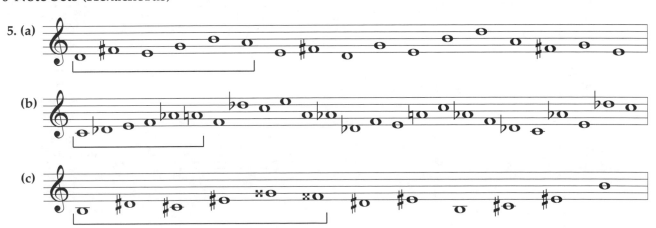

B. Sing each succession of pitches at sight, using whichever system of vocalization is most comfortable for you or is suggested by your instructor. Identify the pitch-class set used in each line.

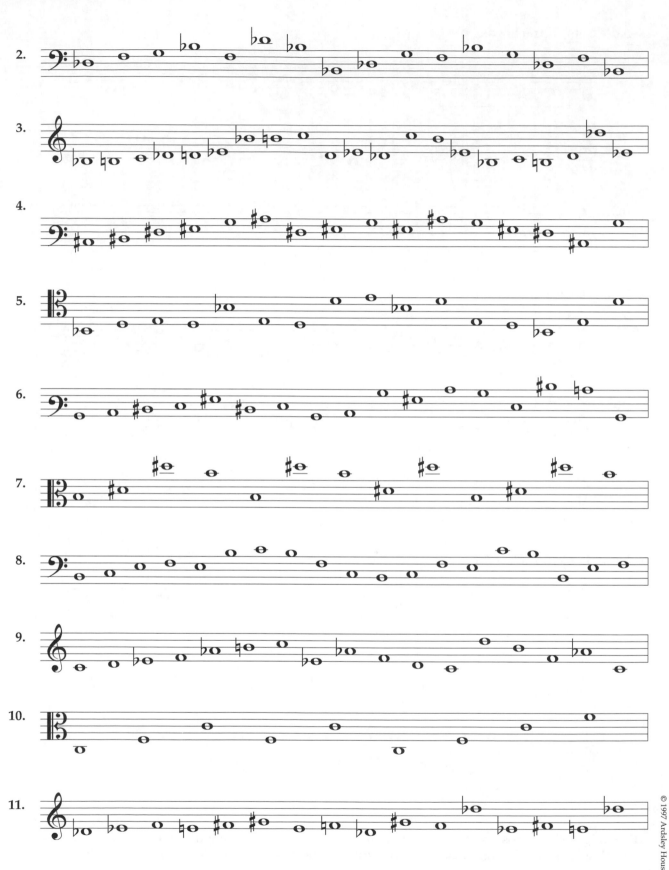

13.

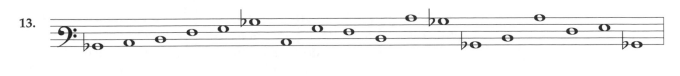

14.

15.

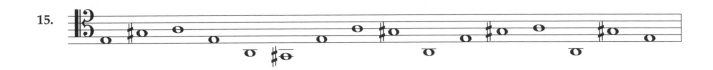

HOME EXERCISES

1 Examine the 2-, 3-, 4-, 5-, and 6-note sets presented in the preceding Class Drills. Determine which sets of pitches could be found in a diatonic major or minor scale, and name those scales. If in a minor scale, indicate the form(s) of that scale. Label each pitch as to which scale degree it would be.

2 In addition to the sets presented in the preceding Class Drills, there are many other possible sets with different interval contents and combinations. Create some of your own sets and write them in source set form (arranged so that the smallest intervals possible exist between the contiguous notes).

Rhythm

UNIT 76

Further Subdivisions and Combinations

Groupings of Five A beat or any of its divisions or multiples are subject to many further subdivisions and rearrangements beyond those that we've practiced. For example, quintuplets of any type are not uncommon; neither are septuplets. To perform one of these subdivisions of a beat requires the easily mastered ability of dividing into five and seven mentally, just as we do with two, three, and four. To perform these divisions across several contiguous beats requires the ability to find least common multiples and to think in terms of groupings of the appropriate division, as we did with 3 against 2 and 3 against 4.

Let's begin with five. Mentally dividing the beat into quintuplets is not in itself difficult; we are simply not as familiar with this subdivision as we are with others. Once you have the basic quintuplet rhythm established in your mind's ear, you should be able to group the subdivisions in a variety of ways. See Example VII.8. Let's stick with these simple arrangements at first until we've achieved a certain level of fluency, not to mention confidence and security.

In Area VII, you will notice that there is a departure from the convention we have followed earlier in the text regarding brackets and tuplet division. For the remainder of the text, the numbers that indicate the identities of the tuplet divisions will *not* be accompanied by a bracket unless the location of the beat(s) divided by the tuplets cannot be clearly indicated and understood from the natural beaming of the grouped tuplets. This more accurately reflects the convention found in the majority of scores that employ these rhythmic devices.

EXAMPLE VII.8 *Various groupings of a quintuplet subdivision*

CLASS DRILLS

Perform the following rhythms using the syllable *ta*. Be aware of both attack and release points.

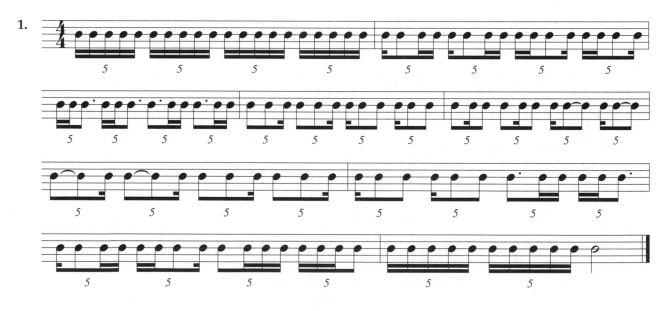

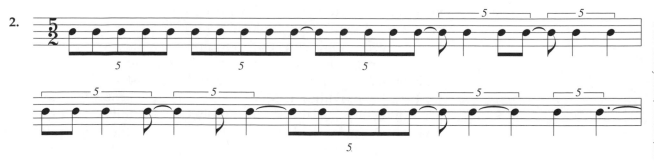

© 1997 Ardsley House, Publishers, Inc.

Ratios Involving Five   In Exercise 5 one set of quintuplet eighths is placed against both beats of the $\frac{2}{4}$ measure. You probably performed it by thinking of the half note as the beat. To perform precisely the 5:2 that is implied, however, we must examine the ratio in musical terms. The least common multiple of 5 and 2 is 10, so there are ten quintuplet sixteenth notes in a pair of sixteenth-note quintuplets. See Example VII.9. We begin by mentally dividing the measure into ten quintuplet sixteenth notes. Then to perform 5:2, all we have to do is regroup the quintuplet sixteenths in pairs, as illustrated in Example VII.10.

The same procedure will hold true for 5:4; but in this case, the least common multiple of 5 and 4 is 20, which is double the least common multiple of 5 and 2. Thus, we regroup the sixteenth-note quintuplets into fours, as shown in Example VII.11.

The 5:3 ratio can be accomplished similarly, using the least common multiple, 15; if eighth notes are desired, then start with three sets of sixteenth-note quintuplets. This can be thought of as 5 against 3 quarter notes or 5 against 6 eighth notes; for the most part, it's easier, somehow, to perform this rhythm by thinking of it as 5 against 3. See Example VII.12.

EXAMPLE VII.9   *Ten quintuplet sixteenth notes in a quarter-note pair*

EXAMPLE VII.10   *Regrouping two sixteenth-note quintuplets into an eighth-note quintuplet*

EXAMPLE VII.11   *Regrouping four sixteenth-note quintuplets into a quarter-note quintuplet*

EXAMPLE VII.12   *Regrouping three sixteenth-note quintuplets into five eighth notes against three quarter notes*

CLASS DRILLS

Perform each of the following rhythms by singing the syllable *ta*.

Groupings of Seven See if you can work out similar strategies involving groups of seven and ratios involving seven. After all, a musician can expect to find divisions of nine, ten, thirteen, or more in the music encountered in today's professional repertoire. We'll begin with groupings of seven, and then proceed to the ratios involving seven.

CLASS DRILLS

Perform each of the following rhythms using the syllable *ta*.

***Reading
Complex Rhythms*** Now let's put it all together and attempt to read some rather complex rhythms. Some formidable mental gymnastics will be called for, but with patience, practice, and understanding, you'll be able to tackle these and most other rhythmic challenges that you encounter during your musical career. Do *not* give up, do *not* say you cannot do it, or that it is *not* important. These are, after all, just ways of saying "I'm afraid," or "I don't want to try," or perhaps worse yet, "I'm afraid of failing." It is true that if you don't try you can't fail; but it is also true that if you don't try, you can't improve.

CLASS DRILLS

Perform each of the following rhythms using the syllable *ta*.

Finally, here are a few two-part rhythmic exercises for practice of all of the preceding concepts, plus ensemble coordination. You will be able to hear cross-rhythms and their resultant composite rhythms when these ratios are performed in two parts. Be aware of this as you perform your part, and do not allow the cross-rhythms to throw you off; instead, listen for the expected composite rhythm as an aid to accurate performance.

CLASS DRILLS

Perform each of the following two-part rhythms in groups of two or more students; it is not important that you be able to perform these rhythms individually (although it would be impressive if you can do so!). Have a third person follow the music and bring to your attention any errors in rhythm or ensemble.

HOME EXERCISES

Locate a copy of the *Fanfare for a New Theater* (*Lincoln Center Fanfare*), which was written for two trumpets by Igor Stravinsky. This piece contains many uncommon divisions of the beat, as well as mixed meter and complex cross-rhythms. The effect, when played correctly, is one of many more trumpets than are actually playing. With another musician, try reading the piece as a rhythmic duet, either singing (which we recommend) or tapping/clapping.

Melodic Constructs

UNIT 77

All-Chromatic Sets

For practice in pure intervallic hearing, nothing beats a **twelve-tone row**! This device consists of a collection of the twelve pitches available from the chromatic scale, ordered by the composer to yield certain predictable results, often in a nontonal context. Perhaps you are familiar with the idea of **twelve-tone music** (a type of **serial music**). But with how many such works are you really acquainted? The sounds of pieces written with serial procedures are as diverse as the composers who write them and the decades from which they come. Compare the Violin Concerto of Alban Berg and the *Requiem Canticles* of Igor Stravinsky with, say, *Le marteau sans maître* of Pierre Boulez and the string quartets of Elliott Carter. An illustration of a twelve-tone row (a serialization of the twelve chromatic steps in an octave) is given in Example VII.13.

As with pitch-class sets, it is not within the purview of this text to delve into such matters. We can, however, use ordered pitch-class

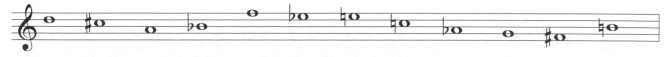

EXAMPLE VII.13 *Row from A. Schoenberg's* Variations for Orchestra

sets containing all twelve tones to practice hearing and performing intervals in a nontonal context—working without a net, so to speak. Some rows will sound as if they have a tonal reference, and others certainly will not. Some rows will exhibit interesting mathematical properties and intervallic relationships; others will exhibit purely melodic characteristics that are compelling in their own right. How *composers* use these tone rows lies solely within their artistic vision, aesthetic, and style. How *we* use them will be as practice for its own sake, to sharpen and test our already considerable skills and, hopefully, to ease the trepidation that many musicians naturally feel when encountering this particular musical language for the first time.

CLASS DRILLS

A. Sing each of the following twelve-tone or ordered pitch-class sets at sight. Use whichever syllable system is most comfortable for you, or the one that your instructor suggests.

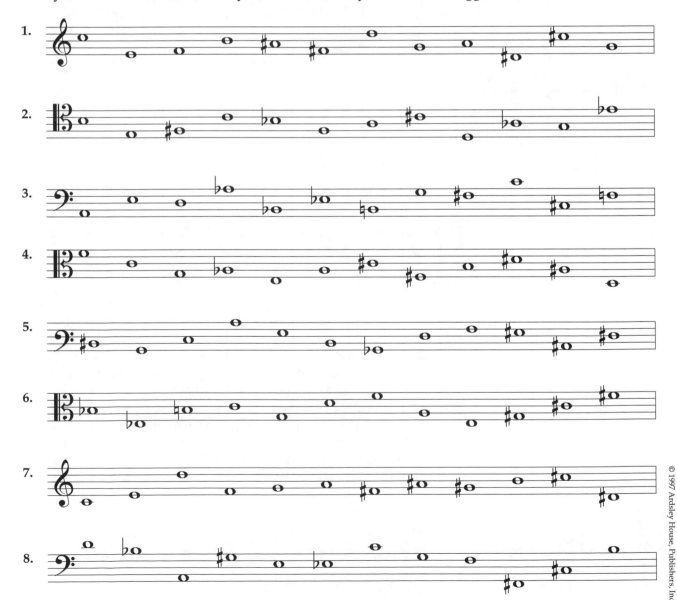

© 1997 Ardsley House, Publishers, Inc.

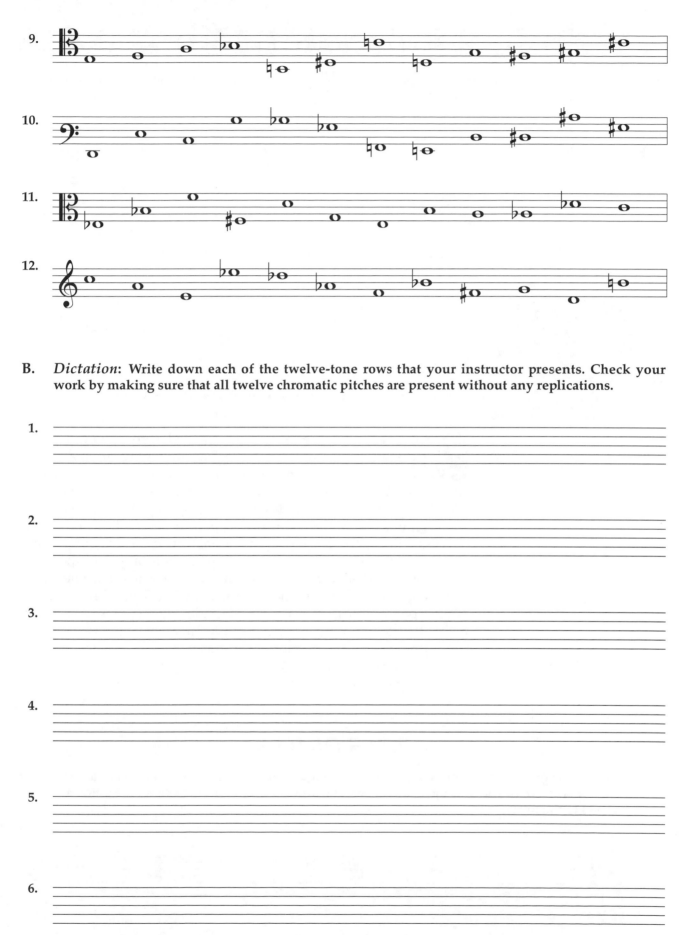

B. *Dictation*: Write down each of the twelve-tone rows that your instructor presents. Check your work by making sure that all twelve chromatic pitches are present without any replications.

1.

2.

3.

4.

5.

6.

HOME EXERCISES

Sing or play the following twelve-tone row, transposed at the perfect 5th below, the major 2nd below, the minor 3rd above, and the minor 7th below (or major 2nd above).

Melody

UNIT 78

Nonfunctional Contexts

*H*ere are a number of advanced melodies for the purposes of sight-singing and dictation. They are highly chromatic, and they may or may not have been composed using serial techniques. They may have a tonal orientation, or they may sound completely atonal. How this music sounds may depend as much upon the listener as upon the composer. In performing each melody, your success will depend largely upon your ability to discern quickly and accurately the intervallic content, although you may find that each piece, once studied, carries its own melodic sense and becomes more "singable" as you become more familiar with it. This is true of much contemporary music. It may seem daunting at first, but with familiarity often comes appreciation. It's unfortunately true that we rarely hear a new piece of contemporary music more than once. So give these your best shot, and find your personal favorites. We hope there will be some!

CLASS DRILLS

A. *Sight-singing*: **Sing the following melodies at sight. Feel free to stop if you make an error, but always start from the beginning again. Repeat the process until you've mastered the piece, and then proceed to the next one.**

S. Tipei

1.

G. Burt

9.

B.   *Dictation*: **Write down the melodies that your instructor plays.**

1.

2.

3.

4.

5.

6.

HOME EXERCISES

Compose a melody using a twelve-tone row, its inversion, its retrograde, and its retrograde inversion. (There are forty-eight notes in all.) Perform the melody on your instrument or at the keyboard until you think you are familiar with it, and then try to sing it. What could you do to increase its singability? Bring the melody to class for others to analyze or perform.

Twelve-Tone Row

Inversion

Retrograde

Retrograde Inversion

APPENDIX

Tables and Exercises in La-based Minor

*W*ithin the movable-*do* solfège system, the use of *la* as the tonic in the minor mode is sometimes preferred. It is particularly convenient when music in the minor mode modulates to the relative major. To accommodate this version of the movable-*do* system, we provide here alternate forms of various tables from Area I as well as exercises from Area I interpreted in *la*-based minor.

THE NATURAL MINOR SCALE

C	D	Eb	F	G	Ab	Bb	C
la	*ti*	*do*	*re*	*mi*	*fa*	*so*	*la*
$\hat{1}$	$\hat{2}$	$\hat{3}$	$\hat{4}$	$\hat{5}$	$\hat{6}$	$\hat{7}$	$\hat{1}$

THE HARMONIC MINOR SCALE

C	D	Eb	F	G	Ab	B	C
la	*ti*	*do*	*re*	*mi*	*fa*	*si*	*la*
$\hat{1}$	$\hat{2}$	$\hat{3}$	$\hat{4}$	$\hat{5}$	$\hat{6}$	$\hat{7}$	$\hat{1}$

THE MELODIC MINOR SCALE

Ascending ———→

C	D	Eb	F	G	A	B	C
la	*ti*	*do*	*re*	*mi*	*fi*	*si*	*la*
$\hat{1}$	$\hat{2}$	$\hat{3}$	$\hat{4}$	$\hat{5}$	$\hat{6}$	$\hat{7}$	$\hat{1}$

←——— *Descending*

C	D	Eb	F	G	Ab	Bb	C
la	*ti*	*do*	*re*	*mi*	*fa*	*so*	*la*
$\hat{1}$	$\hat{2}$	$\hat{3}$	$\hat{4}$	$\hat{5}$	$\hat{6}$	$\hat{7}$	$\hat{1}$

ALTERNATE TABLE I.4 *Three forms of the minor scale in* la-*based minor*

Class Drills and Home Exercises, page 6

11

Major:

fa	*so*	*la*	*ti*
$\hat{4}$	$\hat{5}$	$\hat{6}$	$\hat{7}$

la	*ti*	*do*	*re*
$\hat{6}$	$\hat{7}$	$\hat{1}$	$\hat{2}$

do	*re*	*mi*	*fa*
$\hat{1}$	$\hat{2}$	$\hat{3}$	$\hat{4}$

mi	*fa*	*so*	*la*
$\hat{3}$	$\hat{4}$	$\hat{5}$	$\hat{6}$

ti	*do*	*re*	*mi*
$\hat{7}$	$\hat{1}$	$\hat{2}$	$\hat{3}$

re	*mi*	*fa*	*so*
$\hat{2}$	$\hat{3}$	$\hat{4}$	$\hat{5}$

so	*la*	*ti*	*do*
$\hat{5}$	$\hat{6}$	$\hat{7}$	$\hat{1}$

Minor:

ti	*do*	*re*	*mi*
$\hat{2}$	$\hat{3}$	$\hat{4}$	$\hat{5}$

re	*mi*	*fa*	*si*
$\hat{4}$	$\hat{5}$	$\hat{6}$	$\hat{7}$

si	*la*	*ti*	*do*
$\hat{7}$	$\hat{1}$	$\hat{2}$	$\hat{3}$

mi	*fa*	*si*	*la*
$\hat{5}$	$\hat{6}$	$\hat{7}$	$\hat{1}$

re	*mi*	*fi*	*si*
$\hat{4}$	$\hat{5}$	$\hat{6}$	$\hat{7}$

la	*ti*	*do*	*re*
$\hat{1}$	$\hat{2}$	$\hat{3}$	$\hat{4}$

do	*re*	*mi*	*fa*
$\hat{3}$	$\hat{4}$	$\hat{5}$	$\hat{6}$

so	*la*	*ti*	*do*
$\hat{7}$	$\hat{1}$	$\hat{2}$	$\hat{3}$

mi	*fa*	*so*	*la*
$\hat{5}$	$\hat{6}$	$\hat{7}$	$\hat{1}$

fi	*si*	*la*	*ti*
$\hat{6}$	$\hat{7}$	$\hat{1}$	$\hat{2}$

do	*re*	*mi*	*fi*
$\hat{3}$	$\hat{4}$	$\hat{5}$	$\hat{6}$

fa	*so*	*la*	*ti*
$\hat{6}$	$\hat{7}$	$\hat{1}$	$\hat{2}$

mi	*fi*	*si*	*la*
$\hat{5}$	$\hat{6}$	$\hat{7}$	$\hat{1}$

re	*mi*	*fa*	*so*
$\hat{4}$	$\hat{5}$	$\hat{6}$	$\hat{7}$

fa	*si*	*la*	*ti*
$\hat{6}$	$\hat{7}$	$\hat{1}$	$\hat{2}$

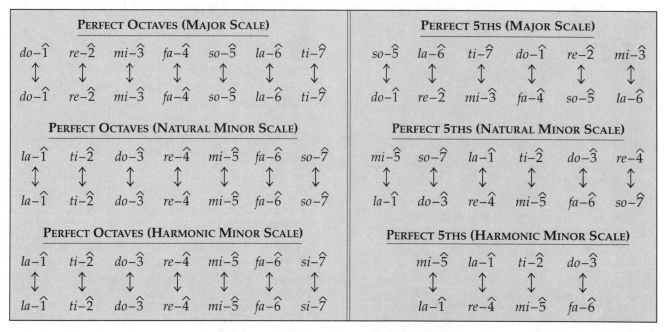

ALTERNATE TABLE I.9 *Diatonic locations of perfect octaves and perfect fifths using la-based minor, where appropriate. Double-headed arrows are placed between the syllables of each interval to indicate that the interval is of identical size and quality, regardless of the direction sung.*

Class Drills and Home Exercises, page 11

ALTERNATE TABLE I.10 *Some interval inversions using la-based minor, where appropriate*

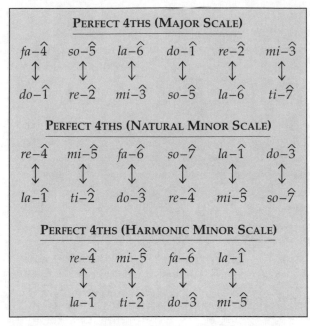

PERFECT 4THS (MAJOR SCALE)

fa–$\hat{4}$ so–$\hat{5}$ la–$\hat{6}$ do–$\hat{1}$ re–$\hat{2}$ mi–$\hat{3}$
↕   ↕   ↕   ↕   ↕   ↕
do–$\hat{1}$ re–$\hat{2}$ mi–$\hat{3}$ so–$\hat{5}$ la–$\hat{6}$ ti–$\hat{7}$

PERFECT 4THS (NATURAL MINOR SCALE)

re–$\hat{4}$ mi–$\hat{5}$ fa–$\hat{6}$ so–$\hat{7}$ la–$\hat{1}$ do–$\hat{3}$
↕   ↕   ↕   ↕   ↕   ↕
la–$\hat{1}$ ti–$\hat{2}$ do–$\hat{3}$ re–$\hat{4}$ mi–$\hat{5}$ so–$\hat{7}$

PERFECT 4THS (HARMONIC MINOR SCALE)

re–$\hat{4}$ mi–$\hat{5}$ fa–$\hat{6}$ la–$\hat{1}$
↕   ↕   ↕   ↕
la–$\hat{1}$ ti–$\hat{2}$ do–$\hat{3}$ mi–$\hat{5}$

ALTERNATE TABLE I.11 *Diatonic locations of perfect fourths using la-based minor, where appropriate*

Class Drills and Home Exercises, page 16

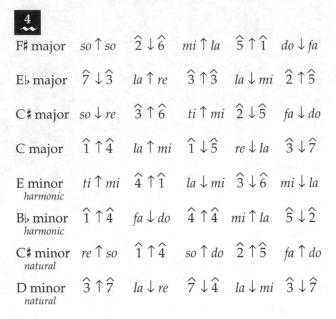

4

F♯ major	so↑so	$\hat{2}$↓$\hat{6}$	mi↑la	$\hat{5}$↑$\hat{1}$	do↓fa
Eb major	$\hat{7}$↓$\hat{3}$	la↑re	$\hat{3}$↑$\hat{3}$	la↓mi	$\hat{2}$↑$\hat{5}$
C♯ major	so↓re	$\hat{3}$↑$\hat{6}$	ti↑mi	$\hat{2}$↓$\hat{5}$	fa↓do
C major	$\hat{1}$↑$\hat{4}$	la↑mi	$\hat{1}$↓$\hat{5}$	re↓la	$\hat{3}$↓$\hat{7}$
E minor *harmonic*	ti↑mi	$\hat{4}$↑$\hat{1}$	la↓mi	$\hat{3}$↓$\hat{6}$	mi↓la
Bb minor *harmonic*	$\hat{1}$↑$\hat{4}$	fa↓do	$\hat{4}$↑$\hat{4}$	mi↑la	$\hat{5}$↓$\hat{2}$
C♯ minor *natural*	re↑so	$\hat{1}$↑$\hat{4}$	so↑do	$\hat{2}$↑$\hat{5}$	fa↑do
D minor *natural*	$\hat{3}$↑$\hat{7}$	la↓re	$\hat{7}$↓$\hat{4}$	la↓mi	$\hat{3}$↓$\hat{7}$

MAJOR 3RDS (MAJOR SCALE)

mi–$\hat{3}$ la–$\hat{6}$ ti–$\hat{7}$
↕   ↕   ↕
do–$\hat{1}$ fa–$\hat{4}$ so–$\hat{5}$

MAJOR 3RDS (NATURAL MINOR SCALE)

mi–$\hat{5}$ la–$\hat{1}$ ti–$\hat{2}$
↕   ↕   ↕
do–$\hat{3}$ fa–$\hat{6}$ so–$\hat{7}$

MAJOR 3RDS (HARMONIC MINOR SCALE)

mi–$\hat{5}$ si–$\hat{7}$ la–$\hat{1}$
↕   ↕   ↕
do–$\hat{3}$ mi–$\hat{5}$ fa–$\hat{6}$

MINOR 6THS (MAJOR SCALE)

do–$\hat{1}$ fa–$\hat{4}$ so–$\hat{5}$
↕   ↕   ↕
mi–$\hat{3}$ la–$\hat{6}$ ti–$\hat{7}$

MINOR 6THS (NATURAL MINOR SCALE)

fa–$\hat{6}$ so–$\hat{7}$ do–$\hat{3}$
↕   ↕   ↕
la–$\hat{1}$ ti–$\hat{2}$ mi–$\hat{5}$

MINOR 6THS (HARMONIC MINOR SCALE)

fa–$\hat{6}$ do–$\hat{3}$ mi–$\hat{5}$
↕   ↕   ↕
la–$\hat{1}$ mi–$\hat{5}$ si–$\hat{7}$

ALTERNATE TABLE I.14 *Diatonic locations of major thirds and minor sixths using la-based minor, where appropriate*

Class Drills and Home Exercises, page 28

5

E major	so ↑ re	6̂ ↓ 4̂	mi ↑ do	4̂ ↓ 1̂	la ↑ fa
A♭ major	3̂ ↓ 1̂	ti ↑ so	2̂ ↑ 5̂	ti ↓ ti	5̂ ↑ 7̂
B major	do ↑ mi	6̂ ↑ 4̂	la ↑ re	4̂ ↑ 6̂	ti ↑ so
D major	1̂ ↓ 3̂	la ↓ la	4̂ ↓ 6̂	ti ↓ so	3̂ ↑ 6̂
A♭ minor *harmonic*	mi ↑ la	5̂ ↓ 7̂	la ↓ fa	3̂ ↓ 5̂	fa ↓ la
E♭ minor *harmonic*	1̂ ↑ 6̂	si ↑ mi	4̂ ↑ 1̂	fa ↑ la	7̂ ↓ 5̂
A minor *natural*	mi ↑ do	2̂ ↑ 7̂	fa ↓ la	4̂ ↓ 7̂	so ↑ ti
F minor *natural*	5̂ ↓ 3̂	fa ↑ la	7̂ ↓ 2̂	so ↓ do	2̂ ↓ 7̂

6

Minor	mi	↓do	↑fa	↑la	↓mi	↓la	
Minor	so	↑ti	↑so	↓do	↑fa	↓mi	↓la
Major	fa	↓do	↑mi	↑do	↓so	↓ti	↑do
Major	so	↑ti	↓mi	↑la	↓fa	↓la	↑re
Minor	mi	↓si	↑la	↓mi	↑do	↑mi	↓la
Major	do	↑fa	↓la	↑re	↑so	↓ti	↑do

MINOR 3RDS (MAJOR SCALE)				MAJOR 6THS (MAJOR SCALE)			
fa–4̂	so–5̂	do–1̂	re–2̂	la–6̂	ti–7̂	re–2̂	mi–3̂
↕	↕	↕	↕	↕	↕	↕	↕
re–2̂	mi–3̂	la–6̂	ti–7̂	do–1̂	re–2̂	fa–4̂	so–5̂

MINOR 3RDS (NATURAL MINOR SCALE)				MAJOR 6THS (NATURAL MINOR SCALE)			
do–3̂	re–4̂	fa–6̂	so–7̂	la–1̂	ti–2̂	re–4̂	mi–5̂
↕	↕	↕	↕	↕	↕	↕	↕
la–1̂	ti–2̂	re–4̂	mi–5̂	do–3̂	re–4̂	fa–6̂	so–7̂

MINOR 3RDS (HARMONIC MINOR SCALE)				MAJOR 6THS (HARMONIC MINOR SCALE)			
do–3̂	re–4̂	fa–6̂	ti–2̂	si–7̂	la–1̂	ti–2̂	re–4̂
↕	↕	↕	↕	↕	↕	↕	↕
la–1̂	ti–2̂	re–4̂	si–7̂	ti–2̂	do–3̂	re–4̂	fa–6̂

ALTERNATE TABLE I.16 *Diatonic locations of minor thirds and major sixths using la-based minor, where appropriate*

Class Drills and Home Exercises, page 35

8

F major	re ↑ fa	3̂ ↓ 5̂	mi ↑ so	3̂ ↓ 7̂	do ↑ la
Db major	6̂ ↑ 1̂	ti ↑ re	4̂ ↑ 2̂	so ↑ mi	7̂ ↓ 2̂
A major	re ↑ ti	4̂ ↓ 2̂	so ↑ mi	1̂ ↓ 6̂	re ↓ fa
G major	6̂ ↓ 1̂	fa ↓ re	2̂ ↑ 7̂	re ↓ fa	5̂ ↓ 3̂
C minor *harmonic*	2̂ ↓ 7̂	do ↓ la	2̂ ↑ 7̂	ti ↓ re	6̂ ↓ 4̂
B minor *harmonic*	re ↑ fa	7̂ ↓ 2̂	la ↓ do	2̂ ↑ 4̂	si ↑ ti
F# minor *natural*	5̂ ↑ 7̂	re ↑ ti	1̂ ↑ 3̂	mi ↓ so	4̂ ↓ 6̂
G minor *natural*	fa ↑ re	7̂ ↑ 5̂	re ↓ ti	3̂ ↑ 1̂	so ↓ mi

16

Major	do	↓la	↑re	↓do	↓so	↓mi ↓do
Major	la	↓fa	↓re	↑ti	↑do	↓fa ↓do
Minor	la	↑do	↑la	↓mi	↑ti	↓so ↑la
Minor	do	↓la	↑re	↑ti	↓la	↓do ↓la
Major	la	↓do	↑fa	↓la	↑ti	↑do
Minor	la	↓re	↑fa	↑re	↓ti	↓so ↑la

MAJOR 2NDS (MAJOR SCALE)

re–2̂	mi–3̂	so–5̂	la–6̂	ti–7̂
↕	↕	↕	↕	↕
do–1̂	re–2̂	fa–4̂	so–5̂	la–6̂

MINOR 7THS (MAJOR SCALE)

do–1̂	re–2̂	fa–4̂	so–5̂	la–6̂
↕	↕	↕	↕	↕
re–2̂	mi–3̂	so–5̂	la–6̂	ti–7̂

MAJOR 2NDS (NATURAL MINOR SCALE)

ti–2̂	re–4̂	mi–5̂	so–7̂	la–1̂
↕	↕	↕	↕	↕
la–1̂	do–3̂	re–4̂	fa–6̂	so–7̂

MINOR 7THS (NATURAL MINOR SCALE)

so–7̂	la–1̂	do–3̂	re–4̂	fa–6̂
↕	↕	↕	↕	↕
la–1̂	ti–2̂	re–4̂	mi–5̂	so–7̂

MAJOR 2NDS (HARMONIC MINOR SCALE)

ti–2̂	re–4̂	mi–5̂
↕	↕	↕
la–1̂	do–3̂	re–4̂

MINOR 7THS (HARMONIC MINOR SCALE)

la–1̂	do–3̂	re–4̂
↕	↕	↕
ti–2̂	re–4̂	mi–5̂

ALTERNATE TABLE I.17   *Diatonic locations of major seconds and minor sevenths using* la-*based minor, where appropriate*

Class Drills and Home Exercises, page 42

8

F♯ major	*la* ↑ *ti*	$\hat{5}$ ↓ $\hat{4}$	*do* ↓ *re*	$\hat{6}$ ↓ $\hat{7}$	*mi* ↑ *re*
E♭ major	$\hat{7}$ ↓ $\hat{6}$	*re* ↑ *do*	$\hat{4}$ ↓ $\hat{5}$	*re* ↑ *mi*	$\hat{6}$ ↓ $\hat{5}$
C♯ major	*so* ↓ *la*	$\hat{7}$ ↑ $\hat{6}$	*so* ↑ *la*	$\hat{1}$ ↑ $\hat{2}$	*re* ↓ *mi*
C major	$\hat{2}$ ↓ $\hat{1}$	*so* ↑ *fa*	$\hat{6}$ ↑ $\hat{5}$	*re* ↑ *mi*	$\hat{4}$ ↑ $\hat{5}$
E minor *harmonic*	*la* ↓ *ti*	$\hat{4}$ ↓ $\hat{3}$	*mi* ↑ *re*	$\hat{2}$ ↑ $\hat{1}$	*do* ↓ *re*
B♭ minor *harmonic*	$\hat{4}$ ↑ $\hat{5}$	*re* ↑ *do*	$\hat{2}$ ↓ $\hat{1}$	*re* ↓ *mi*	*do* ↑ *re*
C♯ minor *natural*	*fa* ↑ *so*	$\hat{2}$ ↑ $\hat{1}$	*so* ↑ *fa*	$\hat{7}$ ↓ $\hat{1}$	*mi* ↑ *re*
D minor *natural*	$\hat{1}$ ↑ $\hat{7}$	*fa* ↓ *so*	$\hat{3}$ ↓ $\hat{4}$	*la* ↓ *so*	$\hat{4}$ ↓ $\hat{3}$

16

Minor	*la*	↑*so*	↓*fa*	↓*do*	↑*mi*	↓*so* ↑*la*
Major	*do*	↓*re*	↑*mi*	↓*so*	↑*re*	↓*la* ↑*do*
Major	*do*	↓*so*	↑*fa*	↓*mi*	↓*la*	↑*re* ↓*do*
Minor	*re*	↑*do*	↓*ti*	↓*so*	↓*fa*	↓*re* ↑*mi*
Major	*fa*	↓*mi*	↑*re*	↑*mi*	↑*fa*	↓*so* ↑*do*
Minor	*mi*	↑*do*	↑*re*	↑*fa*	↓*so*	↑*do* ↓*la*

MINOR 2NDS (MAJOR SCALE)		MAJOR 7THS (MAJOR SCALE)	
fa–$\hat{4}$ ↕ *mi*–$\hat{3}$	*do*–$\hat{1}$ ↕ *ti*–$\hat{7}$	*ti*–$\hat{7}$ ↕ *do*–$\hat{1}$	*mi*–$\hat{3}$ ↕ *fa*–$\hat{4}$
MINOR 2NDS (NATURAL MINOR SCALE)		**MAJOR 7THS (NATURAL MINOR SCALE)**	
do–$\hat{3}$ ↕ *ti*–$\hat{2}$	*fa*–$\hat{6}$ ↕ *mi*–$\hat{5}$	*ti*–$\hat{2}$ ↕ *do*–$\hat{3}$	*mi*–$\hat{5}$ ↕ *fa*–$\hat{6}$
MINOR 2NDS (HARMONIC MINOR SCALE)		**MAJOR 7THS (HARMONIC MINOR SCALE)**	
do–$\hat{3}$ ↕ *ti*–$\hat{2}$	*fa*–$\hat{6}$ ↕ *mi*–$\hat{5}$ *la*–$\hat{1}$ ↕ *si*–$\hat{7}$	*si*–$\hat{7}$ ↕ *la*–$\hat{1}$ *ti*–$\hat{2}$ ↕ *do*–$\hat{3}$	*mi*–$\hat{5}$ ↕ *fa*–$\hat{6}$

ALTERNATE TABLE I.18
Diatonic locations of minor seconds and major sevenths using la-based minor, where appropriate

Class Drills and Home Exercises, page 51

8 ∿

E major	mi↓fa	$\hat{7}$↑$\hat{1}$	mi↑fa	$\hat{4}$↑$\hat{3}$	do↑ti
A♭ major	$\hat{7}$↓$\hat{1}$	fa↑mi	$\hat{4}$↓$\hat{3}$	do↑ti	$\hat{1}$↓$\hat{7}$
B major	fa↓mi	$\hat{7}$↓$\hat{1}$	ti↑do	$\hat{3}$↓$\hat{4}$	do↑ti
D major	$\hat{3}$↓$\hat{4}$	mi↑fa	$\hat{1}$↑$\hat{7}$	fa↑mi	$\hat{7}$↓$\hat{1}$
A♭ minor *harmonic*	si↓la	$\hat{5}$↑$\hat{6}$	ti↓do	$\hat{5}$↓$\hat{6}$	do↓ti
E♭ minor *harmonic*	$\hat{6}$↑$\hat{5}$	la↓si	$\hat{3}$↑$\hat{2}$	la↑si	mi↑fa
A minor *natural*	mi↓fa	$\hat{3}$↑$\hat{2}$	fa↑mi	$\hat{3}$↓$\hat{2}$	ti↓do
F minor *natural*	$\hat{6}$↓$\hat{5}$	do↑ti	$\hat{7}$↑$\hat{1}$	mi↓fa	$\hat{3}$↓$\hat{2}$

16 ∿

Minor	ti	↑re	↑mi	↓fa	↓mi	↑re	↓do
Minor	mi	↑ti	↓do	↑fa	↓so	↑so	↑la
Major	la	↓fa	↑mi	↑fa	↑re	↓so	↓do
Major	ti	↑re	↓do	↑fa	↓mi	↓fa	↑so
Minor	mi	↓si	↑la	↑ti	↓do	↑fa	↓mi
Major	mi	↑la	↓do	↑ti	↓so	↑re	↓do

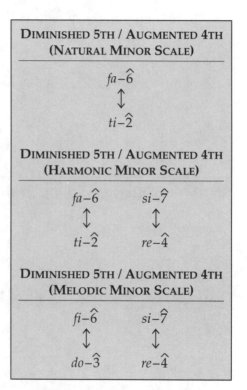

> **DIMINISHED 5TH / AUGMENTED 4TH**
> **(NATURAL MINOR SCALE)**
>
> fa–$\hat{6}$
> ↕
> ti–$\hat{2}$
>
> **DIMINISHED 5TH / AUGMENTED 4TH**
> **(HARMONIC MINOR SCALE)**
>
> fa–$\hat{6}$ si–$\hat{7}$
> ↕   ↕
> ti–$\hat{2}$ re–$\hat{4}$
>
> **DIMINISHED 5TH / AUGMENTED 4TH**
> **(MELODIC MINOR SCALE)**
>
> fi–$\hat{6}$ si–$\hat{7}$
> ↕   ↕
> do–$\hat{3}$ re–$\hat{4}$

> **DIMINISHED 4TH / AUGMENTED 5TH**
> **(MAJOR SCALE)**
>
> ti–$\hat{7}$
> ↕
> fa–$\hat{4}$

ALTERNATE TABLE I.19 *Diatonic location of the diminished fourth and augmented fifth: major scale*

ALTERNATE TABLE I.20 *Diatonic locations of diminished fifths and augmented fourths: minor scale using* la-*based minor*

> **DIMINISHED 7TH**
> **(HARMONIC MINOR SCALE)**
>
> fa–$\hat{6}$
> ↕
> si–$\hat{7}$

ALTERNATE TABLE I.21 *Diatonic location of the diminished seventh using* la-*based minor*

> **AUGMENTED 2ND**
> **(HARMONIC MINOR SCALE)**
>
> si–$\hat{7}$
> ↕
> fa–$\hat{6}$

ALTERNATE TABLE I.22 *Diatonic location of the augmented second using* la-*based minor*

Class Drills and Home Exercises, page 60

[8]

F major	mi↑do	6̂↑4̂	mi↓la	7̂↓4̂	la↓do
D♭ major	7̂↑4̂	ti↓la	3̂↓5̂	fa↑mi	2̂↑7̂
A major	re↓ti	5̂↓3̂	re↓fa	1̂↓6̂	fa↓ti
G major	2̂↓3̂	fa↑ti	4̂↓6̂	ti↑so	6̂↓2̂
C minor *harmonic*	ti↑fa	7̂↑6̂	re↓fa	7̂↑4̂	fa↑si
B minor *harmonic*	7̂↑6̂	re↓si	6̂↓2̂	fa↓si	7̂↓6̂
F♯ minor *natural*	ti↑fa	3̂↑2̂	ti↓fa	7̂↑5̂	fa↓do
G minor *natural*	6̂↓2̂	la↓do	7̂↓4̂	6̂↑2̂	mi↑re

[22]

Major	do	↓ti	↓fa	↓mi	↑la	↓so	↓do
Major	mi	↑fa	↑ti	↑do	↓so	↓ti	↑fa ↓mi
Minor	mi	↑fa	↓si	↑la	↑mi	↑si	↑ti ↓la
Minor	la	↑ti	↑re	↓do	↑mi	↑fa	↑si ↑la
Minor	ti	↓si	↓fa	↓mi	↑re	↓do	↓la
Minor	do	↓do	↑ti	↓mi	↑fa	↓si	↑la

Class Drills and Home Exercises, page 78

Major Keys				
1. Higher pitch: la	2̂	do	4̂	re
Lower pitch: la	7̂	mi	7̂	la
Dictation 1: _____	_____	_____	_____	_____
Dictation 2: _____	_____	_____	_____	_____
Dictation 3: _____	_____	_____	_____	_____
2. Higher pitch: 5̂	do	7̂	fa	1̂
Lower pitch: 4̂	re	3̂	ti	6̂
Dictation 1: _____	_____	_____	_____	_____
Dictation 2: _____	_____	_____	_____	_____
Dictation 3: _____	_____	_____	_____	_____
3. Higher pitch: so	6̂	fa	3̂	so
Lower pitch: ti	1̂	re	3̂	la
Dictation 1: _____	_____	_____	_____	_____
Dictation 2: _____	_____	_____	_____	_____
Dictation 3: _____	_____	_____	_____	_____

4. Higher pitch: $\hat{6}$ re $\hat{7}$ mi $\hat{6}$
    Lower pitch: $\hat{7}$ so $\hat{1}$ re $\hat{4}$

Dictation 1: _____ _____ _____ _____ _____

Dictation 2: _____ _____ _____ _____ _____

Dictation 3: _____ _____ _____ _____ _____

5. Higher pitch: ti $\hat{3}$ re $\hat{3}$ do
    Lower pitch: re $\hat{5}$ fa $\hat{6}$ ti

Dictation 1: _____ _____ _____ _____ _____

Dictation 2: _____ _____ _____ _____ _____

Dictation 3: _____ _____ _____ _____ _____

6. Higher pitch: $\hat{7}$ la $\hat{5}$ fa $\hat{2}$
    Lower pitch: $\hat{4}$ mi $\hat{1}$ la $\hat{3}$

Dictation 1: _____ _____ _____ _____ _____

Dictation 2: _____ _____ _____ _____ _____

Dictation 3: _____ _____ _____ _____ _____

7. Higher pitch: fa $\hat{7}$ do $\hat{3}$ ti
    Lower pitch: do $\hat{6}$ so $\hat{4}$ so

Dictation 1: _____ _____ _____ _____ _____

Dictation 2: _____ _____ _____ _____ _____

Dictation 3: _____ _____ _____ _____ _____

Natural Minor Keys

8. Higher pitch: ti   fa   ti   do   so
    Lower pitch: so   la   mi   la   re

Dictation 1: _____ _____ _____ _____ _____

Dictation 2: _____ _____ _____ _____ _____

Dictation 3: _____ _____ _____ _____ _____

9. Higher pitch: $\hat{5}$ $\hat{4}$ do   fa   so
    Lower pitch: $\hat{2}$ $\hat{7}$ re   fa   la

Dictation 1: _____ _____ _____ _____ _____

Dictation 2: _____ _____ _____ _____ _____

Dictation 3: _____ _____ _____ _____ _____

10. Higher pitch: *re*   *la*   *so* $\hat{5}$ $\hat{4}$

Lower pitch: *fa*   *mi*   *do* $\hat{6}$ $\hat{1}$

Dictation 1:   _____   _____   _____   _____

Dictation 2:   _____   _____   _____   _____

Dictation 3:   _____   _____   _____   _____

11. Higher pitch: $\hat{1}$ *fa* $\hat{1}$ *do* $\hat{2}$

Lower pitch: $\hat{4}$ *so* $\hat{6}$ *do* $\hat{4}$

Dictation 1:   _____   _____   _____   _____

Dictation 2:   _____   _____   _____   _____

Dictation 3:   _____   _____   _____   _____

12. Higher pitch: *so* $\hat{2}$ *do* $\hat{6}$ *mi*

Lower pitch: *ti* $\hat{3}$ *fa* $\hat{5}$ *do*

Dictation 1:   _____   _____   _____   _____

Dictation 2:   _____   _____   _____   _____

Dictation 3:   _____   _____   _____   _____

13. Higher pitch: $\hat{6}$ *mi* $\hat{4}$ *fa* $\hat{3}$

Lower pitch: $\hat{3}$ *so* $\hat{4}$ *ti* $\hat{7}$

Dictation 1:   _____   _____   _____   _____

Dictation 2:   _____   _____   _____   _____

Dictation 3:   _____   _____   _____   _____

14. Higher pitch: *mi* $\hat{6}$ *la* $\hat{3}$ *so*

Lower pitch: *la* $\hat{4}$ *do* $\hat{5}$ *fa*

Dictation 1:   _____   _____   _____   _____

Dictation 2:   _____   _____   _____   _____

Dictation 3:   _____   _____   _____   _____

Harmonic Minor Keys

15. Higher pitch: $\hat{1}$ *ti* $\hat{6}$ *la* $\hat{4}$

Lower pitch: $\hat{4}$ *do* $\hat{7}$ *mi* $\hat{6}$

Dictation 1:   _____   _____   _____   _____

Dictation 2:   _____   _____   _____   _____

Dictation 3:   _____   _____   _____   _____

16. Higher pitch: *do* $\hat{5}$ *do* $\hat{1}$ *si*

      Lower pitch: *la* $\hat{2}$ *re* $\hat{6}$ *mi*

Dictation 1: _____ _____ _____ _____ _____

Dictation 2: _____ _____ _____ _____ _____

Dictation 3: _____ _____ _____ _____ _____

17. Higher pitch: $\hat{4}$ *do* $\hat{7}$ *ti* $\hat{6}$

      Lower pitch: $\hat{5}$ *fa* $\hat{1}$ *fa* $\hat{3}$

Dictation 1: _____ _____ _____ _____ _____

Dictation 2: _____ _____ _____ _____ _____

Dictation 3: _____ _____ _____ _____ _____

18. Higher pitch: *re* $\hat{2}$ *fa* $\hat{7}$ *do*

      Lower pitch: *do* $\hat{5}$ *la* $\hat{7}$ *ti*

Dictation 1: _____ _____ _____ _____ _____

Dictation 2: _____ _____ _____ _____ _____

Dictation 3: _____ _____ _____ _____ _____

19. Higher pitch: *la* $\hat{7}$ *fa* $\hat{4}$ *la*

      Lower pitch: *ti* $\hat{6}$ *re* $\hat{7}$ *do*

Dictation 1: _____ _____ _____ _____ _____

Dictation 2: _____ _____ _____ _____ _____

Dictation 3: _____ _____ _____ _____ _____

20. Higher pitch: $\hat{5}$ *si* $\hat{3}$ *fa* $\hat{1}$

      Lower pitch: $\hat{6}$ *re* $\hat{5}$ *ti* $\hat{7}$

Dictation 1: _____ _____ _____ _____ _____

Dictation 2: _____ _____ _____ _____ _____

Dictation 3: _____ _____ _____ _____ _____

Glossary

Although several terms in this glossary have multiple meanings, only those senses that are intended in the text are defined here.

ABRUPT MODULATION. A swift and complete shift in tonal center with little or no preparation or intimation that such a shift is about to occur.

AEOLIAN MODE. One of the so-called theoretical modes, corresponding to the intervals of the natural minor scale.

AGOGIC ACCENT. An accent whose stress is derived solely from the longer duration of a given note relative to those surrounding it.

AIR DICTATION. A harmonic dictation in which the bass line alone is played; the student must then propose a reasonable harmonic progression that is suggested by the bass line, as if "plucking the chords from the air."

ALTERED CHORD. A chord that contains one or more nondiatonic notes, that does not have a secondary function in the given context, and is not modally borrowed. *See* ALTERED DOMINANT, AUGMENTED SIXTH CHORD, NEAPOLITAN SIXTH CHORD.

ALTERED DOMINANT. A dominant chord in which $\hat{2}$ is chromatically altered by a half step either up or down.

ALTO CLEF. The C-clef that locates middle C on the middle line of the staff.

ANTECEDENT AND CONSEQUENT PHRASES. A pair of musical phrases that are related by similar or complementary rhythmic patterns, melodic structure, and/or harmonic implications. The musical statement made in the first phrase, the *antecedent*, is given a response or reaction in the second phrase, the *consequent*. Together, the antecedent and consequent form a completed musical idea, known as a **PERIOD**, which is always punctuated with an authentic cadence on a stable harmony.

ANTICIPATION. A nonchord tone, usually unstressed, that becomes a chord tone when it is carried over into the harmony that immediately follows.

APPOGGIATURA. A nonchord tone that is approached by leap, generally from below, and that usually resolves by step in the opposite direction.

ARPEGGIATE. To sound the members of a chord in succession, in ascending or descending order, rather than together.

ARPEGGIO. A chord whose members are sounded successively, in ascending or descending order.

ARTIFICIAL SCALE. A scale that differs from the more commonly used scales and modes, particularly one comprising other than seven or twelve notes. It is often contrived by a composer for particular effects, styles, or aesthetics.

ASYMMETRIC METER. Any meter in which the number of beats per measure is a prime number greater than 3.

AUGENMUSIK. Literally, *eye music*. Music notated in such a way as to have appeal or meaning as much for the eye as for the ear.

AUGMENTATION. The restatement of a musical passage using proportionately longer note values.

AUGMENTED INTERVAL. Any interval spanning the same number of scale degrees as a given major or perfect interval, but larger by a half step.

AUGMENTED SIXTH CHORD. An altered chord that exhibits a strong pre-dominant function resulting from the characteristic interval of an augmented 6th found in each of four principal versions. In addition to the augmented 6th formed between $\flat\hat{6}$, always in the bass, and $\sharp\hat{4}$ above it (each resolving to $\hat{5}$, at least an octave apart), each augmented 6th chord incorporates $\hat{1}$, the tonic, which produces a major 3rd above the bass. The root of the ITALIAN SIXTH is $\sharp\hat{4}$, so the harmonic analysis of the chord is iv^{+6}. The GERMAN SIXTH also has the root of $\sharp\hat{4}$, together with an added perfect 5th ($\flat\hat{3}$) above the bass; the German 6th is expressed as iv$^{+6}_5$. The root of the FRENCH SIXTH is $\hat{2}$, which forms an augmented 4th above the bass; the French 6th is expressed as ii$^{+6}_{\;4}$. The root of the DOUBLY AUGMENTED FOURTH is $\hat{2}$, which forms a doubly augmented 4th above the bass; it is therefore expressed as ii$^{+6}_{+4}$.

AUGMENTED TRIAD. *See* TRIAD.

AUTHENTIC CADENCE. A cadence in which the tonic is preceded by its dominant.

AUXILIARY TONE. A nonchord tone that results from stepping away from a chord member before returning by step to the same chord member. Also termed a **NEIGHBOR NOTE**.

BARITONE CLEF. An F-clef that locates the F below middle C on the third line of the staff. A C-clef version that is rarely used locates middle C on the top line of the staff.

BAROQUE. The period in Western music history from approximately 1600 to 1750.

BASS. The lowest sounding member of a chord.

BASS CLEF. An F-clef in which the F below middle C is located on the second line from the top of the staff.

BASS LINE. The lowest sounding horizontal voice, formed by a succession of harmonies.

BEAMED GROUPING. A group of notes (eighth notes or shorter values) whose stems are connected to the same beam for the purpose of organizing the notes into rhythmic cells within a given measure.

BEAT. The principal temporal unit into which a measure is equally divided.

BORROWED. *See* MODAL BORROWING.

BREAK FOR CADENCE. An interruption, or the cessation, of a musical process to effect a cadence.

CADENCE. A musical formula employed to create a sense of closure at the end of a phrase, period, section, or an entire composition.

CADENZA. An elaboration of a cadence in a concerto, inserted to display the skill and virtuosity of a soloist.

CANCRIZANS. Literally, *crablike*. The retrograde inversion of a given subject.

CANON. A contrapuntal device in which a musical line introduced in one voice is restated in one or more different voices according to an established principle or procedure.

CATCH. An English round, usually for three or more unaccompanied voices and usually employing hocket.

C-CLEF. A clef that locates middle C on the staff.

CELL. A small amount of harmonic, rhythmic, or melodic material used to create order and structure in a composition.

CHANGE OF BASS. A movement of the lowest sounding voice (generally to a consonance) that is concurrent with the resolution of a suspension.

CHORD. Three or more tones sounding together—usually a tertiary sonority in which each successive member of the sonority is related to another by a major or minor 3rd.

CHORD PROGRESSION. A succession of harmonies.

CHROMATICISM. The use of nondiatonic pitches for melodic and harmonic purposes.

CHROMATIC MODULATION. A modulation effected through a chord that is chromatically altered in either the initial key or the new key (or both).

CHROMATIC SCALE. A twelve-note scale consisting of equal divisions of an octave. It consists of a series of successive half steps lying within the span of an octave.

CHURCH MODE. *See* ECCLESIASTICAL MODES.

CIRCLE OF FIFTHS. The succession of keys whose roots are related by ascending or descending perfect 5ths.

CIRCULAR PROGRESSION. A harmonic progression that begins and ends on the same chord, usually the tonic.

CLEF. A sign placed at the left end of a staff that indicates the specific pitches and register to be represented by the lines and spaces.

CLOSED PROGRESSION. A harmonic progression that begins with a chord other than the tonic but ends on the tonic. Most cadences are forms of closed progressions.

CLOSELY RELATED KEYS. Keys whose signatures differ by at most one sharp or flat or whose tonic chords are diatonic with respect to the same key. Two keys that are the relative major or relative minor of one another are examples of closely related keys.

CLOSURE. The conclusion, finishing, or ending of a phrase, period, section, or movement with a cadence on a stable harmony.

COLOR. The quality of a chord, determined by the disposition of major and minor 3rds among its members.

COMES. Literally, *follower*. Voices that imitate the musical statements of earlier voices, particularly in a canon or other imitative work.

COMMON CHORD. A chord that exists diatonically in two or more keys.

COMMON-CHORD MODULATION. Modulation that relies on the existence of at least one chord common to both keys. Pivot chords are often used in common-chord modulation.

COMMON-PRACTICE PERIOD. The period of music history from approximately 1600 to 1900.

COMMON TONE. A note that is found in two adjacent chords.

COMMON-TONE MODULATION. A modulation that exploits the way a single tone functions in two different keys. For example, the given tone might function in the first key as $\hat{3}$ and in the new key as $\hat{1}$. A common-tone modulation occurs when the common tone is used in the context of the first key and is then immediately presented with its new function in the context of the second.

COMPOSITE RHYTHM. The rhythm projected by the combined attacks of two or more rhythms sounding simultaneously.

COMPOUND INTERVAL. An interval larger than an octave.

COMPOUND METER. A meter whose time signature has a numerator that is divisible by 3.

CONCERT PITCH. The pitch that results when a given written note is sounded. For transposing instruments, the sounding and written notes are different.

CONSEQUENT. *See* ANTECEDENT AND CONSEQUENT PHRASES.

CONSONANT. A characterization of sounds that are heard as stable and that need no further resolution.

CONSTRUCTIVISM. A compositional practice whose name is borrowed from a fine-art movement that began in the 1920s. Constructivism is characterized as abstract music composed from nonexpressive and geometric or quasi-mathematical elements.

CONTINUO PLAYERS. Musicians who perform from figured bass parts. Depending on the style of music in question, figured bass parts are assigned to various combinations of instruments that reinforce the bass line (cello, viola da gamba, bass viol, bassoon, trombone), that provide the harmonies specified by the figures (organ, harpsichord, lute, theorbo), and that embellish the texture (lute, theorbo, harp, chitarrone, spinet, pandora).

CONTRAPUNTAL. Characterized by counterpoint.

COUNTERPOINT. The combining of two or more distinct melodic lines and the resulting vertical and horizontal interactions when they sound together.

CRAB CANON. A canon in which one voice imitates the other in retrograde inversion.

CROSS-ACCENT. Notated accents that are at variance with the natural pattern of beats specified by the given meter.

CROSS-RELATION. The simultaneous or successive use of a note together with a chromatic variant of that note.

CROSS-RHYTHMS. The simultaneous sounding of two or more rhythms whose natural accents and/or attacks are at variance with one another.

DECEPTIVE CADENCE. A cadence in which the submediant, after dominant preparation, is substituted for the (expected) tonic at the moment of closure.

DECEPTIVE MOTION. Any movement from a dominant-function chord to the submediant or (rarely) the mediant chord.

DIATONIC. Belonging to or being solely derived from a particular major or minor scale of seven notes within an octave.

DIMINISHED INTERVAL. An interval that spans the same number of scale degrees as a given minor or perfect interval but is smaller by a half step. For example, a **DIMINISHED SEVENTH** (nine half steps, such as F♯ to E♭) is equivalent to the interval of a minor 7th (ten half steps) decreased by a half step.

DIMINISHED SEVENTH CHORD. *See* SEVENTH CHORD.

DIMINISHED TRIAD. *See* TRIAD.

DIMINUTION. The restatement of a musical passage using proportionately shorter note values.

DISSONANT. A characterization of sounds that are heard as unstable and that require movement or resolution to consonance.

DOMINANT. The name given to the fifth scale degree and to the chord built upon that degree.

DOMINANT FUNCTION. One of three structural functions that are exhibited by diatonic chords. Chords with a dominant function have a strong tendency to resolve to tonic-function chords.

DOMINANT SEVENTH CHORD. *See* SEVENTH CHORD.

DORIAN MODE. Ecclesiastical mode I, which places its half steps between $\hat{2}$ and $\hat{3}$ and between $\hat{6}$ and $\hat{7}$. This is equivalent to playing the scale from a given D to the D an octave higher, while remaining in the key of C major.

DOUBLY AUGMENTED FOURTH CHORD. *See* AUGMENTED SIXTH CHORD.

DOWNBEAT. The first beat of a measure.

DUPLE METER. Any meter characterized by two or four principal beats per measure. Recurring groups of four beats can also be identified as quadruple meter.

DUX. Literally, *leader*. In imitative polyphony, the voice in which a subject is first stated.

DYAD. An interval; two notes that are heard, written, or performed horizontally (melodically) or vertically (harmonically).

ECCLESIASTICAL MODES. The eight modes recognized by medieval theorists as proper for the composition of liturgical music. Also known as CHURCH MODES.

ÉCHAPPÉE. An escape tone.

ENHARMONIC EQUIVALENT. In an equal-tempered scale, notes or chords that sound identical but are spelled differently, such as G♯ and A♭.

ENHARMONIC MODULATION. A modulation that exploits the properties of enharmonically equivalent notes or chords to change the tonic to that of a distantly related key.

ESCAPE TONE. A nonchord tone, usually falling on a weak beat, that is approached by step from a chord tone and left by leap in the opposite direction, usually to another chord tone.

ETUDE. Literally, *study*. Music intended for explication and practice of a technical problem, or music with a didactic purpose intended for concert performance.

FIGURED BASS. A bass line marked with Arabic numerals (figures) that indicate the accompanying intervals and harmonies to be played.

FIRST INVERSION. *See* INVERSION OF A CHORD.

FOLLOWER. *See* COMES.

FREE COUNTERPOINT. Contrapuntal material devoid of imitative counterpoint.

FRENCH SIXTH CHORD. *See* AUGMENTED SIXTH CHORD.

FUNCTION. The property of directed motion and tendency exhibited by a diatonic note or harmony in a tonal work.

FUNCTIONAL. Pertaining to the function of a note or harmony in a tonal work.

FUNCTION OF COLOR. The property exhibited by certain notes or harmonies that are used for their color value (sound quality, tonal effect), and not necessarily for any contribution they may make to movement towards a musical goal.

FUNCTION OF HIERARCHY. In tonal music, the concept that certain scale degrees and the triads built on those degrees are of greater structural importance than others.

FUNDAMENTAL. The lowest note in a harmonic series of overtones.

GERMAN SIXTH CHORD. *See* AUGMENTED SIXTH CHORD.

GOAL HARMONY. A harmony that constitutes the arrival point of a cadence.

GREAT STAFF. A two-stave system joined by a brace at the left and notated with a treble clef on the top staff and a bass clef on the bottom one.

GREGORIAN CHANT. Early Roman Catholic church music, named for Pope Gregory I, characterized by unaccompanied melodies set to Latin liturgical texts.

HALF CADENCE. A cadence with a dominant-function chord as the goal harmony.

HALF-DIMINISHED SEVENTH CHORD. *See* SEVENTH CHORD.

HALF STEP. The smallest intervallic division in diatonic music, which is the interval of a minor 2nd. In systems utilizing equal temperament, exactly one-twelfth of an octave. Also called a SEMITONE.

HARMONIC. *See* OVERTONE.

HARMONIC FUNCTION. *See* FUNCTION.

HARMONIC INTERVAL. *See* INTERVAL.

HARMONIC MINOR SCALE. The form of the minor scale from which the functional harmonies in the minor mode are derived. In the harmonic minor scale, the half steps are located between $\hat{2}$ and $\hat{3}$, $\hat{5}$ and $\hat{6}$, and $\hat{7}$ and $\hat{1}$.

HARMONIC PERIOD. A statement of at least three chords.

HARMONICS. The various pure tones that make up a composite tone, including the fundamental and its upper partials. The presence and amplitudinal disposition of harmonics are responsible for the unique timbre of any given sound. Also known as OVERTONES.

HEMIOLA. Literally, *one and one-half*. Any instance in which three equal note values are played in the time usually marked by two notes of equal value (the ratio 3:2). *See also SESQUIALTERA*.

HEXACHORD. Any collection of six pitches. For example, a six-note scale, a six-note chord, or, in twelve-tone music, one-half of a twelve-tone row.

HIERARCHY OF FUNCTION. *See* FUNCTION OF HIERARCHY.

HOCKET. A technical device that divides the pitches of a single melodic line between two voices so that one voice sounds during the times the other is silent, and vice versa.

HOME KEY. The key of the original tonic note, especially in music that modulates.

HOMOPHONIC. The characterization of a musical texture in which all the parts or voices move in the same or nearly the same rhythm. A note-against-note or chordal style found in simple chorales and hymns. Also called FAMILIAR STYLE.

HOMOPHONY. Music written in homophonic style.

ICTUS. Literally, *stroke*. The beginning of a note (an accented note). An attack.

IMITATION. The restatement of a phrase or melodic subject by another voice in a contrapuntal procedure.

IMPRESSIONISM. A school of musical style and technique, led by Debussy (and Ravel), that sought to render impressions and moods by various characteristic devices, including the use of exotic scales and modes.

INTERVAL. The distance between two notes, whether successive (melodic) or simultaneous (harmonic), measured by the number of scale degrees, counting both notes as well as those in between. A MAJOR INTERVAL (as differentiated from a *perfect interval*) can be defined as any dyad identical in size, quality, and structure with the imperfect consonances found between $\hat{1}$ and any other scale degree ($\hat{2},\hat{3},\hat{6},\hat{7}$) above it. A MINOR INTERVAL can be defined as any dyad identical in size, quality, and structure with the imperfect consonances found between $\hat{1}$ and any other scale degree ($\hat{7},\hat{6},\hat{3},\hat{2}$) below it in the major scale.

INVERSION OF A CHORD. A chord in which a chord tone other than the root is in the bass, irrespective of the voicing of the other chord tones. When the third is in the bass, the chord is in FIRST INVERSION; when the fifth is in the bass, the chord is in SECOND INVERSION. For seventh chords, if the seventh is in the bass, the chord is in THIRD INVERSION. Whenever the root is in the bass of a chord, it is in ROOT POSITION.

INVERSION OF AN INTERVAL. An interval in which the lower note has been placed an octave or more above its original position. The sum of the sizes of an interval and its inversion is always 9.

INVERSION OF A SUBJECT. A contrapuntal procedure, usually encountered in imitative counterpoint, that makes use of intervallic inversion. The inversion of a theme results in the mirror image of that theme. That is, an interval in the original subject is the inversion of the corresponding interval in the inverted subject. When an inverted subject is used to answer the original one or when the original subject is combined with the inverted version in another voice, small adjustments to the interval of inversion are sometimes made to avoid undesirable dissonances. When this occurs, the inverted version is called TONAL. When such adjustments are not made, the inverted version is called REAL.

IONIAN MODE. One of the so-called theoretical modes, in which half steps are found between $\hat{3}$ and $\hat{4}$ and between $\hat{7}$ and $\hat{1}$; it has the structure of the major scale.

ITALIAN SIXTH CHORD. See AUGMENTED SIXTH CHORD.

JAZZ. Music of African-American origin characterized by syncopated rhythms, extended tertiary harmonies, and improvisation.

KEY SIGNATURE. An arrangement of sharps or flats (or the absence of both) at the beginning of a staff that usually indicates the key of a musical work.

LAW OF THE HALF STEP. The observation that, in most tonal music, those scale degrees separated by a half step tend to gravitate or move toward each other.

LEADER. *See* DUX.

LEADING TONE. The seventh note of a scale, a half step below the tonic, whose tendency is toward the tonic. Occasionally, other notes with strong tendencies to move by step are referred to as leading tones. Also, the chord whose root is the half step below the tonic.

LEAP. A melodic interval larger than a major 2nd.

LEAST COMMON MULTIPLE. The smallest (positive) integer that is evenly divisible by two or more given integers. For example, 12 is the least common multiple of 4 and 6.

LEDGER LINE. A fragment of a line placed parallel to a staff, used to indicate the position of a note above or below the range of that staff.

LOCRIAN MODE. One of the so-called theoretical modes, whose half steps are located between $\hat{1}$ and $\hat{2}$ and between $\hat{4}$ and $\hat{5}$. Equivalent to the scale between a given B and the B an octave higher in the key of C major.

LYDIAN MODE. One of the ecclesiastical modes, whose half steps are located between $\hat{4}$ and $\hat{5}$ and between $\hat{7}$ and $\hat{1}$. Equivalent to the scale between a given F and the F an octave higher in the key of C major.

MAJOR INTERVAL. See INTERVAL.

MAJOR MODE. Any collection of pitches that function like those found in the major scale.

MAJOR SCALE. Any of the seven-note scales consisting primarily of whole steps, but with half steps between $\hat{3}$ and $\hat{4}$ and between $\hat{7}$ and $\hat{1}$.

MAJOR SEVENTH CHORD. See SEVENTH CHORD.

MAJOR TRIAD. See TRIAD.

MEDIANT. See SCALE DEGREE.

MEDIANT TRIAD. The triad whose root is $\hat{3}$.

MELODIC CONSTRUCT. A single-line composition, written for didactic purposes and for practice, that does not necessarily have the characteristics of contour and construction associated with typical melodies.

MELODIC INTERVAL. See INTERVAL.

MELODIC MINOR SCALE. The form of the minor scale that has the sixth and seventh scale degrees raised a half step when ascending, but that is identical with the natural minor scale when descending.

METER. A regularly repeating pattern of successive strong and weak beats found in most Western tonal music.

METRIC ACCENT. The regular emphasis carried by a note derived solely from its placement on a strong beat of a measure.

MEZZO-SOPRANO CLEF. The C-clef that locates middle C on the second line from the bottom of the staff.

MINIPROGRESSION. A three-chord progression that, despite its brevity, exhibits many of the properties of a larger harmonic progression.

MINOR INTERVAL. See INTERVAL.

MINOR MODE. A collection of pitches that function like those found in the various forms of the minor scale.

MINOR SCALE. Any of the three scales that are distinguished from the major scale sharing the same tonic by the presence of a half step between $\hat{2}$ and $\hat{3}$. See HARMONIC MINOR SCALE, MELODIC MINOR SCALE, NATURAL MINOR SCALE.

MINOR SEVENTH CHORD. See SEVENTH CHORD.

MINOR TRIAD. See TRIAD.

MIXED METER. The use of multiple time signatures in the same piece.

MIXOLYDIAN MODE. One of the ecclesiastical modes, whose half steps are located between $\hat{3}$ and $\hat{4}$ and between $\hat{6}$ and $\hat{7}$. Equivalent to the scale between a given G and the G an octave higher in the key of C major.

MODAL BORROWING. The practice of using notes and/or chords found in a parallel minor or major key.

MODE. A general term referring to all of the scales arranged and structured in a similar way.

MODULATE. To effect a modulation from one key to another, frequently by means of a pivot chord that has a specific harmonic function in the initial key but a different one in the new key.

MODULATION. The process of establishing a new key as the tonal center, confirmed by the use of at least one clear authentic cadence in the new key.

NATURAL MINOR SCALE. The form of the minor scale that has a half step between $\hat{2}$ and $\hat{3}$ and between $\hat{5}$ and $\hat{6}$. (It lacks a half step between $\hat{7}$ and $\hat{1}$.)

NEAPOLITAN SIXTH CHORD. An altered chord built on $\flat\hat{2}$ and placed in first inversion, in which there is a minor 3rd and a minor 6th above $\hat{4}$, the bass.

NEIGHBOR NOTE. See AUXILIARY TONE.

NEUTRAL METRICS. In a metered context, the complete avoidance of any natural, implied, or added accents so that all notes are stressed equally.

NEUTRAL SYLLABLE. A syllable without functional significance, such as "ta" or "lu," chosen for its singability over a relatively wide range.

NONCHORD TONE. Any note sounding simultaneously with a given chord that is not a constituent of that harmony.

OCTATONIC SCALE. An artificial scale of eight notes that consists of alternating half steps and whole steps.

OPEN PROGRESSION. A harmonic progression that begins on the tonic and concludes with a chord other than the tonic. HALF CADENCES and ANTECEDENT PHRASES are forms of open progressions.

OSTINATO. A persistently repeated pattern, often of rhythm, in a composition or in a section of a work.

OTTAVA. Playing or sounding in an octave relation to the notes written. Piccolos and contrabasses are ottava instruments.

OVERTONE. A member of an overtone series, often called a HARMONIC or PARTIAL.

OVERTONE SERIES. The attendant higher frequencies above a given fundamental frequency. In a harmonic overtone series these higher frequencies are all integer multiples of the fundamental frequency. They are caused by the manner in which a string or a column of air, for example, vibrates.

PANDIATONIC. A style or system in which all the notes of a given collection are treated more or less equally, especially with regard to consonance and dissonance.

PARALLEL FIFTHS. The simultaneous, similar motion of two voices that maintain the distance of a perfect 5th. Parallel motion between perfect 5ths, octaves, and unisons is generally avoided in traditional counterpoint.

PARALLEL MAJOR. The major key that has the same tonic as a given minor key.

PARALLEL MINOR. The minor key that has the same tonic as a given major key.

PARALLEL UNISONS. The simultaneous, similar motion of two voices that maintain the distance of a perfect unison.

PARTIAL. *See* OVERTONE.

PASSING CHORD. A chord that is used to harmonize what would otherwise be a passing tone in the bass.

PASSING TONE. A nonchord tone that is approached by step from a chord member and that proceeds by step in the same direction, usually to another chord member.

PEDAL (POINT). A nonchord tone, most often encountered in the bass, that begins as a chord tone but is sustained throughout ensuing changes of harmony with which it becomes dissonant. It usually becomes a chord member again.

PENTATONIC SCALE. A scale comprising only five notes. The most familiar pentatonic scale consists of a two-note group separated by a minor 3rd from a three-note group. The two notes of the first group span a major 2nd. In the three-note group, a major 2nd is spanned from the lowest to the middle note and also from the middle to the highest note. This scale in the key of C major is C D F G A.

PERFECT INTERVAL. Any consonant 4th, 5th, octave, or unison. The adjective *perfect* is applied only to the intervals just named (*major*, *minor*, *diminished*, and *augmented* are used to describe the other intervals).

PERIOD. *See* ANTECEDENT AND CONSEQUENT PHRASES.

PERPETUAL CANON. A canon, usually imitative in procedure, that repeats indefinitely, since a final cadence is not provided. A round.

PHRASE. A relatively brief musical unit made up of one or more melodic motives or harmonies, analogous to a sentence in speech.

PHRYGIAN MODE. One of the ecclesiastical modes, in which half steps are located between $\hat{1}$ and $\hat{2}$ and between $\hat{5}$ and $\hat{6}$. Equivalent to the scale between a given E and the E an octave higher in the key of C major.

PICARDY THIRD. A major 3rd placed in the final tonic chord of a piece otherwise in the minor mode, thus changing the final chord from tonic minor to tonic major.

PITCH. The word given to the subjective perception of a sound frequency; often used interchangeably with NOTE.

PITCH CLASS. The collection consisting of all notes of a particular name in all octaves.

PITCH-CLASS SET. A collection of from two to twelve pitch classes.

PIVOT CHORD. In a common-chord modulation, the chord that is heard as common to both the initial key and the new key.

PLAGAL CADENCE. A harmonic cadence in which a subdominant chord, rather than a dominant harmony (as in an authentic cadence), precedes the tonic.

PLAGAL FORM OF A MODE. The form of an ecclesiastical mode in which the final note (the *FINALIS*) is preserved, but the range (the *AMBITUS*) is higher or lower.

PRE-DOMINANT FUNCTION. One of three principal structural functions exhibited by diatonic chords. Chords with a pre-dominant function (that is, those built on $\hat{2}$, $\hat{3}$, $\hat{4}$, or $\hat{6}$) have a strong tendency to move toward either a dominant-function chord or toward another pre-dominant-function chord.

PREPARATION. The first part of a suspension, in which the note of suspension begins as a chord tone, often on a weak beat or a portion of a beat.

PRIME NUMBER. An integer greater than 1 that is divisible only by itself and 1. The smallest primes are 2, 3, 5, 7, 11, and 13.

PROGRESSION. A succession of two or more chords.

PROLONGATION. The process of emphasizing the importance of a musical event, particularly by embellishing a chord with secondary-function harmonies.

PULSE. A regular beat.

QUALITY. The characteristic sound of an interval or chord that is derived from the relative amount of tonal space spanned by the pitches involved.

RANGE. The span of pitches capable of being played or sung by a given instrument or person.

REGISTER. A division or portion of the total range of pitches available for a given voice or instrument in which all the notes share similar characteristics.

RELATIVE MAJOR. The major key that displays the same key signature as a given minor key and whose tonic lies a minor 3rd above the tonic of the minor key.

RELATIVE MINOR. The minor key that displays the same key signature as a given major key and whose tonic lies a minor 3rd below the tonic of the major key.

RENAISSANCE. The period of Western music history from approximately 1430 through 1600, which saw a great flourishing of music, art, and learning.

RESOLUTION OF A SUSPENSION. The movement down, by step, of a suspended note, after the preparation and the suspension itself, to a chord tone.

RESOLUTION OF A TENDENCY. The movement from a tendency (dissonant) tone to a note of greater stability and weaker tendency (consonance).

RETARDATION. Similar to a suspension, except that the resolution of the nonchord tone is up, rather than down, by step.

RETROGRADE. Literally, *proceeding backward*. The form of a given theme in which the order of the notes is reversed.

RETROGRADE INVERSION. The form of a theme in which the intervals presented in the retrograde are inverted.

RHYTHM. The patterns created by the occurrence of sounds in time.

RHYTHMIC VOCABULARY. The variety of note lengths that make up a given rhythm.

ROOT OF A CHORD. The note upon which 3rds are stacked to create a chord.

ROOT POSITION. *See* INVERSION OF A CHORD.

ROOT RELATIONSHIP. The intervallic relation between the roots of two or more chords, regardless of the actual notes in the bass (that is, regardless of the inversion).

ROUND. A perpetual canon at the unison in which each voice, in turn, sings the subject and returns to the beginning of the canon, *ad infinitum*.

SATB. Shorthand for soprano, alto, tenor, bass, used to indicate the distribution of voices, from top to bottom, in many four-part choral textures.

SCALE. A series of consecutive notes spanning an octave.

SCALE DEGREE. The specific numbered position of a pitch within a given scale. In each major and minor scale there are seven scale degrees. These scale-degree numbers, indicated by carets ($\hat{\ }$), are frequently called by the names that follow: $\hat{1}$, TONIC; $\hat{2}$, SUPERTONIC; $\hat{3}$, MEDIANT; $\hat{4}$, SUBDOMINANT; $\hat{5}$, DOMINANT; $\hat{6}$, SUBMEDIANT; $\hat{7}$, LEADING TONE. Chords built on each scale degree are also called by the names given to the corresponding scale degrees.

SECONDARY DOMINANT. A chord borrowed from the key of a diatonic scale degree other than $\hat{1}$ that has a dominant function in that key.

SECONDARY FUNCTION. A tonic, pre-dominant, or dominant function with regard to a diatonic chord or note other than the tonic.

SECONDARY PRE-DOMINANT. A chord borrowed from the key of a diatonic scale degree other than $\hat{1}$ that functions as a supertonic, mediant, subdominant, or submediant in that key.

SEMITONE. A half step.

SEQUENCE. Repetition of brief melodic and/or harmonic units, at successively higher or lower pitch levels.

SERIAL MUSIC. Music based on the precompositional ordering of any or all parameters, including pitch, register, rhythm, dynamics, and articulation. These ordered sets of musical parameters are manipulated and combined by a composer in various ways to create a serial composition. *See* TWELVE-TONE MUSIC.

SESQUIALTERA. The simultaneous combination of three equal divisions of a unit against two equal divisions of the same unit. *See* HEMIOLA.

SEVENTH CHORD. A triad with an added 7th above the root. The quality of the 7th in conjunction with the quality of the triad gives seventh chords their unique sound. There are five distinct qualities found among diatonic seventh chords: The MAJOR SEVENTH CHORD is made up of a major triad with a major 7th. The MINOR SEVENTH CHORD is made up of a minor triad with a minor 7th. The DOMINANT SEVENTH CHORD, the most important of these chords, consists of a major triad with a minor 7th. The DIMINISHED SEVENTH CHORD consists of a diminished triad with a diminished 7th. The HALF-DIMINISHED SEVENTH CHORD is made up of a diminished triad with a minor 7th.

SIGHT-READING. The ability to play or to hear internally a piece of music when seeing it for the first time.

SIGHT-SINGING. The ability to sing a piece of music when seeing it for the first time.

SIMPLE INTERVAL. An interval of an octave or less.

SOLFÈGE SYSTEM. A system of referring to and singing notes with syllable names (rather than letter names), which, for didactic purposes, assigns single syllables to the notes of a given scale.

SOURCE SET FORM. A collection of notes arranged in such an order that the smallest interval possible occurs between the notes.

SPELLING. The way in which notes and chords are expressed using combinations of letters, sharps, and flats.

STABILITY. The relative degree of consonance heard in a note or chord.

STRUCTURAL FUNCTION. The property of chords that governs an entire phrase and constitutes its basic framework.

SUBDOMINANT. *See* SCALE DEGREE.

SUBMEDIANT. *See* SCALE DEGREE.

SUPERTONIC. *See* SCALE DEGREE.

SUSPENSION. A note that is first prepared as a chord member (that is, as a consonant tone) and that is then sustained or repeated into another harmony, where it becomes a nonchord tone or dissonant tone (the suspension). It is then usually resolved down by step to a chord tone.

TEMPO. The relative rate, usually measured in beats per minute, at which beats recur or are felt.

TEMPORAL. Pertaining to time and thus, in music, to tempo and rhythm.

TENDENCY. The property of a note or chord that makes it gravitate toward another.

TENOR CLEF. A clef used to designate the tenor range on the staff. The tenor C-clef locates middle C on the second line from the top of the staff. The ottava tenor clef is a treble G-clef indicating sounds an octave lower than written.

TENSION. The property of a sound or of groups of sounds that creates tendency and the expectation of movement toward a musical resolution or stability.

TETRACHORD. Any collection of four pitches, especially four contiguous pitches in a given scale or twelve-tone row.

THEORETICAL MODES. The modes other than the eight ecclesiastical modes; that is, those modes with tonics other than D, E, F, and G.

THEORY. The principles, identified through the processes of observation and analysis, that describe and explain the ways in which sounds interact and music is structured.

TIMBRE. The tone color of a single sound, derived from the presence and relative amplitudes of the harmonics in its overtone series.

TIME SIGNATURE. The marking placed at the beginning of a work or a section of a work to indicate the meter of the measures that follow.

TONAL. Pertaining to music written within a diatonic system or to music in which a sense of tonal hierarchy is otherwise established.

TONE POEM. A single-movement symphonic genre, developed during the nineteenth century, that seeks to depict, with sometimes specific, sometimes general, musical means, the spirit, impressions, or action of an accompanying narrative or title.

TONIC. *See* SCALE DEGREE.

TONIC FUNCTION. One of three principal structural functions exhibited by diatonic chords. Chords that carry a tonic function frequently serve as points of departure and goals of harmonic progressions because the tonic function is the most stable and least active function.

TONICIZATION. Momentary emphasis of a note other than the tonic, without modulating, through the use of harmonies with secondary function.

TRANSPOSITION. The process of playing or notating music at a pitch other than that written. Transposing instruments transpose any written note automatically.

TREBLE CLEF. A G-clef that locates the G above middle C on the second line from the bottom of the staff.

TRIAD. Any collection of three different notes, but generally used to mean a three-note chord configured so that a 3rd separates the lowest (the ROOT) from the middle pitch (the THIRD) and the middle from the highest pitch (the FIFTH). The root and 3rd of MAJOR and AUGMENTED TRIADS are separated by a major 3rd. The root and 3rd of MINOR and DIMINISHED TRIADS are separated by a minor 3rd. The root and 5th of major and minor triads are separated by a perfect 5th. The root and 5th of an augmented triad are separated by an augmented 5th, whereas those of a diminished triad are separated by a diminished 5th.

TRICHORD. A group of three notes forming part of a twelve-tone row; also, any collection of three notes.

TRIPLE METER. Any meter that contains three principal beats per measure.

TRITONE. Any interval spanning three whole steps; hence, an augmented 4th or diminished 5th.

TWELVE-TONE MUSIC. Music written according to a technique that is based on an arbitrary arrangement of the twelve notes of the chromatic scale. This twelve-tone row becomes the principle that unifies a musical work and that generates all of the musical material in the composition.

TWELVE-TONE ROW. An ordered arrangement of the twelve notes of the chromatic scale.

UPPER LEADING TONE. The term given to a note of a chord that has a strong tendency to resolve down by half step, usually to the 3rd of a chord whose root lies a perfect 5th below that of the chord containing the upper leading tone.

VOICE CROSSING. The instance when a part that was previously lower than another becomes the higher part, and vice versa.

VOICE LEADING. The movement of two or more parts in a contrapuntal texture according to the natural tendencies of the notes in each part.

VOICING. The manner in which the notes of a particular chord are distributed vertically.

WHITE-NOTE MUSIC. A somewhat pejorative term given to music that remains arbitrarily diatonic.

WHOLE STEP. The intervallic distance spanned by two adjacent half steps.

WHOLE-TONE SCALE. An artificial scale of six notes within the span of an octave, in which a whole step separates each member of the scale.

Index

••• Index of Composers Cited ••••••••••••••••••••••••